[redacted]

GENDER AND DIFFERENCE IN ANCIENT ISRAEL

GENDER AND DIFFERENCE IN ANCIENT ISRAEL

Peggy L. Day, *editor*

FORTRESS PRESS Minneapolis

GENDER AND DIFFERENCE IN ANCIENT ISRAEL

Book design: Publishers' WorkGroup

Library of Congress Cataloging-in-Publication Data

Gender and difference in ancient Israel / Peggy L. Day, editor.
p. cm.
Bibliography: p.
Includes index.
ISBN 0-8006-2393-2
1. Women in the Bible. 2. Bible. O.T.—Criticism, interpretation, etc. 3. Feminism. I. Day, Peggy Lynne.
BS1199.W7G46 1989
221.6'082—dc20 89-36038
CIP

The paper used in this publication meets the minimum requirements of American National Standard for Information Sciences—Permanence of Paper for Printed Library Materials, ANSI Z329.48-1984.

Manufactured in the U.S.A. AF 1-2393

93 92 91 90 89 1 2 3 4 5 6 7 8 9 10

CONTENTS

CONTRIBUTORS

PEGGY L. DAY is Assistant Professor of Religious Studies at the University of Winnipeg. She is the author of *An Adversary in Heaven: śāṭān in the Hebrew Bible.*

SUSAN ACKERMAN is Assistant Professor in the Department of Near Eastern Studies, University of Arizona. She is currently preparing for publication a book-length work on Israelite "popular" religion in the sixth century and its relation to the priestly and prophetic cults.

PHYLLIS BIRD is Associate Professor of Old Testament Interpretation at Garrett-Evangelical Theological Seminary. She is the author of *The Bible as the Church's Book,* and a number of essays on women in ancient Israel and on sexual differentiation in the Genesis creation texts. She is currently working on two books, *Harlot and Hierodule in Old Testament Theology and Anthropology* (tentative title) and a study of ancient Israelite religion from the perspective of women's experience and participation.

DEBRA A. CHASE is a doctoral candidate in the Department of Near Eastern Languages and Civilizations at Harvard University. She has published studies on Kuntillet ʿAjrud and on disease in the ancient world. She has been a staff member of several archaeological expeditions in the Levant and is completing a dissertation on Phoenician religion.

JO ANN HACKETT is Assistant Professor of Religious Studies at Indiana University. She is author of *The Balaam Text from Deir ʿAllā,* and is currently working on a book on the polemic against foreigners contained in a variety of ancient Near Eastern texts.

PAULA S. HIEBERT is a doctoral student in Old Testament at Harvard Divinity School currently writing a dissertation on Psalm 78. She has taught at Salve Regina College, Newport, Rhode Island, and Louisiana State University.

SUSAN TOWER HOLLIS is the Director of the Humanities Internship Program and Assistant Professor of Humanities at Scripps College in Claremont, California. Her dissertation on the ancient Egyptian "Tale of Two Brothers" will be published by the University of Oklahoma Press under the tentative title *The Oldest Fairy Tale in the World.* Her current research concerns the ancient Egyptian goddesses Neith, Nut, Hathor, and Isis in the Third Millennium.

MARY JOAN WINN LEITH is a doctoral candidate in the Department of Near Eastern Languages and Civilizations, Harvard University. She has taught numerous courses on myth and religion, and in 1988–89 she was Assistant Professor of Religious Studies (sabbatical replacement) at Stonehill College. She has been a staff member on a number of archaeological excavations in North Africa and the Levant and is currently completing her dissertation on the Wadi ed-Daliyah seal impressions and fourth-century B.C.E. Palestine.

CAROL A. NEWSOM is Associate Professor of Old Testament at the Candler School of Theology, Emory University. Author of *Songs of the Sabbath Sacrifice: A Critical Edition,* she is currently at work on a study of character and community in the literature of the Dead Sea Scrolls.

SUSAN NIDITCH is Associate Professor of Religion at Amherst College. She is the author of *The Symbolic Vision in Biblical Traditions; Chaos to Cosmos: Studies in Biblical Patterns of Creation;* and *Underdogs and Tricksters: A Prelude to Biblical Folklore.*

EILEEN SCHULLER is Associate Professor of Old Testament and Hebrew at Atlantic School of Theology, Halifax. She is the author of *Post-Exilic Prophecy* and *Non-Canonical Psalms from Qumran: A Pseudepigraphic Collection.*

SIDNIE ANN WHITE is Assistant Professor of Religion at Albright College in Reading, Pennsylvania. She is a contributing editor to *Discoveries in the Judean Desert,* the vehicle for the ongoing publication of the Dead Sea Scrolls.

ABBREVIATIONS

AB1	Anchor Bible
AB	*Abingdon Bible*
AfR	*Archiv für Religionswissenschaft*
AHW	W. von Soden, *Akkadisches Handwörterbuch*
ANET	J. B. Pritchard, ed., *Ancient Near Eastern Texts*
Ant	Josephus, *The Jewish Antiquities*
AOAT	Alter Orient und Altes Testament
AOS	American Oriental Series
AS	Assyriological Studies
ATD	Das Alte Testament Deutsch
BA	*Biblical Archaeologist*
BASOR	*Bulletin of the American Oriental Society*
BDB	F. Brown, S. R. Driver, and C. A. Briggs, *Hebrew and English Lexicon of the Old Testament*
Bib	*Biblica*
BibAnt	Pseudo Philo, *Biblical Antiquities*
BKAT	Biblischer Kommentar: Altes Testament
BN	*Biblische Notizen*
BZAW	Beihefte zur *Zeitschrift für die alttestamentliche Wissenschaft*
CAD	*The Assyrian Dictionary of the Oriental Institute of the University of Chicago*
CBQ	*Catholic Biblical Quarterly*
CBQMS	Catholic Biblical Quarterly—Monograph Series
CIS	*Corpus inscriptionum semiticarum*
CRAIBL	*Comptes rendus de l'académie des inscriptions et belles-lettres*

CTA	A. Herdner, ed., *Corpus des tablettes en cunéiformes alphabétiques*
ETL	*Ephemerides Theologicae Lovanienses*
Gilg	The Epic of Gilgamesh
GKC	Gesenius' Hebrew Grammar, ed. E. Kautzch, tr. A. E. Cowley
GRBS	*Greek, Roman, and Byzantine Studies*
HALAT	W. Baumgartner, et al., eds., *Hebräisches und aramäisches Lexikon zum Alten Testament*
HAT	Handbuch zum Alten Testament
HR	*History of Religions*
HSM	Harvard Semitic Monographs
HTR	*Harvard Theological Review*
HUCA	*Hebrew Union College Annual*
ICC	International Critical Commentary
IDB	G. A. Buttrick, ed., *Interpreter's Dictionary of the Bible*
IDBSup	*Interpreter's Dictionary of the Bible,* Supplementary Volume
IEJ	*Israel Exploration Journal*
JAAR	*Journal of the American Academy of Religion*
JAOS	*Journal of the American Oriental Society*
JB	A. Jones, ed., *Jerusalem Bible*
JBL	*Journal of Biblical Literature*
JEA	*Journal of Egyptian Archaeology*
JFSR	*Journal of Feminist Studies in Religion*
JJS	*Journal of Jewish Studies*
JNES	*Journal of Near Eastern Studies*
JPOS	*Journal of the Palestine Oriental Society*
JPSV	*Jewish Publication Society Version*
JQR	*Jewish Quarterly Review*
JSJ	*Journal for the Study of Judaism*
JSOT	*Journal for the Study of the Old Testament*
JSOTSup	Journal for the Study of the Old Testament—Supplement Series
JSS	*Journal of Semitic Studies*
Jub	Jubilees
KAI	H. Donner and W. Rollig, *Kanaanäische und aramäische Inschriften*
KAT	E. Sellin, ed., Kommentar zum Altes Testament

KB	L. Koehler and W. Baumgartner, *Lexicon in Veteris Testamenti libros*
LXX	Septuagint
MDOG	*Mitteilungen der deutschen Orient-Gesellschaft*
MIO	*Mitteilungen des Instituts für Orientforschung*
MLCOT	T. H. Gaster, *Myth, Legend and Custom in the Old Testament*
MT	Masoretic Text
MVAG	*Mitteilungen der vorderasiatisch-ägyptischen Gesellschaft*
NAB	*New American Bible*
NEB	*New English Bible*
OB	Old Babylonian period
Or	*Orientalia*
OTL	Old Testament Library
PEQ	*Palestine Exploration Quarterly*
PN	Personal name
PRU	*Le Palais Royal d'Ugarit*
PTMS	Pittsburgh Theological Monograph Series
RB	*Revue biblique*
RES	*Répertoire d'épigraphie sémitique*
RHA	*Revue hittite et asianique*
RivB	*Rivista Biblica*
RScR	*Revue des sciences religieuses*
RSV	Revised Standard Version
SBL	Society of Biblical Literature
SBLDS	Society of Biblical Literature Dissertation Series
SBLMS	Society of Biblical Literature Monograph Series
SBT	Studies in Biblical Theology
SIDIC	*Service International de Documentation Judeo-Chrétienne*
ST	*Studia theologica*
TDNT	G. Kittel and G. Friedrich (eds.), *Theological Dictionary of the New Testament*
TDOT	*Theological Dictionary of the Old Testament*
TEH	Theologische Existenz heute
THAT	Theologisches Handwörterbuch zum Alten Testament
UF	*Ugarit Forschungen*
UT	C. H. Gordon, *Ugaritic Textbook*
Vg	Vulgate

VT	*Vetus Testamentum*
VTSup	*Vetus Testamentum,* Supplements
WVDOG	Wissenschaftliche Veröffentlichungen der deutschen Orientgesellschaft
ZA	*Zeitschrift für Assyriologie*
ZAW	*Zeitschrift für die alttestamentliche Wissenschaft*
ZPE	*Zeitschrift für Papyrologie und Epigraphik*

PREFACE

This volume is a response to a pressing need for gender-nuanced biblical scholarship. It is a departure from much previous work that has focused on gender-related issues in that it is primarily non-theological. Instead, the contributors apply methods and insights gleaned from fields such as sociology, anthropology, psychology, history, literary criticism, folklore, and women's studies. And because the chapters raise different issues and ask different questions, they frequently focus on aspects of texts that traditional biblical scholarship has deemed peripheral, uninteresting, or invisible. These chapters are offered as examples of the kinds of questions that need to be asked and the various methodological strategies that can be deployed to answer them.

We intend this volume to be accessible to people who have been introduced to critical biblical scholarship, but we do not presume initiation into the greater mysteries of the discipline. We do, however, also want to reach those with a higher degree of expertise—so the essays treat clearly defined topics in depth, with footnotes providing a place for more technical arguments and discussions. For all readers we hope that the chapters serve as methodological models and in that capacity have the potential for application beyond the specific texts and topics they treat.

I would like to thank the contributors for making my role as editor a truly enjoyable and rewarding experience. I would also like to thank my research assistant, Jacqueline R. Isaac, and the University of Toronto's Humanities and Social Sciences Grant-in-Aid Program for making her assistance possible.

Toronto, Canada
June 23, 1989

PEGGY L. DAY

1 INTRODUCTION

PEGGY L. DAY

The essays in this volume present a range of strategies for formulating and addressing gender-nuanced questions. These strategies vary according to what the respective authors think best addresses the particular text or topic each has chosen to discuss. Most of these strategies are informed by theoretical propositions put forward and methodological advances made in disciplines such as sociology, anthropology, psychology, literary criticism, history, classics, folklore studies, and especially women's studies. All are informed by a critical consciousness that maintains that gender is a significant aspect of social identity[1] and therefore must be recognized and addressed when discussing biblical texts and the communities that produced them. Although each essay treats a clearly circumscribed text or topic, the methodologies employed can serve as models for approaching similar types of texts and topics.

Unlike, for example, Letty M. Russel's *Feminist Interpretation of the Bible*,[2] the contributors to this volume are not united by a shared theological stance vis-à-vis the value, or indeed the relevance, of the biblical texts in the modern world. While several of the contributors to this volume discuss possible theological implications of their work, the focus of the collection is on adapting and applying feminist critical approaches developed in the secular humanities and social sciences to the field of biblical studies. To date, feminist theologians have been the most active and visible participants in the discussion of gender in the biblical texts,[3] for obvious and important reasons. But it is equally important to realize that feminist theologians have incorporated and applied feminist insights in a way that is particularly appropriate to the theological enterprise. This theological distillation does not represent the only way that feminist insights can be applied to the biblical texts. For example, feminism affirms the reality and importance of female experience. Feminist theologians apply this tenet by asserting that whenever the biblical text or interpretation of it falsifies or denies women's experience, the biblical text does not have the authority of authentic revelation and does not function as the word of God. This particular application is wholly appropriate to theological reflection. It acknowledges that the biblical texts as well as subsequent interpretations of them are products of patriarchal societies in which men dominated if not monopolized public discourse; therefore both text and interpretation reflect predominantly male experience. For feminist theologians, it is only when male experience does not contradict or deny female experience that the text can be expected to contain theological truth.

The ongoing dialectic between tradition and experience that results in a reinterpretation of tradition in the light of experience is as old as the texts themselves. Biblical sources collected traditions and shaped them in a meaningful way, and later redactors reshaped and reinterpreted earlier sources in order to make them relevant in new contexts. This process of reshaping and retelling traditional stories in a way that is consistent with the worldview of the interpreter and is relevant to the intended audience has produced a plethora of widely divergent interpretations, as anyone familiar with the history of biblical interpretation knows. What feminist theologians have rightly pointed out is that these interpretations have been a dialectic between the text and male experience, and have functioned to preserve male authority. Thus when feminist theologians reshape biblical traditions and retell biblical stories in a way that assigns importance and imparts dignity to female characters, or affirms gender equality, or deplores the denigration of women, they are doing what the theological tradition has always done, which is to read the text and retell the story in light of contemporary experience and as an affirmation of values and worldview. If the goal is to actualize the biblical text theologically, feminist theologians have applied the tenet of female experience in a highly appropriate way. They have claimed female experience as a yardstick of theological truth.

This kind of theological dialectic, however, is not the only valid application of the feminist tenet of the importance of female experience. For feminist theologians, the importance of female experience has been closely tied to rejection of the notion of objectivity,[4] which provides theoretical leverage for denying the truth of androcentric biblical interpretation and placing female experience on par with male in constructing theological discourse. But for feminist historians, for example, absolute rejection of objectivity has not been a central plank in the platform. As historian Linda Gordon put it: "It is wrong to conclude, as some have, that because there may be no objective truth possible, there are no objective lies. There may be no objective canons of historiography, but there are degrees of accuracy; there are better and worse pieces of history."[5] The challenge for feminist historians has been to find ways of insisting upon the importance of female experience that are appropriate to historical inquiry. This has been accomplished, for instance, by writing social[6] and social-science[7] history. In this way feminist historians have made female experience the object of historical inquiry, and in so doing have redefined what writing history means. Advocacy for the importance of female experience is incorporated into the nature of the questions asked, just as historians of past generations have implicitly advocated the importance of male-centered experience and activity by the kinds of historical questions they have chosen to ask. This type of advocacy for the importance of female experience should not be confused with reading feminist values into past and distant cultures. We need to ask feminist questions, but we must be prepared to obtain answers that do not directly confirm the values we hold in the modern world.

By asking gender-nuanced questions and focusing on female experience, the contributors to this volume play a part in the process of redefining biblical scholarship. As M. Z. Rosaldo has pointed out, "what we know is constrained by interpretive frameworks which, of course, limit our thinking; what we *can* know will be determined by the kinds of questions we ask."[8] The essays in this volume offer concrete examples of the kinds of questions that need to be asked when attention is paid to gender. With regard to modern biblical scholarship, they question the value and sometimes the validity of previous studies that have not taken gender into account, document instances wherein gender biases typical of the modern, western worldview have been inappropriately read into the material under study,[9] and implicitly challenge the interpretive frameworks that have characterized and limited the discipline's formulation of questions. Recognition of the gender-related role asymmetries present in the communities that produced the biblical texts and the implications this has for the contents and orientation of the texts themselves aids in the formulation of new questions. These questions articulate the perspectival biases of the sources and explore their implications as well as move beyond letting these biases define and delimit what we consider to be meaningful knowledge. Whereas we may not want entirely to abandon positivistic thought and disregard categories intrinsic to the texts and communities under study, neither should we let these categories restrict us. For, as Phyllis Culham put it, "it is surely necessary that the modern scholar not be unconsciously trapped in the categories of those social actors [under study] and thus remain blinded to the possibility of meaningful groupings [of data] to which those actors themselves were blinded."[10] Full realization of the fact that gender-related role asymmetry is a social product contributes to the formulation of questions directed toward "demystifying" the social factors that both produced and perpetuated gender asymmetry in Israelite society.[11] Thus we maintain that the "syntax of social relationships"[12] is an important aspect of historical inquiry. In short, once we appreciate that unstated, broadly political components are implicit in all interpretive frameworks,[13] we can work toward constructing frameworks that reflect our own historical interests rather than tacitly accepting the agendas of others.

Insisting that there is a subjective and therefore broadly political component built into the process of question formulation (questions themselves are, after all, interpretive frameworks) should not be mistaken as a clarion call to abandon the rigorous pursuit of accuracy. As social and social-science historians of the biblical world, one of our fundamental tasks is to generate a reliable body of knowledge about that world and specifically about gender-related roles and statuses that comprised that world. Two essays in this collection directly address this task. Phyllis Bird explores the meaning of the Hebrew root *znh,* and demonstrates that only the noun *zônâ* refers to a professional prostitute, while the verb *zānâ* refers more broadly to females who engage in extramarital sexual relations. Bird notes the fundamentally female profile of both activities as defined in Israel, in spite of the fact that both require the active participation of men and may be initiated by men. Bird links this conceptual asymmetry to a general pattern of gender-related asymmetries characteristic of patriarchal societies, thus demonstrating a concrete application of the point made above about demystifying the social dynamics that produce and perpetuate gender asymmetries. Bird further demonstrates that neither the noun *zônâ* nor the verb *zānâ* refers in their primary uses to cultic activity, and this leads her to question whether the notion of "sacred prostitution" accurately describes an actual cultic activity. She concludes that no such cultic role existed in ancient Israel, and thus makes a valuable contribution toward constituting a body of reliable knowledge about Israelite gender roles.[14]

The essay by Paula Hiebert investigates another Israelite social status, the *ʾalmānâ*, "widow." Hiebert argues that an *ʾalmānâ* was a woman whose husband had died and who had neither sons nor a father-in-law to assume economic responsibility for her. What, then, were the economic resources available to the Israelite widow? Hiebert utilizes cross-cultural data and social-scientific models to develop a theoretical framework for investigating possible sources of economic support. Her essay demonstrates a methodological strategy for filling gaps in the biblical text and thus fleshing out the cultural profile of the Israelite widow.

The distinction between biblical text and Israelite culture is important.[15] The text may claim to speak for the culture, but it is neither coextensive with nor equivalent to the culture. While the text presents us with an androcentric perspective on Israelite culture, women were nevertheless part of that culture and experienced it from a different perspective. Thus inquiry into women's activities without adopting the text's perspective on those activities is an appropriate and necessary task. This brings us back to the point about not allowing the perspectival biases inherent in the text to delimit and define the range of questions one can ask. Israelite women *did exist* in Israelite culture, and if we take that fact as our point of departure rather than grant the text the authority to speak on women's behalf, then we have every reason to try to ascertain, from a *female's* perspective, the realities of female existence.

Susan Ackerman's essay illustrates this practice. Ackerman takes as her starting point the observation that Israelite women were worshiping the Queen of Heaven (Jer. 7:16–20; 44:15–19, 25). Although the biblical text condemns this activity, Ackerman explores the question of why at least some women chose to give cult to the Queen. Ackerman's strategy acknowledges that the text transmits accurate information insofar as it tells us that this cult practice was taking place, but she refuses to accept the text's judgment of the practice. Rather, Ackerman investigates extrabiblical evidence for additional clues as to the nature of the Queen's cult and women's roles in it. Ackerman's study underlines the disparity between religion as it was popularly practiced and the theological imperialism that characterizes many of the biblical texts.

In my own contribution to this volume, I discuss the story of Jephthah's daughter (Judg. 11:29–40) from the perspective of the role it played in an annual women's ritual observance which, I argue, was a life-cycle ritual. Although the text offers evidence to support this argument, the ritual itself is not the text's focal point. The text recounts the story as a tragic episode in the life of Jephthah, but the story's function as a foundation legend for a female rite of passage from childhood to physical maturity provides a different vantage point from which to view the story. By exploring the stories of two other "dying maidens" (Iphigeneia and Kore) and the customs instituted to commemorate their deaths, I establish the probability that, like them, Jephthah's daughter was an initiatory figure and culture heroine. In the process I underline the fact that women and men in a given culture generate, interpret, and appropriate myths and symbols in gender-distinct ways.

Attention to symbols in relation to gender is an area treated by many of the essays, in various fashions. Carol Newsom and Mary Joan Winn Leith explore the dimensions of woman as symbolic "other." Newsom focuses on the image of the strange woman and the female personification of wisdom in Proverbs 1—9. In these chapters, the author summons his readers to take the subject position of a son who is being counseled by his father. Newsom maintains that this summons to take up a subject position in relation to a particular discourse and one's response to the summons—a process that Newsom calls "interpellation"—is never ideologically neutral. It is within the context of the patriarchal family as symbol of the authority structure of wisdom that readers of Proverbs 1—9 are interpellated, and this has important ideological implications. The father, the speaking voice of the text, lays claim to the abstract notions of righteousness, justice, and equity while vilifying rival discourses. As the discourse unfolds, the reader is continually reinterpellated as subject to the authority of the father, thus perpetuating the authority of the father as head of the patriarchal family unit and urging the son to replicate the patriarchal family so that, in time, he too can become an authoritative father figure. The image of the strange woman, a woman outside the confines of the patriarchal family and implicitly a threat to it, is the father's primary symbol of rival discourse. Moreover, in discourse in which the self is defined as male, woman is the quintessential other. The father identifies the strange woman with the ultimate boundary, death, thereby placing her at the symbolic margin between patriarchal man and chaos. Because normative humanity is defined as male, woman is an available symbol of the frontiers. The strange woman is the gate to Sheol, and wisdom, personified as female, is projected outward to reside on another margin, the gate to heaven. Newsom's analysis is a caution to those who wish to embrace the "positive" figure of female Wisdom, for she, like her antithesis, the strange woman, is the symbolic product of a worldview wherein the male is normative and central.

The prophet Hosea's use of woman as symbolic other is the topic of Mary Joan Winn Leith's essay. Leith argues that Hosea 1—3 is structured on the pattern of a rite of passage, which the prophet employs to communicate his vision of an Israel purged of sinful worship and reunited with Yahweh. The first step in this transition is the negation of Israel's identity, which the prophet accomplishes by a series of image reversals. Portraying Israel as an adulterous woman is one of the ways that the prophet deprives Israel of its normative, male identity. Leith notes that this is consistent with certain treaty curses that threaten the signatories with loss of their masculine identity; they are threatened with becoming women and prostitutes. Israel as woman is transported to the wilderness, where she is promised a new beginning. Here Hosea draws upon the wilderness as a traditional symbol of the liminal or transitional period preceding Israel's emergence as the people of Yahweh. In other words, the woman Israel is transported, not only spatially but also temporally, back to the time of Israel's beginnings, and there is reborn. Her transformation is described as a new betrothal, signaling a renewed covenant. In drawing upon these metaphors of transformation and rebirth, Hosea implicitly rejects the "divine warrior" tradition of creation and styles Yahweh as intimate spouse rather than triumphant fighting man.

Susan Tower Hollis also treats the figure of the adulterous woman, but in the text she focuses on, Gen. 39:7b–20, the sexual overtures proffered by the married woman are rejected by the male protagonist. The married woman is Potiphar's wife, and Hollis examines the effect Joseph's encounter with her has on Joseph's life fortunes. Hollis notes that discussions of the encounter typically focus on the negative actions of the female toward the male, and this results in styling the female as a wholly negative figure. Hollis argues that, viewed from the perspective of the effect Potiphar's wife has on Joseph's life, this seemingly inimical figure actually effects a positive change. Joseph goes to jail, and it is during his confinement that events occur that serve, in the end, to elevate him to a status much higher than the one he occupied as a slave in Potiphar's house. Moreover, Joseph's new status was not only of benefit to himself but also served to benefit the descendants of Abraham and Sarah by effecting their continued existence. The transition to a higher status is set in motion by the powerful and apparently destructive woman who, nevertheless, is the catalyst for long-term gain. She partakes of both the negative and the positive and as such is an ambivalent figure, perhaps a type of mother figure.

The ambivalence that men feel toward the mother figure plays a key role in Susan Niditch's discussion of Jael, the woman who offered sustenance and security to the fleeing Sisera and then felled him by driving a tent peg through his temple. Both nurturing and bloodthirsty, Jael embodies the two competing images of the feminine that, in the male psyche, comprise the mother archetype: the womb that devours and kills, and the protecting originator and sustainer of life. The linkage of sexuality and slaughter inherent in the former image pervades the description of Jael's assassination of the Canaanite Sisera. Niditch examines in detail both the vocabulary and the visual depiction of the murder scene. The violent and phallic image of tent peg and hammer leads to a scene of sexual submission, the warrior slumped between the legs of the erotic, death-dealing female. This nurturer turned killer, the embodiment of man's worst fears, is turned outward, against the enemy, thus providing confidence and reassurance to the Israelite author and his audience. The woman Jael's victory over the Canaanite foe serves as inspiration for the poorly armed Israelite peasants battling against their well-provisioned enemies. Jael has identification power for this audience because she represents the marginal's victory over the powerful.

Like Jael, the female characters treated by Jo Ann Hackett (Hagar) and Sidnie Ann White (Esther) were intended by the authors who created them to evoke identification. It is instructive that in all three cases the audiences intended to identify with these women were in a subordinate sociopolitical position. This is clearly the case for the original audience of the book of Esther. Living in a minority status amongst gentiles and politically dependent, the Jews of the Diaspora were both vulnerable and relatively powerless. White argues that Esther functioned for these Diaspora Jews as a model of the characteristics necessary for survival in a precarious world. White disagrees with many previous commentators who have maintained that Mordecai, not Esther, is the character presented for emulation. Where Mordecai proves inflexible and incurs the wrath of Haman, thus imperiling all the Jews under Persian rule, Esther bends and negotiates, and by working within the system succeeds in making the system work for her. White argues that the skills of cooperation and negotiation are survival skills that women have honed through long years of being in a subordinate status, and that these are precisely the skills that the author of Esther advocates as crucial for the survival of Diaspora Jewry in a predominantly gentile world.

By comparing the story pattern evidenced in the two stories about Hagar (Genesis 16 and 21) with Canaanite and Mesopotamian tales that follow the same pattern, Jo Ann Hackett discerns that the scene depicted in the biblical text is about the capricious use of superior power. All these stories feature a vulnerable protagonist who demeans a being of superior power, who in turn reacts out of reasonable proportion and demands that the underling be severely punished. Hagar plays the role of protagonist in her story, and Hackett argues that the force of the general story line is to make the hearer or reader identify with the vulnerable underling. The story is meaningful for those who have experienced the abuse of superior power, as Hagar has. In recognizing that Hagar is the hero of her story, Hackett challenges previous commentators who have seen Abraham as the focal character.

The final essay in this collection is by Eileen Schuller, who examines biblical retellings of the opening chapters of the book of Exodus. As Schuller notes, these chapters veritably abound with women: the midwives Shiphrah and Puah, the mother and sister of Moses, Pharaoh's daughter, and Zipporah, Moses' wife. All of these women are in various ways instrumental in preserving Moses' life and thus play crucial roles in the unfolding drama of Israel's release from slavery. Schuller's paper examines how these women fared in retellings of this drama during the Second Temple period. Although the women feature prominently in the biblical text, Schuller points out that the text was not the sole nor perhaps even the primary source from which the communities of that period drew their understanding of these foundational stories. It is important to ask, therefore, just how these stories were retold in these communities. How were they embellished? What was altered or left out? Were the women bracketed out and subtly deleted, or were their roles preserved or even magnified? Schuller finds that there is a tendency to name Moses' father and give him an expanded role in preserving his infant son, at the expense of the women credited with this action in the biblical text. Zipporah, the foreign wife of Moses, is generally glossed over or omitted entirely. The midwives have disappeared in all except Josephus' rendition, where they are portrayed as minions of the Egyptian Pharaoh. While certain incidents featuring women do receive attention, Schuller's overall appraisal is that the strong female presence of the biblical text has been muted. As a result, these female characters early in the history of tradition lost much of their potential power to influence the lives and imaginations of people throughout the centuries.

NOTES

1. Cf. M. Z. Rosaldo, "The Use and Abuse of Anthropology: Reflections on Feminism and Cross-cultural Understanding," *Signs: Journal of Women in Culture and Society* 5 (1980): 389–417; Judith Shapiro, "Anthropology and the Study of Gender," in *A Feminist Perspective in the Academy: The Difference it Makes,* eds. Elizabeth Langland and Walter Gove (Chicago: University of Chicago, 1981), 110–29.

2. Philadelphia: Westminster, 1985.

3. The Hebrew Bible bibliography at the end of this collection includes references to recent works that are clearly feminist, but not primarily theological.

4. See, for example, Rosemary Radford Ruether, *Sexism and God-Talk: Toward a Feminist Theology* (Boston: Beacon, 1983), chapter 1.

5. Linda Gordon, "What's New in Women's History," in *Feminist Studies/Critical Studies,* ed. Teresa de Lauretis (Bloomington: Indiana University, 1986), 22.

6. Cf. Jo Ann Hackett, "Women's Studies and the Hebrew Bible," in *The Future of Biblical Studies: The Hebrew Scriptures,* eds. Richard Eliot Friedman and Hugh Williamson (Atlanta: Scholars, 1987), 143–64.

7. Cf. Phyllis Culham, "Ten Years After Pomeroy: Studies of the Image and Reality of Women in Antiquity," in *Rescuing Creusa: New Methodological Approaches to Women in Antiquity,* ed. Marilyn Skinner, *Helios* n.s. 13 (Lubbock, Tex.: Texas Tech University, 1987), 17–19.

8. Rosaldo, "Use and Abuse," 390.

9. We should not assume that the particular configuration of values and attitudes that characterize the sexism of modern, western societies is precisely the same as that which characterized the texts and cultures under study.

10. Culham, "Image and Reality," 12–13.

11. Nancy Jay, "Sacrifice as Remedy for Having Been Born of Woman," in *Immaculate and Powerful: The Female in Sacred Image and Social Reality,* eds. Clarissa W. Atkinson et al. (Boston: Beacon, 1985), 283.

12. Culham, "Image and Reality," 10.

13. Marilyn Skinner ("Introduction," *Rescuing Creusa,* 3) refers to this as

"deciphering the 'hidden agenda' underlying the ongoing production of information about antiquity."

14. Bird's conclusion is supplemented by Mary Joan Winn Leith's discussion of ethnic boundary marking, a phenomenon characterized by charging others with supposed but not necessarily real improprieties in order to distinguish detestable "them" from righteous "us." Leith sees the insinuation of cultic sexual indecency suggested by the prophet Hosea's thematic pairing of Baal cult with whoring as an example of an ethnic boundary marker at work. Hosea manipulates the marker in order to indict Israelite males on charges of subverting Yahwistic cult practice.

15. Cf. Culham, "Image and Reality," 16–17.

2 REHABILITATING HAGAR: FRAGMENTS OF AN EPIC PATTERN*

JO ANN HACKETT

The two stories about Hagar in Genesis 16 and Genesis 21 generally are thought to be doublets: there is a pattern discernible in each of her stories, and it is the same pattern. Scholars have often pointed to the similarities and noted that the version in chapter 16 is from the Yahwist and the version in chapter 21 from the Elohist.[1] I would like to suggest, however, that this pattern is not unique to the Hagar stories, and that by comparing the Genesis stories to other traditions where this same pattern is used, we can hope to generate more information about what an ancient audience would have seen in Hagar as a character and in her story as it stands in two places in Genesis.

In the J version in Genesis 16, we read that Sarai, Abram's wife, "bore him no children," but that she had an Egyptian slave named Hagar. Sarai tells Abram that Yahweh has kept *her* from having children, but that if Abram can impregnate Hagar, Sarai might, literally, be "built up," or established, "from" or "through" Hagar. And Abram agrees.[2]

Hagar does get pregnant, and when the import of that fact hits her, that is, when she understands that she is in some ways in a better position than her mistress, her owner, Sarai, then Hagar apparently flaunts her new status; she begins to treat Sarai differently. The RSV translation, "Hagar looked on Sarai with contempt," is a bit harsh, as is the NEB, "she despised her mistress." The Hebrew can mean simply that Sarai, her mistress, became less, became diminished in Hagar's eyes.

* Several persons have read or commented on earlier versions of this chapter; in particular I would like to thank John Huehnergard and Ron Hendel for their insights and contributions.

This diminished status angers Sarai, and it seems that it riles her more than it should. Commentators often point to the unreasonableness of her outburst that follows. Skinner says that Sarai's "self-respect [finds] vent in a passionate and most unjust imprecation."[3] Speiser says Sarai is "frustrated and enraged."[4] Driver says that Sarai is "imperious and unreasoning," that she blames Abram "passionately and unjustly."[5] Both von Rad[6] and Gunkel[7] interpret the situation to mean that Sarai's status and power as wife and mistress are threatened by this new situation, that is, that Hagar is now Abram's concubine and soon to be the mother of his child, so that Sarai's outburst is remarkable, but understandable given the legal situation.

Von Rad and Gunkel are closer to the mark with their analyses at this point, in that they have at least looked at the conflict from the women's points of view. Within the society described, the status of a woman like Sarai can come from two features of her life, and these are features that concern life in the domestic sphere, her private life revolving around the home. First, she is the wife of a wealthy pastoralist—the chief wife, at least, and perhaps the only legal wife. The second feature is a consequence of the first—that her sons would be Abram's heirs. But she has no sons, and so her status is somewhat tenuous. She might assume that if she herself provides a woman to bear children for Abram, this new arrangement would not decrease her status. It might be, however, that the narrative assumes it was her duty to provide such a woman (other ancient Near Eastern materials imply that this was often the case in actual societies), and so her own status would still be a matter of question. That is to say, Sarai's society might actually force upon her her loss of status, until the point where she herself would bear children.[8]

Hagar, on the other hand, has her own problems. Up until this point, she has been merely a slave. Then she is given to Abram, with no attention paid to her opinion on the matter. Gunkel points this out as well, but he assumes, as do other commentators, that it would have been a great honor for such a woman to sleep with the patriarch.[9] She is represented as a woman who would for the first time have some status in this society because she is pregnant with the child we logically assume to be Abram's heir. This type of situation would bring tension into any household, and in our story we see Sarai feeling slighted by the new arrangement.

I have included this explanation by way of an attempt to counter one trend within Genesis scholarship that is no doubt unconscious, but that nevertheless trivializes the experiences of female characters like Hagar and Sarai by summing up the episode in question as a matter of Abram's being caught between two inconveniently squabbling women. Speiser, as I reported earlier, says that Sarai was "frustrated and enraged," but his complete description of the triangle is this: Sarai—frustrated and enraged; Hagar—spirited but tactless; and Abram—caught in the middle (to paraphrase) between his personal feelings and the legal rights of his wife.[10] Gunkel remarks later in his commentary,[11] and von Rad quotes him,[12] that Abram "plays an unhappy role between these two headstrong women." Gunkel also refers to the "contentious wife" sayings in wisdom literature to support his point that Israelite men often felt put upon by their wives.[13]

Hagar is always "defiant," and Sarai is "passionate" and raging, and Abram lives between them. Painting the picture this way, however, without further comment, simply invites or confirms an interpretation that belittles the female characters and the roles they play in the narrative.

The point I want to return to is that the intensity of Sarai's reaction here has been cause for much speculation. Sarai does seem to explode to Abram with a phrase that is usually translated something like: "May this wrong that has been done to me be on your head." And later she says: "May Yahweh judge between you and me," as if the whole thing had been Abram's fault, as if he is to blame for the way Hagar has acted toward her since getting pregnant.[14] Abram responds with apparent calm, although with no sensitivity whatsoever to Hagar's plight, and tells Sarai that Hagar is in her power, "in her hand," literally. She has his permission to do whatever she wants to Hagar. This episode ends by telling us that Sarai proceeded to oppress Hagar (*wat-təʿannêhā*), and the Hebrew verb generally carries the connotation of physical harm: it can mean to rape, or to oppress as slaves (it is used about Israel in Egypt this way), as well as simply to humble or humiliate.

We know the end of this story. Hagar flees (an interesting thing for her to do since her name may mean something like "flight." It is the same root as is used of Muhammad's Hijrah). She is found in the wilderness by "Yahweh's messenger," who questions her, tells her to go back to Sarai and submit to her abuse, and then aggrandizes her by promising her that *her* descendants will be "greatly multiplied," that they will be innumerable. This is said in language typical in the Genesis narratives of what is usually called "the promise to the patriarchs," a divine promise of descendants and often land. The surprising thing here, however, is that the promise is made to a woman. This is the only case in Genesis where this typical J-writer promise is given to a woman rather than to a patriarch, and so we sit up and take notice. No less interesting, this promise is followed by the first occurrence in the Hebrew Bible of a well-known annunciation speech. (See also Judg. 13:5; Isa. 7:14.) The "messenger" says to Hagar: "Now you are pregnant and you will have a son and name him Ishmael."

Finally, we have a description of Ishmael, an etiological passage about why he was named Ishmael, "God hears, or has heard," and a somewhat garbled but remarkable passage in which the J writer tells us that Hagar gave a name to "Yahweh who spoke to her" (the first time we learn that it was really Yahweh rather than his messenger, as so often happens in biblical passages).[15]

Here the J narrative leaves Hagar, and the end of this portion of the story has been added or substituted by the P writers. The tone is somewhat different: "Hagar bore a son *to Abram,* and *Abram* named *his* son, which Hagar bore, Ishmael."

It will be useful to back up at this point and outline a pattern in verses 4 through 6, the verses in this story that we will focus on from now on.

1. Hagar embarrasses Sarai in some way, looks down on her, belittles her.
2. Sarai becomes extremely exercised over this incident or this attitude.
3. Sarai takes out her anger first, not on Hagar, but on her seemingly relatively innocent husband, Abram. Her outburst seems, in context, not unprovoked perhaps, but overdone.[16]
4. Sarai's anger comes in the form of a curse or a threat: that this whole episode is on Abram's head and that Yahweh will judge her in the right and him in the wrong.
5. And finally, Abram responds rather easily that Sarai can do whatever she wants with Hagar.

We will not deal as fully with the E version in chapter 21, but it is worth pointing out that the stories are similar in plot and theme, and the pattern is much the same. For our purposes we start in verse 9, after we are told that Isaac has been born, has grown, and has been weaned. Verse 9 in the Hebrew reports simply that Sarah[17] saw Hagar's son playing. The Hebrew does not even say "playing with her own son Isaac"; it simply says "playing."[18] And once again Sarah takes a complaint to Abraham that seems to be relatively unprovoked in the text. She demands that he banish Hagar and Ishmael, because she is worried that Ishmael will share Isaac's inheritance.[19]

Although Abraham eventually does what Sarah asks, this time he at least shows some concern—not for Hagar, the text tells us, but for Ishmael who was, after all, his son, and his first-born at that. He does not this time calmly tell Sarah to do whatever she wants; he worries about his son's welfare. At this point, however, God steps in and tells Abraham to do what Sarah asks, and assures him that there will be no harm done: Isaac is to be his real heir, and besides, God will take care of Ishmael, too. "And I will make the son of the slave woman into a nation also," he says, "for he is your seed." This assurance is, of course, quite a step down for Hagar from the "promise to the patriarchs" in the last story. Here in chapter 21 the focus is Abraham, Isaac, and Ishmael, and her role is simply to have borne one of them to another.[20] Abraham then does as Sarah asks, but only after being assured that it is proper, and only after providing Hagar and Ishmael with food and water. To finish the story, the food and water run out, and God saves Hagar and Ishmael at the last minute. Again a well is involved in the story. Finally, we are told that Ishmael, who earlier had been left "the distance of a bowshot" away by his mother, grew up to be an expert archer.

Again, we have a pattern in this story very similar to the one in Genesis 16.

1. Hagar's son Ishmael does something that looks innocent to us, but that is apparently threatening to Sarah.
2. Sarah reacts with harshness and anger.
3. The person she makes her angry demands to is not Hagar or Ishmael, but Abraham.
4. This time Sarah does not curse or threaten, she simply demands. The verb is in the imperative: *gārēš*, "cast out" these two because their very existence here threatens the future wealth of my son.
5. Abraham does not easily go along with Sarah this time. This time his child is involved, not just a woman pregnant with his child, and for the sake of the child he needs God's assurance before he provides them with food and water and sends them away.

For decades now, scholars have discussed these stories in the context of certain laws and contracts from other ancient Near Eastern societies that deal with situations remarkably similar to the ones we have here in Genesis 16 and 21.[21] Any or all of these suggestions may be appropriate, but commentators have had to stretch what is actually in the text, or in the legal material, to find legal justifications for the actions the characters in these Hagar stories take.[22] There is, furthermore, a methodological problem with explaining mythic material by appeal to legal material, a problem that is exacerbated when the legal material is taken from very differently structured, even though neighboring, cultures. A different kind of suggestion for interpreting these stories in their ancient Near Eastern context is in order.

The two stories of Hagar are enough alike that we can propose that the southern (J) and northern (E) traditions have shaped a common story about Hagar being forced out of Sarah and Abraham's household. As is generally true of oral formulaic literature, there would have been several variations on the basic story, but that basic story can be outlined, given the evidence of the J and E sources in Genesis. The story would have begun with some innocent or at least only mildly incriminating incident, and then moved on to Sarah's overreaction, and her storming in to Abraham to make her demands. Abraham would acquiesce to Sarah's demands, but perhaps only after taking some precautions.

I have taken some pains to point out the incongruities in these stories, and to emphasize that other scholars also have felt a need to propose explanations from outside the biblical text for what seem to be odd turns in the stories as we have them. Scholars generally have looked to the emotional or legal spheres for the motivations of the characters, but there is a simpler explanation. These incongruities in the text perhaps can be explained by reference to a familiar ancient Near Eastern mythic scene, one that shows up in the Gilgamesh epic, in the epic of Aqhat from Ugarit, and even in a certain sense in a fragment of a Canaanite myth written in Hittite—that is, the scene of the young goddess, who, after being insulted in some way by a human or divine hero, storms into the king of the gods, usually her father, threatening him, and demanding that something outrageous be done to her antagonist. The wording, the plots, the characters are all different, but the basic pattern is the same, and furthermore they all contain some of the same incongruities.

The Akkadian version of this story is perhaps the most familiar because it occurs in the Gilgamesh epic. Gilgamesh and Enkidu have just finished off Huwawa in the cedar forest.[23] Gilgamesh has washed himself and put on new clothes, and he catches the goddess Ishtar's eye. She comes right to the point with him and suggests that he become her lover. Gilgamesh refuses, but does so in such an insulting way that he angers Ishtar. He questions her about her past lovers: a couple were killed or hurt, one she turned into a wolf, another she turned into a mole, and so forth. He points out to her that being her lover is not necessarily a good deal. Ishtar is so angered by this recital of her past sins that she immediately goes to her father Anu, the god of heaven, and complains.

There are some very difficult places in this text, but the gist of the story is that Ishtar reports that Gilgamesh has insulted her, whereupon Anu tells her that she deserved the insults. Then she asks Anu for the Bull of Heaven with which to kill Gilgamesh. She does not just ask for the Bull, though; she actually threatens Anu. If he does not give her the Bull of Heaven, she says she will smash something, perhaps the doors of the underworld, based on parallel passages in another Mesopotamian myth, usually called "The Descent of Ishtar."[24] She then threatens to bring the dead up to eat the living, to make the dead outnumber the living. Why is Ishtar voicing her threats to Anu when he is not to blame, and why a threat of such violence?

Anu is not completely cowed; before he gives her the Bull of Heaven, he makes sure that she has stored up enough food for the people on earth. Apparently releasing the Bull will mean famine in Uruk. Having been reassured that Uruk would not be hurt by this personal feud between Ishtar and Gilgamesh, Anu apparently simply gives her the Bull.

There are fewer incongruities in this story than in the Canaanite version I will discuss next. Ishtar's anger can hardly be said to be unprovoked, given that Gilgamesh went on and on about her many unfortunate lovers. Still, we might hope that that insulting performance would not be enough for Ishtar to open up the underworld to let the dead prey on all of the living. Yet that is what she threatens to do as an alternative to being allowed to punish Gilgamesh personally. So, while Gilgamesh might have predicted that he was getting himself into big trouble with his recitation, still Ishtar's reaction blows the whole episode out of proportion, and we come off thinking that she, like Sarah, is extremely spoiled. She cares little for anything but her own pride and her own desires, and she is bratty toward Anu, who is, after all, the king of heaven.

We also wonder why she is so vicious toward Anu, how and why she has the nerve to threaten him when we would assume he could crush her if he wanted. There is something of an explanation here: she may have been upset because Anu tells her she has no right to get angry since they were arguing, after all, and nothing Gilgamesh said was untrue.

Given that Anu thinks that way, we are a little surprised to see him hand over the Bull at the end of the scene, rather than telling her to go away and cool off. Still, this is a society where it was believed that the gods sent a flood to destroy all of humankind because we make too much noise, so perhaps we should not be surprised that the punishment hardly seems to fit the crime here.

The second use of this scene is from the Aqhat epic in Canaanite literature, discovered at the ancient city of Ugarit.[25] The young goddess Anat has asked our hero Aqhat for his bow and arrows, made for him by the god of craft, Kothar wa-Hassis, but Aqhat has refused. He has, furthermore, like Gilgamesh, gone out of his way to be insulting to her. "Bows are for soldiers. Do women hunt?" he says.[26]

Anat's response to all this is to threaten Aqhat, then to go to El, the head god and her father. First, she prostrates herself; then she apparently recounts the episode with Aqhat.[27] Next, she proceeds to threaten El. "I'll make your gray hair flow with blood, your gray beard with gore," she says to him. She goes on to suggest that El might find some help in Aqhat, that he might want to rely on the young human to save him from her anger. El's answer is remarkably calm and is an attempt to soothe her. He is first described as kind and compassionate, two of his usual epithets; then he says, "I know, daughter, that you can be likeable, but goddesses have no restraint. Leave now, since you will do whatever blasphemous thing you want anyway."

In the end she has Aqhat killed. At the risk of being repetitious, let me say once more that this is a story of a human male angering a young goddess. Her anger is to a certain extent understandable since he has insulted her, but to a certain extent it is excessive, since he had every right, we would think, not to give up his magical bow and arrows. Her response is, first of all, to threaten him, but then, to our surprise, to go to El her father, and threaten *him* with severe bodily harm. Why should she be angry with El? She implies he is on Aqhat's side. He responds to her threats in a surprising manner. He recognizes that she is overreacting, but he nevertheless gives her his permission to do, as the Ugaritic says, "whatever is in [her] heart." Actually it says "liver," but we would say "heart." And so she does.

I propose that the scene between Sarah and Abraham over Hagar (or Hagar and Ishmael) is in fact another instance of the use of a motif now familiar from ancient Near Eastern myth.[28] We have the exact pattern: First, in these myths, as in the Genesis narratives, there is some insult or humiliation, even though it may seem slight to us.

Second, the goddesses become exceptionally angry, like Sarai/Sarah in both Genesis episodes, angrier than seems reasonable given the context. This feature has already been treated at some length. Third, Ishtar goes to Anu, and Anat goes to El, just as in Genesis 16 Sarai's anger is directed first toward Abram. Even in Genesis 21 she goes first to Abraham and takes her complaints to him, rather than dealing with Ishmael directly. Fourth, in the myths the anger takes the form of a threat of violence. The fifth and last element in the mythic pattern is the calm acceptance by the patriarch god of the goddess's overreaction and his acquiescence to her plans, even though he realizes they are excessive. In Genesis 16 Abram acquiesces immediately, saying that the slave woman is, literally, in Sarai's hand, a phrase that sounds something like El's "whatever you desire, you will do" at Ugarit.

At this point I would like to make three further suggestions about the Genesis stories, based on a comparison of these narratives and the other mythic material.

1) Let me expand on the insult or humiliation element of the pattern in Genesis 21. Although I have argued that Hagar's sin in Genesis 16 was fairly minor and in context somewhat understandable, still it was *hubris* if anything, and her apparent motive was to raise herself up in relation to Sarai. In Gen. 21:9, Ishmael was playing—just playing in the Hebrew text, but I am not alone in worrying that there is a piece missing here.[29] The original story must have said that he did something to rile Sarah, to make her think or to remind her that he was also in a position to inherit, since that is her complaint to Abraham later in the episode.

Another possibility is that the text is complete as it stands, and we simply must read it correctly. The Hebrew word for what Ishmael was doing is *məṣaḥēq*. It is from the root *ṣḥq*, which is the same root from which Isaac's name is taken. One meaning of this root is "to laugh." It is used in that sense in the play on words when Isaac is named earlier in chapter 21: Sarah says in verse 6, "Elohim has made *laughter* for me; all who hear will *laugh* at me [or for me]." This also goes back to the report that Sarai *laughed* when she overheard Yahweh telling Abram in chapter 18 that she would become pregnant. Besides "to laugh," the root also means "to play" (e.g., RSV Exod. 32:6). In our story, it is important not just that the root means "to laugh" or "to play," but also that it has been pointed out to us again and again that it is the basis for Isaac's name. So when Ishmael is *məṣaḥēq*, he is not just laughing or playing—he is also

"Isaac-ing." And this is perhaps what Sarah is complaining about in the next verse, that she noticed Ishmael doing something to indicate he was just like Isaac, that they were equals, and it is this that threatens her so. If we are meant to read so much into the Hebrew word here, then we might say that Ishmael's "sin" also was *hubris,* striving for a social and familial position that was not his to take.

2) In the myths from Mesopotamia and Ugarit, the young goddesses threaten violence to the patriarch gods. This element of the pattern is not as clear in the Genesis stories, but there is one possible occurrence of it. In Gen. 16:5 the Hebrew for the phrase in question is *ḥămāsî ʿālêkā,* literally "my violence on you," "let my violence be on you, on your head," or "my violence is your responsibility," or "is against you." Any of those is possible. Commentators always have to play with the word "violence" here. Speiser translates "this outrage," and writes that it is "a strictly legal term," but he cites only Gen. 6:11 from the Bible and no extrabiblical texts where he thinks *ḥāmās* is used in a "strictly legal" sense.[30] Von Rad says the phrase means "my wrong is your responsibility," and continues: "the cry was the customary legal formula with which one appealed for legal protection," again with no citation of evidence of this "custom."[31] The "my" on the word is always assumed to be an objective genitive: the wrong done *to me,* but it could just as easily be a subjective genitive, the violence done *by me.* Likewise, the preposition *ʿal-* means "on, upon," and so the translation "on you," as in "it is on your head." But it could just as easily be translated "against." It is possible, then, that we have been misreading this phrase all along in searching for an idiomatic translation, and that in fact Sarai, like Anat and Ishtar in the myths we considered, is threatening violence: either violence that is against Abram or violence that is against Hagar but is, she claims, Abram's responsibility.

3) Finally, there may be a reflex in the biblical stories of another of the elements from the Gilgamesh pericope. In Genesis 21, Abraham pauses because what Sarah is asking is going to be harmful, perhaps even fatal, to his own son Ishmael; but after being assured that Ishmael will not die, and, significantly, after getting together provisions for Hagar and Ishmael, he also acquiesces to Sarah's potentially violent wish. The pausing and the concern with food (although not precisely for the victim of the anger) is also a feature of Anu's response to Ishtar, before he gives her the Bull of Heaven. Unfortunately, the Gilgamesh text is broken at this point and we do not know what Anu said to Ishtar as he gave in to her.

If it is convincing that there is a pattern in the Hagar doublet in Genesis that is the same as the pattern for these scenes in Gilgamesh and Aqhat (and perhaps the Hittite myth), just what does that mean? I will not argue that Sarah and Abraham were deities in some early form of the story, although their names certainly are suggestive.[32] In these Genesis stories, a human social situation of polygyny and an extended household, including all the tension such a situation normally means for the women of the household and indirectly for their children, is a perfectly understandable home for the interaction described. We need not suggest that this story was "originally" about deities and has been "brought down" to human level in Genesis; rather, we can simply say that several authors have made use of a typical or formulaic scene within several oral narrative traditions.[33]

Given our knowledge of other ancient Near Eastern narratives, what does the pattern suggest about the Genesis stories? This is a scene about the capricious use of superior power. Aqhat and Gilgamesh, as human beings, cannot compete with Anat or Ishtar, or El and Anu, and so are in a position of vulnerability, even to the point of being in danger for their lives. The young men in this scene had more than their share of nerve, to insult a powerful goddess, and yet one can imagine that the audience would have been cheering them along when they take on the goddess. These men are the protagonists of their stories, and they also are human like us and at the mercy of the whims of the gods, certainly a theme in Mesopotamian literature. Who would not like to shake a fist at those gods and hope to live through the experience? Even the patriarch gods, who are kind and compassionate like El, or worried about famine on earth as Anu is, are in the end indulgent of their own kind, even when that means undeserved suffering for the upstart human beings in the story.[34]

The force of this general story line is to make us sympathetic toward the underling and to emphasize the moral gap that often exists between the absolutely powerful and the rest of us. Beyond this, the stories point in slightly different directions.[35] We would think that challenging the gods or the more powerful would spell disaster for the challenger, and indeed Anu and Ishtar do unleash the Bull of Heaven, and Anat manages to have Aqhat killed in the Canaanite myth. Gilgamesh and Enkidu gain the upper hand for a moment; they slaughter the Bull of Heaven, but in the end Enkidu is cut down for his part in the affair. Enkidu is more expendable in the story than Gilgamesh, and he is the one to die. Perhaps we are to see this as part of one of the larger lessons of the Gilgamesh epic: that we are only human and that human life is not fair when compared to what the gods have set up for themselves, but that we simply cannot cross those boundaries between heaven and earth, we cannot dare to be divine or even to defeat the divine without expecting to suffer for it. So in the end, in the Gilgamesh version of our scene, the whole episode was the cause of eventual, predictable disaster for the less powerful human beings involved.

The use of the scene in the Aqhat epic is more difficult to spell out. The immediate result of Aqhat's standing up to Anat, of course, is that Anat has him killed. But from that point onward, the Aqhat story looks like a dying-and-rising god myth, even though Aqhat is human. After Aqhat's death, vegetation withers, Aqhat's sister mourns for him, his father finds his remains and buries them, and at the end of the part of the legend that is preserved, Aqhat's sister is trying to kill the cohort of Anat who actually killed Aqhat. It has often been assumed that if we had the end of the story, there would be a revival of Aqhat, and that revival would bring about renewed fertility in the fields. It has recently been argued, however, that this part of the Aqhat story that we are concerned with should be compared not to dying-and-rising god myths, but instead to a widespread pattern of a confrontation between a goddess of the hunt and a young hunter, which inevitably ends in the hunter's death.[36] Such a story is, in fact, *about* death. This makes more sense than the interpretation that sees Aqhat rise again, since he is a human being and not a deity in this story. So, following more recent commentators, here again our formulaic scene foreshadowed disaster for the less powerful human who challenged the absolute power of divinity.

Like the Gilgamesh and Aqhat narratives, where the less powerful person is actually the protagonist and the hero of the story, Hagar in Genesis 16 and Ishmael in Genesis 21 are the protagonists in these stories, and not Abraham as most commentators would have us believe. That is to say, one result of the use of this stock scene is to focus attention on the uppity underling; that character is traditionally the central one in the narratives where this scene is used.

This suggestion gains credence when we note that the rest of the story in each case does in fact emphasize Hagar and Ishmael. Hagar, as was pointed out earlier, receives an unexpected promise in Gen. 16:10 that her "seed" will be multiplied beyond number. Then there is the annunciation speech; and finally the narrative about the naming of Yahweh and of the well. This really does seem to be a story about Hagar, only incidentally tied into the Sarah and Abraham cycle. The doublet in Genesis 21 has as its protagonist not Hagar, but Ishmael. It is Ishmael who plays at being Isaac; it is Ishmael who represents the threat to Sarah; and in this chapter it is Ishmael, because he is Abraham's "seed," who is to be made into a nation. Again, we are confirmed in calling Ishmael the focus of the story, in that the end of this story, also in the desert, concerns Ishmael's later life. So our analysis gives the insight that the use of this scene signals from the beginning that we have here an interlude where Hagar or Ishmael is going to be at the center of things.

Further, some disaster in the life of the protagonist is foreshadowed by the use of this scene, although the disaster need not be absolute or terminal. As we have seen, Hagar and Ishmael actually survive after they leave Sarah and Abraham in each story. So the scene serves to bring tension to the narrative (because disaster is foreshadowed for the hero), a tension that is here resolved through divine intervention in an aggrandizement of the protagonist in each story.

Recognizing this scene as the equivalent of the ones in the myths also suggests that we are correct to feel sympathy for Hagar or Ishmael because this scene is at its heart a classic portrayal of the abuse of absolute power: the power that owners have over their slaves, or deities have over human beings. Our immediate reaction that there is something unfair and uncalled for in Sarah's response is appropriate.

The J writer has given a twist to the story, perhaps, by making the protagonist female. (We have already noticed that Hagar was given the promise typically given to a male.) We do not know how integral it was to our formulaic scene that the protagonist be male, even though in Gilgamesh and Aqhat and even in the broken Hittite version that is the case. But in the J narrative, we do not have a goddess trying to seduce a male and then abusing her power over him because of a sexual rejection. Rather, we have one human female abusing another, another who has all the problems a female slave would have: she has no power even over her own sexuality and no status in the household in which she lives. Whereas Gilgamesh and Aqhat could at least turn down Ishtar and Anat, Hagar did not have that choice in her story, as was discussed at the beginning of this paper. The point is that she, as a female and a slave, was even more powerless than her counterparts in the myths we have been discussing. The J narrative, then, is sensitive not just to power relationships, but also to gender relationships and is, further, not above making a female, a particularly powerless one at that, the hero of this story.[37] As was admitted earlier, we do not have a big enough sample to say that this is a startling innovation, but that is a possibility. The Israelite version of this story can be seen to make a point about the kind of power some human beings have over other human beings, and perhaps especially over a human being who is in the most vulnerable position possible: female, slave, and foreign.

NOTES

1. For instance, S. R. Driver, *The Book of Genesis* (London: Methuen & Co., 1904), 180, 210–13; Hermann Gunkel, *Genesis*, HAT, 1902 (Reprint: Göttingen: Vandenhoeck and Ruprecht, 1977), 184, 226–27; Gerhard von Rad, *Genesis*, rev. ed., trans. John H. Marks, from the 9th ed. of *Das Erste Buch Mose, Genesis*, 1953–56, OTL (Philadelphia: Westminster, 1972), 191; John Skinner, *Genesis*, ICC (Edinburgh: T. & T. Clark, 1962), 285, 321; E. A. Speiser, *Genesis*, AB (Garden City, NY: Doubleday, 1964), 116, 119, 153, 156–57. See Claus Westermann, *Genesis 12—36, A Commentary*, trans. John J. Scullion, from *Genesis*, vol. 2, BKAT, 1981 (Minneapolis: Augsburg, 1986), 237, 338, for a dissenting opinion.

2. See Gen. 30:3, where Rachel says the same thing to Jacob when she gives her slave Bilhah to him for the same reason.

3. Skinner, *Genesis*, 286.

4. Speiser, *Genesis*, 120.

5. Driver, *The Book of Genesis*, 181.

6. Von Rad, *Genesis*, 186.

7. Gunkel, *Genesis*, 185.

8. See, e.g., law #146 in the code of Hammurapi (*ANET* 172), where it is possible that such a provision is alluded to.

9. Gunkel, *Genesis*, 185.

10. Speiser, *Genesis*, 120.

11. Gunkel, *Genesis*, 192.

12. Von Rad, *Genesis*, 192.

13. Gunkel, *Genesis*, 186. He cites Prov. 25:24 and 27:15, as well as Sir. 25:16–26 and 26:6–7.

14. This incongruity was noticed by ancient authors as well, e.g., *Gen Rabbah* 45:5.

15. She calls him "a god of seeing," or perhaps "being seen," presumably because she is amazed that she has seen God and is still alive to tell about it. The Hebrew is very difficult here, however, and this interpretation of the name she gives Yahweh is actually simply suggested by the name given to the well in the next verse, "the well of the living one who sees me," or some such, where living and seeing are juxtaposed.

16. That is no doubt the reason the English translations make Hagar's attitude sound harsher than it really is in Hebrew: they are looking for a reason for Sarai's anger.

17. Her name has been changed from Sarai to Sarah since chapter 16, as has Abram's been changed to Abraham, in both cases probably just dialectal differences in the names.

18. The Septuagint and Vulgate have, in addition, "with her son." The Syriac and Targum Onkelos follow the MT.

19. We do not know what Ishmael's inheritance rights would actually have been. The evidence within the Hebrew Bible is contradictory, as is evidence from legal materials from other ancient Near Eastern societies. (Cf., e.g., laws 170 and 171 from the code of Hammurapi [*ANET*, 173] with laws 25 and 27 of the Lipit-Ishtar lawcode [*ANET*, 160].) It *is* clear in this case, however, that Sarah thinks that as long as Ishmael is in the household, he has some inheritance rights.

20. See Nancy Jay, "Sacrifice, Descent and the Patriarchs," *VT* 38 (1988): 60, for E's concern with a clearly patrilineal descent.

21. Gunkel, von Rad, and Speiser in their commentaries (all cited in n.1, above) particularly come to mind. These stories are often compared to various laws, especially in the code of Hammurapi (*ANET*, 163–80), where, e.g., a *nadītu* priestess supplies her husband with a slave woman for bearing children, and where a slave woman is punished for considering herself the equal of her mistress. See above, nn. 8 and 19, also.

22. Several recent works have been critical of the use of second-millennium legal material to justify motivations or to explain the setting of the stories of the Ancestors in Genesis. See especially John Van Seters, *Abraham in History and Tradition* (New Haven: Yale University, 1975), and Thomas L. Thompson, *The Historicity of the Patriarchal Narratives*, BZAW, 133 (Berlin: Walter de Gruyter, 1974).

23. See the translation by E. A. Speiser (with additions by A. K. Grayson) in *ANET*, 72–99, 503–7.

24. Also translated in *ANET*, 106–9.

25. See the translation in Michael D. Coogan, *Stories from Ancient Canaan* (Philadelphia: Westminster, 1978), 27–47.

26. Anat is a deity who absolutely delights in gore, so such a comment would be especially insulting. See, for instance, her behavior in the Baal myth: Coogan, *Stories*, 90–91.

27. There was a break in the text between her recounting of her exchange with Aqhat and her threatening El, so it is possible that he (like Anu in the Gilgamesh epic) took Aqhat's side against Anat and that those lines are simply lost to us.

28. It is possible that we have the same pattern in a very broken Hittite text, called "El, Ashertu and the Storm-god" in *ANET* (p. 519). This is a very fragmentary text, but again we have a goddess, this time Ashertu, the wife of the chief god Elkunirsha, complaining about an underling, this time

also divine (the storm god). Her complaint, although it is not preserved in the broken text, is presumably that she has been insulted by the storm god. We expect, based on the two other myths we have examined, that she has gone so far as to threaten Elkunirsha, but we have no evidence of that. After a break in the text, we see her seducing him instead. Elkunirsha's response is also by now predictable. "Do whatever you want to him. I'm placing him in your power," or something like that. For full treatments, see Heinrich Otten, "Kanaanäische Mythen aus Hattusa-Bogozköy," MDOG 85 (1953): 27–38, and "Ein ranaanäischer Mythus aus Boğazköy," MIO 1 (1953): 125–50; H. A. Hoffner, "The Elkunirsa Myth Reconsidered," *RHA* 76 (1965): 5–16.

29. Several commentators have seen the pun, and Gunkel: *Genesis,* 228, even believed that the passage developed out of the pun on Isaac's name. None, however, uses the pun to explain what Ishmael might have been doing, and why it would have angered Sarah so. (See also n. 18 above.)

30. Speiser, *Genesis,* 117.

31. Von Rad, *Genesis,* 192.

32. Sarai or Sarah could be a short form for a longer name like Ummu-šarra, "the (divine) mother is queen" (see Ignace J. Gelb, *Computer-Aided Analysis of Amorite*, AS 21 [Chicago: Oriental Institute, 1980], 73) and Abram or Abraham would be "the (divine) father is exalted," or in the alternate form Abi-ram, "my (divine) father is exalted" (cf. the PN Abiram in Num. 16 and elsewhere).

33. For references on type-scenes or formulaic scenes, Albert B. Lord, *The Singer of Tales* (Cambridge: Harvard University, 1960); Robert Alter, *The Art of Biblical Narrative* (New York: Basic Books, 1981); Robert C. Culley, *Studies in the Structure of Hebrew Narrative* (Philadelphia: Fortress; Missoula: Scholars, 1976); and the references in Ronald S. Hendel, *The Epic of the Patriarch* (Atlanta: Scholars, 1987), 13 n. 53.

34. I have been leaving out the Hittite myth because it is so fragmentary, but some of the same elements are there. The storm god, though not human, is nevertheless inferior to Ashertu and Elkunirsha, the *most* powerful gods, we assume. He is apparently seduced, without himself instigating the seduction at all, then gives in on the advice of Ashertu's husband, and then is apparently to be handed over to her wrath simply because he did what the more powerful deity advised him to do. So the powerful characters in that myth are also capricious and indulgent to a fault, and the less powerful is presumably harmed because of that.

35. Here we must rely only on Gilgamesh and Aqhat; we do not have the end of the Hittite myth.

36. See Hendel, *Epic,* 73–81, and references there.

37. On the differences between Pentateuchal sources' treatment of lineages see Jay, "Sacrifice, Descent and the Patriarchs."

3 THE WOMAN IN ANCIENT EXAMPLES OF THE POTIPHAR'S WIFE MOTIF, K2111

SUSAN TOWER HOLLIS

At least since the publication of Hermann Gunkel's *Das Märchen im Alten Testament* in 1917,[1] if not with the third edition of his *Genesis* in 1910,[2] there has been little question in biblical circles that various folktales, more accurately, folktale motifs, have counterparts within the Hebrew Bible. Perhaps the oldest known example came to light with the partial publication in 1852 of a translation of the ancient Egyptian "Tale of Two Brothers,"[3] the first episode of which closely parallels Gen. 39:7b–20, the story of Joseph and Potiphar's wife. Early designated "the oldest fairy tale in the world," the Egyptian narrative excited interest among Egyptologists, folklorists, and Biblicists alike,[4] albeit for different reasons. In fact, the episode of Joseph and Potiphar's wife has entered folklore studies in Stith Thompson's motif-index as Motif K2111, Potiphar's Wife.[5]

By definition, "[a] *motif* is the smallest element in a tale having a power to persist in tradition."[6] Thus, the inclusion of this episode in the motif-index speaks to its widespread presence in traditional narratives generally, not just in the ancient Near East. Examples of it abound in classical and other ancient sources.[7]

The earliest examples of this motif include Gen. 39:7b–20 and the Egyptian "Tale of Two Brothers." Certain aspects of Ishtar's invitation to Gilgamesh in Tablet VI of the Gilgamesh epic place it too among examples of the motif. An examination of each of these episodes in its total narrative context and within the contexts of the history, political ideology, and religion of its respective civilization shows that the destructive evil female character also plays a positive role in relation to the hero and his culture. Such a study can also lay the foundation for studies of the motif in later materials and of the perception of women in the cultures that are heir to these early narratives.

Although the motif-index presents the motif's structure very simply—"woman makes vain overtures to a man and then accuses him of attempting to force her,"[8]—an examination of each of the examples cited as well as most of those from the classical world and other ancient Near Eastern contexts shows that the motif is more complex than its outline suggests. At minimum, one must add that the man is unjustly punished for his alleged attempt to seduce the woman, for I know of no example of the motif that lacks this third part. When this part is included, the motif may also act as a tale type, that is, a tale in itself, for there exist some examples of it as an independent narrative, e.g., Child Ballad 291, "Child Owlet."[9] The tale type index provides no such type, however, and as Redford observed, "The motif was probably never used as a self-contained narrative, but rather as an introductory device with which to begin a composite tale . . . it is 'open-ended' with purpose."[10] If such a type had been identified, it might have been entitled the "Calumniating Wife/ Woman" or even the "Calumniated Male."[11]

A fuller description of the motif, following the outline suggested by Delbert Hillers,[12] shows the following general characteristics: a young, virile male is approached by an older female, human or deity, who is in a position of power or authority with relation to him and who attempts to seduce him. The male refuses her overtures. At this point the female exercises her power and falsely accuses him, generally bringing severe punishment upon him. This punishment is carried out by an authoritative male, usually a type of father figure, and effectively removes the supposed male seducer from action, sometimes even killing him. In many, though not all, examples, the hero ultimately returns in a kind of resurrection.

The usual discussions of this motif focus on the negative actions of the female toward the male, the latter being placed in an impossible situation in which whatever he does is wrong, a true catch-22. In such discussions the female is termed a negative figure and is presented only in that light. Athalya Brenner provides an excellent example of this approach when she characterizes Potiphar's wife as a negative temptress[13] and a negative foreign woman.[14] I will argue that it is also possible to view this "negative" woman as effecting a positive change when the narrative includes a return or resurrection. Indeed, when one views each of the three narratives in question in its appropriate historic and religious/ideological context, such a conclusion appears obvious and serves to highlight the ambiguous light in which women are generally viewed,[15] particularly in the ancient Near East.[16] Ironically, Brenner herself alludes to such a possibility when she notes that Joseph's banishment to jail "serves to elevate him to a position much higher than the one he occupied in his master's household."[17] Thus it can be said that the "evil" woman effects a positive transformation of the hero. Furthermore, in each of these narratives, the change carries ramifications that extend beyond the hero himself. In fact, in a recent discussion, J. Robin King suggested that the Joseph narrative is among a number of ancient Near Eastern texts that relate to a dynastic struggle in which the hero is exiled to later return home for "the good of all."[18] In other words, characteristically the episode can be said to lead to changes that affect not only the hero involved but also the community of which he is a part.

Both King's article and one by Carol Fontaine in *Semeia* 42[19] use analytical approaches to look at Joseph and Ishtar (though not specifically at the Gilgamesh episode in Tablet VI) respectively, which approach a fuller description of the actions than is present in the folkloric description of the motif, or even in Hillers's discussion. Because of his focus on emasculation, Hillers limits his analysis to the seduction episode alone, not placing it in its wider context. This wider placement is needed since, as was noted previously, the episode generally serves as an introductory episode. It is the action of the "negative" woman, be she human or deity, that gets the narrative underway and without which the necessary changes and transformations could not take place.

As I will attempt to show, each of the examples under consideration includes this problematic woman who initiates action by means of attempted seduction that leads to the transformation of the hero and the eventual profit of the community.[20] In a schematic form, the pattern takes the following shape:[21]

1. A male, usually young and without exception virile, coexists with an older female who is in a position of authority.
2. The female, attracted by the male, attempts to seduce him or offer him marriage.
3. The male refuses for reasons appropriate to his culture and place.
4. The female falsely accuses him of attempting to seduce her.
5. Severe punishment is inflicted, usually administered by another male in an authority position.

6. Exile, analogous to death, results.
7. An exilic challenge is issued.
8. An exilic battle takes place.
9. The outcome, victory, effects a return from exile to reconciliation.
10. The male assumes another status from that in which he was when exiled.
11. The community benefits.

Before continuing, I must note that this pattern, which could be classified as a tale type as previously noted, functions only as a guide; like any narrative pattern, it is a tool for analysis. As such it will appear in various forms, sometimes with parts missing and/or with significant variations on the presentation of the different parts. Further informing the present discussion is the general conception of the rite of passage as observed by van Gennep[22] and elaborated by Victor Turner.[23] Although the pattern also follows the general flow of folktale morphology as analyzed by Propp,[24] I have chosen not to analyze the present narratives in such a fashion, seeing such to be superfluous. A psychoanalytic approach also could be taken, but the speculativeness of such an analysis would add little to this discussion. Finally, due to space limitations, I will not be able to treat sections seven through eleven in detail and hope and trust that the reader will choose to work them out through her or his own reading.

Beginning with the episode from which the motif takes its name, even though chronologically its appearance in writing makes it the latest of the examples under consideration, one notes that the actual Potiphar's wife episode in Genesis 39 is one chapter in a longer narrative treating Joseph (Genesis 37—50), itself part of an even longer narrative about the Israelite patriarchs (Genesis 12—50). Some scholars consider it to be a later addition to this overall tale, probably having had an independent existence apart from the patriarchal saga,[25] while others take the view that it fits nicely into the whole.[26] In this chapter, Joseph, already exiled to Egypt due to the jealousy of his older half brothers, has been bought by Potiphar, an Egyptian official. In time, Potiphar gave Joseph full responsibility for running his household, in the exercise of which the Israelite had the full run of the house. Potiphar's wife thus had ample opportunity to see him and, finding him attractive [1],[27] made multiple efforts to get him to sleep with her [2]. Joseph repeatedly denied her, stating that to sleep with her would be wicked and a sin against God [3]. One day, however, during one of these attempts, she managed to grasp his garment, which he left behind in her hand as he fled. She then called the servants and claimed that he had attempted to seduce her [4]. On hearing his wife's tale, Potiphar had Joseph arrested and thrown into prison [5], effectively removing him from his position of status [6].[28]

The following chapters of Genesis relate that Joseph, who had had an earlier reputation for the successful interpretation of dreams (Genesis 40), subsequently used this talent to correctly interpret two dreams had by the king. They foretold a severe and lengthy famine, and Joseph advised the king to choose an able administrator to plan against it (Gen. 41:33–36). It was Joseph, freed from prison, whom the king eventually chose to fill the job, and from this position, the Israelite, graced by the presence of God, acted as the salvation for his own family when the famine-affected Israelites sought grain in Egypt (Gen. 41:37—46:7).[29]

Set in this fuller context, one can see that the apparently negative effect of the wife's accusation actually resulted in the positive elevation of Joseph into a position to help his own family, the descendants of Abraham, and thus ensured the continuation of the Israelite people. In addition, the episode, when set within the patriarchal stories, served as continued evidence to the Israelites that they were the chosen people of God.

While there is no question that Semitic peoples, including Israelites, lived in Egypt during the second millennium B.C.E. and that famines occasionally occurred, some lengthy, the actual historicity of the episode cannot be proved or disproved. Most significantly there is no attestation of Joseph or Potiphar in Egyptian sources, although the name *Pꜣ-di-pꜣ-Rꜥ* (*Pa-di-pa-Re*) is known from the late period.[30] Nevertheless, such an episode could have occurred, and the Israelites understood that it did, its features most likely being transmitted orally before being included within the Genesis narrative and written down.

It is important to observe that in its overall presentation, the Potiphar's wife episode constitutes the first part of a rite of passage according to the classic tripartite formulation of Arnold van Gennep.[31] Such a rite of passage, the effect of which is to move an individual from one social status to another within the community, consists of separation, transition, and incorporation. Considering the pattern I presented previously, parts one through five represent the separation, six through eight the transition, and nine through eleven, the incorporation.

In the Genesis narrative Joseph was separated from his secure, comfortable position in the Egyptian official's household by a powerful woman and sentenced to prison. His imprisonment is analogous to death: he was removed from the land of the living, that is normal existence, such as occurs in an initiatory rite of passage.[32] In the continuation of the biblical narrative, Joseph was eventually released from jail and placed in a position of responsibility over the whole land. Clearly, this sequence fits the initiatory rite of passage by means of which an individual is moved from one stratum of society to another.

Dating in written form to the last years of the thirteenth century B.C.E.,[33] the ancient Egyptian "Tale of Two Brothers," presents the earliest known exemplar of the motif. The tale's origin, however, is the subject of debate. Michael Astour has suggested that it and the biblical narrative represent an adaptation of a Phoenician topic,[34] while Donald Redford feels the two reflect "a common motif, eminating *[sic]* originally from Egyptian folklore, which became popular all over the Levant."[35] In fact both these ideas are speculative, for there is no documentary evidence for either concept. The most that one can state definitively on the issue is that the two narratives exhibit many similarities and that the motif reflects a common human situation.

The Egyptian tale[36] tells of two brothers, the older of whom is married and acting as a father to the younger. The family farms and herds cattle, typical of Egyptians in the Delta area, the northern section of the land. As the story opens, the annual inundation has receded enough to start the planting. At this point, the younger brother Bata, "a beautiful young man" (d'Orbiney 1,3) [1], who normally tends the cattle, assists his older brother Anubis with the planting, and when more seed is needed, Anubis sends Bata back to the barn to get it. Seeing him set out with the bags of extra seed, his sister-in-law, who was attracted to him and "desired to know him as a man" (d'Orbiney 3,6), asks him how much seed he is carrying. Apparently further impressed with his five-bag load, she then takes hold of him and invites him to sleep with her [2], asserting it will be good for him and promising him clothes. Bata becomes very angry, telling her that she and her husband are like parents to him [3] and directing her never to speak of the matter again, as also he will not. The implication is that such a suggestion is morally and ethically wrong. She apparently does not trust him and, like Potiphar's wife, reverses the action of the incident in relating it to her husband [4].[37] Anubis, in a rage, seeks to kill his brother, chasing him with a sharpened spear [5] until the god Pre-Harakhty, petitioned by Bata, rescues him by placing a river with crocodiles between the two men.

The next day, Bata tells Anubis what really happened. Following his report, the younger brother severs his phallus, throws it into the river where a fish eats it, and sets off for the Valley of the Pine, actually central Syria [6].[38] In this place, reminiscent of the necropolis areas of Egypt and thus representing not only exile[39] but also a kind of death of the young man,[40] Bata sets up housekeeping. In time he undergoes several more deaths at the hand of a divinely formed wife given him by the gods and is finally reborn from her as crown prince, eventually acceding to the throne of Egypt.

As was seen in the biblical narrative, in the Egyptian tale, the actions of a vindictive and scared woman effected the move of a young man from his safe and secure situation into a death and then a rebirth at a higher stratum of society. The female in each case acts in a negative fashion with ultimately positive results. In fact, the Egyptian variant of the motif shows such close parallels to the biblical narrative that some have suggested that the biblical version represents a borrowing of the older Egyptian tale[41] or at least the use of a narrative in general circulation.[42] In 1898, in an extreme example, Charles Moldenke suggested that Moses, the presumed author of the Joseph narrative, "certainly knew and studied the (Egyptian) story at the University of Heliopolis and must have had the wording in mind while writing the Joseph story."[43] Although this statement is laughable to the modern biblical scholar,[44] one cannot escape the parallels of the Egyptian and Hebrew expressions of the motif: both men are young and very attractive; both live in a household with an older woman and her husband; both are approached sexually by the older woman; both refuse the woman on moral grounds; both are falsely accused by her; both are separated from the household into exile/death; and both eventually return from their exile/death to rule over much more than had been theirs previously.

Like the Hebrew tale, the Egyptian tale points far beyond what is apparent, but an examination of its reflexes shows how very different a purpose it served in its cultural and religious/ideological context from that of the Genesis narrative. While the latter tells of humans and human behavior, the former relates the actions of gods, albeit gods living on earth like humans. Furthermore the gods involved, Bata and Anubis, relate clearly and directly to the mortuary realm. Anubis was the mortuary god par excellence in ancient Egypt, the deity responsible for the successful transition of the deceased to the next world, most especially the king. In this tale Anubis demonstrates every facet of this activity in his relation to Bata.[45] Bata, on the other hand, appears to have been an ancient underworld god[46] and represents the Horus/Osiris succession. Bata's loss of his phallus, eaten by a fish, a motif in the Osiris myth, followed by his death, rebirth, and accession to the throne, affirm the tale as a parallel. In both the narrative about Bata and that of Osiris, a woman is central to the transformation needed for the succession to the kingship, but the light in which she appears depends on which narrative dominates. In the traditional Osiris narrative,[47] the death of the hero, i.e., Osiris, occurs at the hands of a male, his brother Seth, and the revivification takes place by means of the ministrations of a female, his sister-wife Isis, who conceives the new king Horus by him. The female thus appears in a wholly positive light. In contrast, in the Bata narrative, Bata's death is effected through the actions of a female, not a male, while his rebirth to eventual kingship occurs normally by means of a female. Thus in this ancient example of the Potiphar's wife motif, one finds that the female figure is presented ambivalently, in both an obviously positive role as well as a clearly negative one.

It is quite possible that the Egyptian narrative contains reflexes of an actual historical situation. There exists debate among scholars over who succeeded Merneptah in the last years of the Nineteenth Dynasty when the tale was written down.[48] This modern confusion may itself reflect an ancient confusion over who was the next legitimate king, and it is possible that this tale could have served as a kind of legitimation by focusing on one particular aspect of succession: the transformation of Osiris into Horus through the wife-mother figure. In our tale, the dead Bata becomes his own father through his wife-mother, an ancient and venerable Egyptian concept for the proper succession to the kingship in which the woman's action makes her the means of transformation.[49]

With specific regard to the role of the women in the Egyptian tale, Leonard Lesko has suggested recently that this tale, along with the "Contendings of Horus and Seth" and the "Blinding of Truth by Falsehood," two other New Egyptian tales,[50] reflects not only the succession to kingship but also presents a negative attitude toward queens.[51] He argues that the strength of Hatshepsut and Eighteenth Dynasty queens in general led to the attempt by the Nineteenth Dynasty to avert any challenge to the throne by their surviving relations.[52] Though he has a point, I am inclined to think the issue is far more complex and refers even more strongly to the basic ambivalence toward women in all times and all places.

Finally, like the biblical narrative, the Egyptian tale presents a rite of passage with regard to its hero. The young shepherd, separated from his comfortable life through the destructive act of a mother figure, goes through a series of deaths, to be reborn into a higher stratum of society in true van Gennep fashion.

At first glance the Babylonian Gilgamesh narrative seems to be, and in fact is, very different from the other two tales, but on close examination, certain parallels become obvious. The sixth tablet of the Epic of Gilgamesh[53] tells of Ishtar's attempt to entice Gilgamesh into marriage [2], she being most attracted by his beauty and demeanor [1] following his triumphal return with Enkidu from killing Huwawa in the cedar forest. She tries to seduce him with goods, just as Anubis's wife did with Bata, promising him all kinds of good things, even total world power (VI:7–21). Gilgamesh, like Bata and Joseph, refuses the female's overtures [3]. At this point, the Babylonian tale clearly diverges from the other two, for Gilgamesh's refusal does not revolve around a moral or ethical issue. Rather, he gives a three-part answer, beginning by asking what he can bring to this relationship, the implicit answer being nothing, since she has it all. He then notes that her offers tend to be deceptive, and finally he observes that previously she has transformed and destroyed her lovers. Thus Gilgamesh refuses Ishtar's offer of marriage,[54] as a result of which Ishtar retaliates by setting the Bull of Heaven against him and his friend Enkidu [5].[55] Together they kill the Bull in order to prevent widespread annihilation and famine in the land, and as a final insult, Enkidu throws the severed thigh of the Bull before Ishtar (VI:161). These actions, rather than leading to Gilgamesh's death, ultimately result in the death of Enkidu, his alter-ego or soul mate [6]. Gilgamesh's devastation at his friend's death leads to his unsuccessful search for immortality and the ultimate realization of his own humanity.

Unlike the other two stories, one of which has human characters and the other of which has divine characters, the protagonists in the Babylonian epic combine the divine and human worlds: Ishtar is the powerful goddess of love and war; Gilgamesh, king of Uruk, is understood to be two-thirds god and one-third man; and Enkidu is a man created by the gods from clay. Furthermore, instead of a servant-type person like Joseph and Bata, Gilgamesh, who is quite impressed with himself, begins as a king—he can move no higher—and he seems to deliberately offend the goddess with his insulting response to her invitation (VI:44–79). I would note that, like Joseph and Bata, no matter what the answer that Gilgamesh might give, he would suffer from it—the catch-22. Similarly Ishtar's reaction is one of intense anger, but she, unlike the other females, takes direct action herself in procuring and then setting the Bull of Heaven against Gilgamesh and Enkidu. Finally the death here is not that of the hero per se, as in the other narratives, but that of his intimate. When the results are examined closely, however, one sees that Gilgamesh's devastation at Enkidu's death and his subsequent actions represent a death to his old ways, arrogant at best and destructive at worst, and the humanization of his view of himself. Thus Ishtar's negative action effects a positive change and, as in the Egyptian and biblical examples, represents the separation part of a rite of passage, albeit showing an internal rather than an external transformation.

Like the other two narratives, the Epic of Gilgamesh can and should be placed in the context of its civilization and history for the fullest possible understanding. Significantly its hero was an actual king, a historical figure who ruled in the second quarter of the third millennium B.C.E. and who received cult as King of the Netherworld as early as the twenty-fourth century.[56] By the end of this period, he appeared as the hero in a cycle of tales in Sumerian, some of which were included in the longer epic that began to appear in the Old Babylonian Period, around the eighteenth century. Gilgamesh clearly was one who was remembered and honored by the Mesopotamians throughout their history, to wit the existence and continued revisions of this very epic.[57]

The literary history of the attempted seduction episode is problematic. Because the epic itself underwent a long period of development and the finds of the cuneiform tablets containing it have been irregular and sporadic, it is virtually impossible to know the date when the episode under scrutiny appeared and was integrated into it. Possibly the scene originated in the Akkadian versions,[58] but it is also possible that the lack of its evidence in the older versions is due to chance.[59] What is clear is that at the point when the seduction scene becomes a definite part of the whole, it is integral to Gilgamesh's appreciation of his true earthly kingship, the assumption of his proper status as a human being— and this status is effected through the powerful and apparently destructive female.[60]

Before concluding, it is important to note that the differences between Tablet VI of the Gilgamesh epic on the one hand and the biblical and Egyptian narratives (with their other ancient analogues) on the other, make it a dubious proposition to include the Babylonian episode under the Potiphar's wife motif. Indeed, I think it should not be done save from the perspective that in Tablet VI, one finds the basic pattern:

a virile man, an attempted seduction, and a death, the whole effecting a positive transformation of the hero through the actions of a female who is presented in negative form.

Thus in conclusion, in each of these narratives the male finds himself in a typical no-win or catch-22 situation: He will be destroyed if he accepts the proposition and he will be destroyed if he does not accept it. He risks virtual death no matter what his choice, and the powerful female puts him in this position. In many respects, her actions closely resemble those of the evil stepmother of so many folktales, again seen as an evil figure. Yet when each of these ancient episodes is followed to its conclusion, the male returns in a transformed state, at a new stratum of society in the case of Joseph and Bata and with a new knowledge and understanding of himself in the case of Gilgamesh. Each thus forms the first part of a typical tripartite rite of passage. In each of the three cases, the narrative relates to the beliefs and ideologies of its culture, and each also touches in some way on its culture's history. Thus one can see that the apparently destructive female in fact effects long-term positive results that affect not only her male target but also his people. Clearly the Potiphar's wife motif encloses more substance than is at first apparent, and this knowledge may challenge commentators to look more deeply into other apparently negative or destructive women.

NOTES

1. Recently translated into English: Hermann Gunkel, *The Folktale in the Old Testament* (Sheffield: Almond, 1987). For this history, see Gunkel's introduction.

2. Gunkel, *The Folktale,* 14.

3. The tale, written in hieratic in the New Egyptian dialect, is found in the Papyrus d'Orbiney, BM 10183. For a translation of the tale, see one of the following: *ANET*[3], 23–25; Miriam Lichtheim, *Ancient Egyptian Literature* vol. 2 (Berkeley: University of California, 1976), 200–211; William Kelly Simpson, *The Literature of Ancient Egypt* (New Haven: Yale University, 1972), 92–107; Adolf Erman, *The Ancient Egyptians: A Sourcebook of their Writings* (New York: Harper Torchbooks, 1966), 150–61.

4. Cf. Susan Tower Hollis, "The New Egyptian 'Tale of Two Brothers': A Mythological, Religious, Literary, and Historico-Political Study of the Papyrus d'Orbiney" (Ph.D. diss., Harvard University, 1982), chap. 1 for a history of the scholarship and related issues.

5. Stith Thompson, *Motif-Index of Folk-Literature* (Bloomington, Ind.: Indiana University, 1955–58), 4:471.

6. Stith Thompson, *The Folktale* (Berkeley: University of California, 1977 [1946]), 415.

7. Cf. John D. Yohannan, *Joseph and Potiphar's Wife in World Literature: An Anthology of the Story of the Chaste Youth and the Lustful Stepmother* (New York: New Directions, 1968); Theodor H. Gaster, *Myth, Legend, and Custom in the Old Testament* (New York: Harper & Row, 1969), 217–18; Emma Brunner-Traut, "Papyrus d'Orbiney," *Lexikon der Ägyptologie* (Wiesbaden: Otto Harrassowitz, 1982), vol. 4, col. 703, n.19; and Delbert R. Hillers, "The Bow of Aqhat: The Meaning of a Mythological Theme," in *Orient and Occident: Essays Presented to Cyrus H. Gordon on the Occasion of his Sixty-fifth Birthday,* ed. Harry A. Hoffner, AOAT 22 (Neukirchen-Vluyn: Neukirchener, 1973), 74–75, for examples and sources.

8. Thompson, *Motif-Index,* 4:471.

9. Cf. Francis James Child, *English and Scottish Ballads* (New York: Dover, 1965), 5:156–57.

10. Donald B. Redford, *A Study of the Biblical Story of Joseph (Genesis 37—50),* VTSup 20 (Leiden: Brill, 1970), 93.

11. On the gender biases of the two indices, see Torborg Lundell, "Gender-Related Biases in the Type and Motif Indexes of Aarne and Thompson" in *Fairy Tales and Society,* ed. Ruth Bottigheimer (Philadelphia: University of Pennsylvania, 1986), 151–63.

12. Hillers, "The Bow of Aqhat," 76–78.

13. Athalya Brenner, *The Israelite Woman: Social Role and Literary Type in Biblical Narrative* (Sheffield: *JSOT,* 1985), 111. See also James G. Williams, *Women Recounted: Narrative Thinking and the God of Israel*, Bible and Literature Series, 6 (Sheffield: Almond), 88–92, 107–9.

14. Brenner, *The Israelite Woman,* 121.

15. Cf. Erich Neumann, *The Great Mother: An Analysis of the Archetype,* 2d ed., Bollingen Series XLVII (Princeton: Princeton University, 1963).

16. Carol Fontaine, "The Deceptive Goddess in Ancient Near Eastern Myth: Inanna and Inaraš," *Semeia* 42 (1988): 97.

17. Brenner, *The Israelite Woman,* 121.

18. J. Robin King, "The Joseph Story and Divine Politics," *JBL* 106 (1987): 577–78.

19. See note 16 above.

20. Although I have not studied in detail each of the examples of the motif cited in Yohannan, Gaster, and Hillers, on a casual reading of them, the ultimate return of the hero to the benefit of his community is not generally a feature as it will be shown to be for the narratives discussed in this paper. My sense is that in the later translation and use of the motif, it may have served a different function in the narrative from what it does in the oldest sources, which are those with which we are dealing.

21. Cf. Hillers, "The Bow of Aqhat," 76–78; King, "The Joseph Story," 580–85.

22. Arnold van Gennep, *The Rites of Passage* (Chicago: University of Chicago, 1960).

23. Victor Turner, *The Forest of Symbols: Aspects of Ndembu Ritual* (Ithaca, N.Y.: Cornell University, 1967).

24. Vladimir Propp, *Morphology of the Folktale* (Austin, Tex.: University of Texas, 1968).

25. Redford, *A Study*, 183; W. Lee Humphreys, *Joseph and His Family: A Literary Study* (Columbia, S.C.: University of South Carolina, 1988), 204.

26. G. Coats, *From Canaan to Egypt: Structural and Theological Context for the Joseph Story*, CBQMS 4 (Washington, D.C.: Catholic Biblical Association, 1976), 28–29.

27. The numbers in brackets designate the part of the pattern to which the description refers.

28. Normally death, not prison, was the sentence for adultery in Egypt, and few commentators on Genesis 39 fail to mention this fact. Von Rad, for instance, feels that the narrator, if questioned, would have explained the situation simply by saying, "Yahweh was with Joseph" (Gerhard von Rad, *Genesis: A Commentary*, 3d rev. ed., OTL [London: SCM, 1972], 367), and Speiser points out that one should not "overlook the simple point that had Joseph been subjected to the [normal] fate . . . the Joseph story itself would have died an untimely death" (E. A. Speiser, *Genesis: A New Translation with Introduction and Commentary*, 3d ed., AB 1, [Garden City, N.Y.: Doubleday 1987], 304).

29. See Louis Ginzberg, *The Legends of the Jews*, vol. 2 (Philadelphia: The Jewish Publication Society, 1910), 39–58 for a legendary account of the Joseph and Potiphar's wife episode; and Thomas Mann, *Joseph and His Brothers* (New York: Knopf, 1971), 667–840, for a novelistic rendering of the episode, perhaps reflecting the legendary account.

30. Joseph Vergote, *Joseph in Égypte: Genèse Chap. 37–50 à la lumière des études égyptologiques rëcentes* (Louvain-Leuven: Publications Universitaires/ Institutuut voor Oriëntalisme, 1959), 146–48. Cf. also Hermann Ranke, *Die ägyptische Personennamen*, vol. 1 (Glückstadt: J. J. Augustin, 1935), 123:11; and Adolf Erman and Hermann Grapow, *Wörterbuch der ägyptischen Sprache*, vol. 1 (Leipzig: J. C. Hinrichs'sche, 1925), 492:6.

31. See note 22 above.

32. For a fine discussion of transition in terms of symbolic death, see Turner, *Forest of Symbols*, chap. 4, 93–111.

33. Cf. Brunner-Traut, "Papyrus d'Orbiney," col. 697, and n.2, col. 703, for dating. My own study of the tale (see n. 4 above) suggests it had a specific purpose in the time and space in which it was written down, though features in it, notably the terms for the wife, can be seen to reflect an earlier period (cf. Lise Manniche, "The Wife of Bata," *Göttinger Miszellen* 18 [1975]: 33–38).

34. Michael Astour, *Hellenosemitica: An Ethnic and Cultural Study in West Semitic Impact on Mycenaean Greece*, (Leiden: Brill, 1965), 258.

35. Redford, *A Study*, 93.

36. For a translation of the tale, see one of the sources in n. 3 above.

37. Vergote notes that the respective reactions of Potiphar's wife and Anubis's wife "were the only means of defense of these women who knew only too well what awaited them if their husbands learned the truth" (Vergote, *Joseph in Égypte,* 23). Clearly neither woman trusted the object of her desire despite the reassurance by each young man that he would say nothing.

38. Hollis, "The New Egyptian 'Tale of Two Brothers,'" 180.

39. The end of the Middle Egyptian tale about Sinuhe, for which see *ANET*[3], 18–22; Lichtheim, *Ancient Egyptian Literature,* vol. 1, 222–35; Simpson, *Literature,* 57–74; or Erman, *The Ancient Egyptians,* 14–29, expresses very well the Egyptian feeling about being away from his/her land in exile.

40. Hollis, "The New Egyptian 'Tale of Two Brothers,'" 203–4.

41. See Redford, *A Study,* 93, n. 1; and Claus Westermann, *Genesis: A Practical Commentary* (Grand Rapids: Eerdmans, 1987), 273.

42. Coats, *From Egypt to Canaan,* 30, cf. also 81.

43. Hollis, "The New Egyptian 'Tale of Two Brothers,'" 25.

44. Westermann, *Genesis,* 273 states that "[t]he author of the Joseph story made the Egyptian narrative (which has a different conclusion) into an episode in his story, with appropriate changes."

45. Susan Tower Hollis, "Anubis' Mortuary Functions in the 'Tale of Two Brothers'" (Paper presented at the Annual Meeting, American Research Center in Egypt, Washington, D.C., 18 April 1986).

46. Hollis, "The New Egyptian 'Tale of Two Brothers,'" 92–101.

47. Although references to this myth appear in all periods of Egyptian history, no complete rendition of it dates earlier than that of Plutarch about 120 C.E. For a translation and commentary, see J. Gwyn Griffiths, *Plutarch's De Iside et Osiride* (Cardiff: University of Wales, 1970), chaps. 12–20.

48. David O'Connor ("New Kingdom and Third Intermediate Period, 1552–664 B.C." in *Ancient Egypt: A Social History,* eds. B. G. Trigger, B. J. Kemp, D. O'Connor, and A. B. Lloyd [Cambridge: Cambridge University, 1983], 223) states that Amenmesses usurped Seti II's position as king for a time during the latter's reign, while K. A. Kitchen (*Pharaoh Triumphant: The Life and Times of Ramesses II* [Mississauga, Canada: Benben, 1982], 216) suggests that Amenmesses, probably a lesser son, ruled for a very short time before Seti II, the crown prince (see the colophon to the papyrus), acceded to the throne.

49. Cf. Neumann, *The Great Mother,* especially chap. 15, though Neumann's emphasis differs somewhat from that of the present paper. For a discussion of the wife-mother figure, see Helmut Jacobsohn, *Die dogmatische Stellung des Königs in der Theologie der alten Ägypter,* Äg. For. 8 (Glückstadt: J. J. Augustin, 1939), especially pp. 13–22, and also his "Kamutef," *Lexikon der Ägyptologie,* vol. 3 (1978), cols. 308–9.

50. The "New Egyptian" dialect represents the vernacular of Dynasties XVIII–XXIV in which letters and business documents as well as some literary works, such as these, were written.

51. Leonard Lesko, "Three Late Egyptian Stories Reconsidered" in *Egyptological Studies in Honor of Richard A. Parker. Presented on the Occasion of His 78th Birthday, December 10, 1983,* ed. Leonard Lesko (Providence: Brown University, 1986), 101.

52. Lesko, "Three Late Egyptian Stories Reconsidered," 102. See also Barbara S. Lesko, "Women of Egypt and the Ancient Near East" in *Becoming Visible: Women in European History,* 2d ed., eds. Renate Bridenthal, Claudia Koonz, Susan Stuard (Boston: Houghton Mifflin, 1987), 52. For another more popularized discussion of women in ancient Egypt, see B. S. Lesko, *The Remarkable Women of Ancient Egypt,* 2d rev. ed. (Providence: B. C. Scribe, 1987). For a discussion of queens and the mythology surrounding them, see Lana Troy, *Patterns of Queenship in Ancient Egyptian Myth and History,* BOREAS 14 (Uppsala, 1986).

53. For translations of this tablet, see *ANET*[3], 83–85 and 505; or John Gardiner and John Maier, *Gilgamesh: Translated from the Sîn-Leqi-Unninni Version* (New York: Vintage, 1984), 148–65. The entire epic may be read in either of these sources.

54. For an interesting discussion and a different interpretation of this tablet, see Tzvi Abusch's recent discussion, "Ishtar's Proposal and Gilgamesh's Refusal: An Interpretation of *The Gilgamesh Epic,* Tablet 6, Line 1–79," (*HR* 26 [1976]: 143–87) in which he argues that Ishtar invited Gilgamesh to marry her and become King of the Netherworld, the role that Gilgamesh eventually filled and for which he was first known. As Joan Goodnick Westenholz has pointed out, however (personal conversation), Ishtar was not an underworld deity for Gilgamesh to marry. I would note that there are those who see Ereshkigal, the Queen of the Underworld, as Ishtar's "neglected side" or dark side (cf. Diane Wolkstein in Diane Wolkstein and Samuel Noah Kramer, *Inanna, Queen of Heaven* [New York: Harper & Row, 1983], 155–63).

55. Note that section 4 of the pattern does not occur in Gilgamesh.

56. Thorkild Jacobsen, *The Treasures of Darkness: A History of Mesopotamian Religion* (New Haven: Yale University, 1976), 209–11.

57. Cf. Jeffrey H. Tigay, *The Evolution of the Gilgamesh Epic* (Philadelphia: University of Pennsylvania, 1982).

58. Tigay, *The Evolution,* 70.

59. Tigay, *The Evolution,* 122.

60. It is possible to see the narrative as an affirmation of the nondivinity of Akkadian kingship. Near the end of the third millennium, kings in Mesopotamia tended to consider themselves divine as is evidenced by the inclusion of the divine determinative with their names, and William L. Moran has proposed that this epic dealt a death blow to the concept by affirming that kings were human, not divine (William L. Moran, Lectures in Folklore and Mythology 109, "The Traditional Epic," 28 February and 1 March 1984).

4 EROTICISM AND DEATH IN THE TALE OF JAEL

SUSAN NIDITCH

Associations between eroticism and death and between sex and violence are old and intimate ones reverberating in the various cultural artifacts of western and nonwestern tradition, reflecting and, in turn, affecting the essential nature of human self-consciousness. Eroticism or the sex act itself may be equated with dying as in Song of Songs 8:6,[1] or slaughter with sexuality as in the battle imagery of the ancient Greeks explored brilliantly by Emily Vermeule.[2] Death itself may be imagined as a gay seducer, a male lover, as in the "harlequin" tradition explored psychoanalytically by David C. McClelland[3] while other equally powerful traditions portray erotically charged and sexually potent goddesses as violent warriors who wade through the bodies of slain soldiers,[4] who wreak vengeance on the enemies of their beloved,[5] or who threaten the love objects themselves even while making offers of immortality and bliss.[6] Attraction and revulsion, longing and fear—images of love and death.

It is beyond the scope of this essay to explore the origins of this association. Freud's speculations on the forces of Eros and Thanatos, the loving, receiving and the aggressive, destructive sides of ourselves, remain relevant,[7] as do Jungian suggestions about competing sides of the unconscious. Erich Neumann, for example, suggests that the archetype of the mother has at a ground level two competing images of the feminine: the devouring, constricting womb who suffocates and kills, arresting development, and the nurturing, fertile, protecting originator and sustainer of life.[8] For Neumann these are the two sides of the unconscious, which is identified with the feminine. The conscious mind for him is to be identified with male symbolism in one western version of the yin/yang.[9]

Closer to my own field, Delbert Hillers has been influenced by Neumann in his intriguing study of the bow of Aqhat.[10] The Canaanite tale tells of a king's longing for a son to be born to him. The gods finally answer Daniel's prayers, and the divine artisan Kothar gives the beautiful young man a fine bow and arrows as a gift. The bow—a magic, special weapon to be compared with Achilles' shield and the weapons prepared by Kothar for Baal—is coveted by the goddess Anat, who has Aqhat slain when he refuses her offer of immortality for the bow.

Noting that the bow has explicitly sexual resonances elsewhere in ancient Near Eastern literature as a symbol of masculinity,[11] and drawing fine parallels with tales of Adonis, Attis, Gilgamesh, and other handsome manly lads who suffer at the hands of a goddess who holds or desires sexual power over them, Hillers suggests that Anat threatens Aqhat sexually. Aqhat's "bow" is his masculinity.[12] Influenced by Erich Neumann's studies of the Great Mother, Hillers writes that "the mythological theme springs from man's experience of woman as attractive, yet threatening to his sexuality and his life."[13] The end of the Aqhat tale, which exists only in fragmentary form, describes Paghat, Aqhat's sister, acting in the Anat role to Baal, dressing as a male warrior to avenge the death of her brother (CTA 19 iv 206). In another line (208) she appears to cover her armor and assumed maleness with the finery and make-up of an alluring woman presenting the intriguing liminal portrait of a woman dressed as a man dressed as a woman, a symbolization of other related aspects of her duality as seducer and killer, loving sister and merciless assassin. Hillers, again working from Neumann, suggests that Anat and Paghat are two models of womanhood, two archetypal levels of the feminine: the frightful killer-womb earth mother—the terrible aspect of archetypal feminine, a symbolization of the unconscious; and the loyal, loving sister—the anima, who occupies an archetypal level closer to the ego and the conscious mind. As articulated in Neumann's earlier work, the theory suggests that whereas the woman child identifies with her mother and the mother archetype, maturing to integrate the archetypal feminine within her, the male child never can become his mother and risks remaining in a love/fear relationship with all women; he is able to overcome his fear with the help of the solid and more fully positive image of the anima, the sister and/or wife.[14]

It might well be suggested that this theory of human development is based on outmoded notions of male and female psychology and child development. The relationship between the archetypal symbols explored by Neumann and actual human development is problematical. Neumann himself nuances his discussion of the relation of the archetypes to the psychology of real men and women in his later work, *The Great Mother.*[15] Here he more clearly emphasizes that the unconscious, reflected in a dual feminine archetype, is fundamental to the psyches of men and women; consciousness is male in the psyches of both genders. Neumann thus attempts more strongly to "depersonalize" his archetypes. The woman develops her "male" side too as she matures into consciousness. Of course such identifications between the unconscious and the feminine, and consciousness and the masculine, and suggestions that the female anima is not a star but a supporting actress in the drama of human development, make one, as a woman, wince. One senses that Neumann is ultimately concerned with men's development and cannot see women apart from their roles in men's lives, a theme to which we will return as we explore tales of Jael. Hillers himself might be faulted for too strongly dichotomizing the sister image from that of the devouring mother, and the terrible mother from the good mother. In *The Great Mother,* Neumann pays more attention to portrayals that share traits of various aspects of "the feminine," coming closer to describing what Lévi-Strauss would suggest is a mediating portrait, partaking of both sides of a dichotomy. Aqhat's loving sister is, after all, Yatpan's killer-seductress.[16] As Ronald Hendel notes, the tale of Aqhat contains many dynamics or dichotomies: male and female, hunter and hunted, appearance and disguise, sex and death.[17] It is against this interplay of themes that we must also appreciate the figure of Jael in Judges 4, 5 and more specifically the exquisite artistry of Judg. 5:27.

Other scholars such as J. Glenn Taylor have drawn comparisons between Jael, assassin of Sisera, and ancient Near Eastern goddesses, in Taylor's case the Canaanite Athtart.[18] Jael, however, is not derivative or modeled after ancient Near Eastern goddesses, but like such figures is heroic and liminal, a warrior and seducer, alluring and dangerous, nurturing and bloodthirsty.

In his study of the prose account of Jael, Robert Alter beautifully traces nuances of mother, lover, and killer.[19] Jael offers to the vulnerable, fleeing Sisera, food, choice food, protection, and warmth—a rug under which to hide and sleep. She comes to him secretly (*bl'ṭ*) (Judg. 4:21). The coming verb is often used in sexual entry contexts (see BDB *bw'*, "e"); the *l'ṭ* word evokes mystery, even romance. So Ruth comes to

Boaz *blṭ* (Ruth 3:7). Jael comes to Sisera and kills. Alter is strangely anxious to contrast the portrait of Judges 4, rich in images of sex and death, with the poetic account of Judges 5 in which he sees the dominant image to be Jael as strong hammerer.[20] Themes of seductress are not for him found in Judges 5, and yet he does acknowledge sexual nuances of Sisera's position at death, describing the "image of the Canaanite general felled by the hand of a woman, lying shattered between her legs in a hideous parody of soldierly assault on the women of a defeated foe."[21] Jael is "standing over the body of Sisera, whose death throes between her legs—he's kneeling then prostrate—may be perhaps, an ironic glance at the time-honored martial custom of rape."[22]

Like Mordecai Levine some years before him, Alter notices the ironic connection between Sisera's position "between Jael's legs," the legs being a euphemism for sexual organs (so the afterbirth emerges), and his mother's hopes for women booty—called *raḥam raḥămātayim* whose literal, root meaning is "womb."[23] Levine, somewhat less eloquently than Alter, sees in this "montage" the ironic juxtaposing of the warrior's loyal mother's thoughts and his assassin's actions, a veritable polemic against rape. The montage of mother and assassin contributes further to the counterpoint between beloved and assassin, genuine loyalty and false loyalty, feigned affection and nurturing care. Images of love and battle, of victor and vanquished, vie with one another creating tension, discomfort, and uncertainty. Who is the winner, who is the loser, and where is the reader's sympathy? Powerful emotions clash uncomfortably, creating exquisite uncertainty and tension. These themes and images are as strongly found in Judges 5 as in Judges 4. The same offer of best nourishment is coupled with an "aggressively phallic" assassination. The "driving through of the tent peg" into the ground at 4:21[24] is matched in 5:26 by the image of reaching for peg and hammer and "piercing his temple," *ḥlp* being a motion verb literally meaning "to pass through." The poetry is necessarily more telegraphic than prose, but the short-hand impressionistic imagery presents the same "myth" as in Judges 4. The impression, if anything, is more instantaneous than in the slower unrolling of the prose account. Themes of sex and violence, death and seduction are particularly strong in v. 27.

Alter's translation is by far the best and most sexually evocative of all I have seen, so much stronger than other recent examples.

Alter:

Between her legs he kneeled, fell, lay
between her legs he kneeled and fell
where he kneeled, he fell, destroyed[25]

Lindars:

He sank, he fell, he lay still at her feet;
at her feet he sank, he fell
where he sank, there he fell dead[26]

Lindars desexualizes the passage completely. So too Michael Coogan:

Between her feet he collapsed, he fell, he lay;
between her feet he collapsed, he fell
in the place he collapsed, there he fell in ruins[27]

Boling:

At her feet he slumped. He fell. He sprawled.
At her feet he slumped. He fell
At the place where he slumped, there he fell. Slain.[28]

Soggin:

Between her feet he sank, he fell, he lay;
there where he was struck, fallen, dead.[29]

Judges 5:27 evokes a powerful scene of eroticism and death. Its language is charged with sexuality, sexual submission intertwined, doubling with language of defeat and death, associations found elsewhere in Scripture, but nowhere as exquisitely or compactly.[30] My own translation and exegesis is as follows:

Between her legs he knelt, he fell, he lay
Between her legs he knelt, he fell
Where he knelt, there he fell, despoiled.

bên raglêhā, "BETWEEN HER FEET"

Translations "at her feet, between her feet" obscure the visceral sexual quality of the imagery. Like the hand, *yād*, the *raglayim*, "legs" or "feet," are used in Scripture as euphemisms for male or female organs. *Śaʿar hāraglāyim* in Isa. 7:20 refers to pubic hair. Urination is referred to as "pouring out his *raglāyw* (Judg. 3:24; 1 Sam. 24:3). As noted above, in a birthing context, the afterbirth comes out from between her "legs" (Deut. 28:57). The phrase "between her legs" can be erotic enough even without specific reference to private parts as in Ezek. 16:25, one of the classic passages in which the unfaithful Israel is described as a harlot: "and you parted your legs wide."

kāraʿ nāpal, "HE KNELT, HE FELL"

The kneeling word has connotations of defeat and death of one's enemies in Ps. 20:9 where it is paired with *nāpal* as in Judg. 5:27.

They will kneel and fall
But we will rise and be restored.

It also is used in a visceral sexual context at Job 31:10 paired with another sexual image, which is not always recognized as such.

My wife will "grind" for another
Upon her will kneel others.

Some suggest that the wife's grinding or milling for others is a sign of her humiliation and servitude. Kittel's suggestion of "sensu obscoeno" like that of the Rabbis (b.Soṭa 10a) and Marvin Pope[31] is more likely the case as confirmed by Isa. 47:2.

Take millstones and grind flour
Remove your veil
Strip off (your) skirt
Reveal the thigh
Pass through rivers
Your nakedness will be revealed
Also will your shame be seen.

Babylon, the virgin, becoming the unhappy spoils of war, is to be sexually humiliated and abused. Thus kneeling and grinding create strongly sexual imagery in Job as kneeling between her legs in our Judges passage produces a synonymous image of eroticism and death. The image is further strengthened by the next verb in the chain of Judg. 5:27 *nāpal.* Falling, a lowering of self, is the posture of petition and humility. So Haman who falls upon Esther's couch (Esth. 7:8), so the grateful Shunammite who falls at Elisha's feet (2 Kgs. 4:37) in obeisance. The falling word is also a popular one for death in battle or defeat (2 Sam. 1:4; 2 Sam. 1:25; 2 Sam. 2:23; Isa. 21:9).

At Judg. 5:27 images of vulnerability, petition, and ignominious defeat in battle intertwine. Jael, the beautiful woman who lures the enemy with a fecund bowl of rich curds and gentle promises of comfort, is the warrior who fells the unsuspecting Sisera with a massive blow to the head. In sexual posture, in the posture of a would-be lover, a vulnerable petitioner, he falls.

šākab, "HE LAY"

Images of sexuality, defeat, and death continue in the following verb of the chain *škb*, "to lie." Some references to lying are to legitimate sexual relations as in the conception of Solomon (2 Sam. 12:24) or in Micah 7:5. (You will not be able to trust even the one who lies in your bosom, your beloved.) See also Uriah's noble explanation to David as to why he does not wish to spend the night with his wife while his troops are in an open field on battle alert (2 Sam. 11:11). The vast majority of biblical uses of *škb* in a sexual context refer to illegitimate relations in rape, incest, ritual impurity, adultery, and so forth. It is not clear whether most biblical discussions of sex concentrate on problem situations—hence the negative associations of *škb*—or whether this particular term has special crass nuances. In any event, it appears in the contexts of rape and incest [Gen. 19:32, 34, 35 (Lot and his daughters); Gen. 34:2, 7 (the rape of Dinah); 2 Sam. 13:11, 14 (the rape of Tamar)]; of wife-stealing [Gen. 35:22 (Reuben's taking Bilhah); 2 Sam. 12:11 (the punishment of David that others will lie with his wives)]; of promiscuity [1 Sam. 2:22 (the activities of Samuel's sons)]; of seduction or adultery [Gen. 39:10, 12, 14 (Potiphar's wife)]; and a host of other forbidden sexual relationships [Lev. 20:11, 12, (father's wife and daughter-in-law); Lev. 20:13 (homosexuality); Lev. 15:24 and 20:18 (an unclean woman); Lev. 20:20 (aunt)].[32] Could these crass uses of *škb* color the scene in which Leah buys Jacob's conjugal services from Rachel for the price of some mandrakes (Gen. 30:15, 16)? Jacob is the hired lover, told with whom he will lie.

Like *nāpal*, the *škb* word also has significant associations with death and defeat. A mundane phrase for dying is to lie or sleep with one's ancestors (1 Kgs. 1:21, 2 Kgs. 14:22, etc.). The dead are those who sleep or lie in the grave (Ps. 88:6). Lying/sleeping/resting parallels are found in Job 3:13. See also Job 14:12. Battle death images employing *škb* apply to Meshech and Tubal (Ezek. 32:29) and Egypt (Ezek. 32:21). Via *škb* Judg. 5:27 brings together the nuances of improper sexual intimacy, death, and the warrior's defeat.

šādûd, "DESPOILED"

Finally we come to the word *šādûd*, "dealt violently with, despoiled, devastated." A common context of *šdd* words is the destruction of cities and of various enemies in war (e.g. Isa. 15:1, 23:1; Jer. 47:4). Jeremiah 4:30, however, provides a fascinating metaphor relevant to Judg. 5:27.

> And you are despoiled[33]
> What are you doing in dressing in scarlet
> in decking yourself with golden ornaments
> in widening your eyes with make-up
> In vain you make yourself beautiful
> Your lovers despise you.
> They seek your life.

As in Hosea 2, Ezekiel 16, Jeremiah 2, and Isaiah 57 images of harlotry intertwine with images of the unfaithful people, whose lovers are really her enemies. Israel the people is devastated and destroyed by the allies she trusted; Israel the loose woman, still beautifying herself with flashy clothes, trinkets, and make-up is sexually despoiled and ruined. The same double meaning attaches to Judg. 5:27.

> Between her legs he knelt, he fell, he lay
> Between her legs he knelt, he fell
> Where he knelt, there he fell, despoiled.

The verse itself has the intoning repetitive quality of sacrificial or ritual death. The brief parallel phrases, the staccato verbs, the refrain, *kāraʿ/nāpal,* knelt/fell, build to the singly used passive participle despoiled/utterly destroyed.[34]

Double meanings of violent death and sexuality emerge in every line. He is at her feet in a pose of defeat and humiliation; he kneels between her legs in sexual pose. He falls and lies, a dead warrior assassinated by a warrior better than he; he is a supplicant and a would-be lover. This one verse holds an entire story. The final twist and nuance of the tale awaits the last line, which nevertheless retains the doubleness of meaning. He is despoiled/destroyed. The woman Jael becomes not the object of sexual advances, with the improper nuances of *škb,* and not the complacent responder to requests for mercy, but herself is the aggressor, the despoiler.

Eroticism and death especially in the context of battle is a theme explored by Emily Vermeule.[35] As in the "bow" material discussed by Hillers in which death is likened to emasculation and/or sexual humiliation, so here the defeated soldier is the woman, the one subdued, raped, and made love to.

> *Damazo* or *damnemi* have similar values, working in three related spheres of action: taming an animal, raping a woman, killing a man. In a duel, an isolated world inside the main battle, one soldier must be the female partner and go down, or be the animal knocked down.
>
> Homer's habit of playing on sex and war is not new with him, one imagines, but is common war talk and wartime humor.[36]

Vermeule points to "the ambiguity of slaughter and sex" as it appears in Greek battle painting of Amazons and Greek soldiers and notes that Homer has "a habit, at mocking moments, of treating enemies as lovers, fusing the effects of Eros and Thanatos."[37]

> The *oaristus* of war, the manipulated bodies, the lily-white fallen enemy stripped on the field with the spear lusting to taste him, the marriage with death, those "jeux meurtriers" which have struck some as a curious prelude to Alexandrian bad taste, seem rather very archaic and inevitable in war slang of all cultures."[38]

The Song of Deborah presents just such an epic battle context and, I suggest, the same juxtaposition of slaughter and sex. Here, however, the duelers are not two men, but a male warrior and a woman assassin disguised as a protector and ally, disguised as a "mere" woman. A man is not rendered womanish by another man, but is despoiled by a woman. He, in a pose to make love, is felled by her. And again as Neumann, Hillers, Hendel, and others' studies of portrayals of mythic warrior women suggest, such an ambivalent role of woman as potential nurturer become killer is not unique to this characterization of Jael. She participates in a broader archetype fusing in Freud's terms Eros and Thanatos. So Vermeule finds the same constellation of motifs in representations of the female man-eater, raptor sphinx that Alter finds in Jael, "a mother with her young? A lady with her love? A hungry predator."[39]

We conclude thus far then that language in Judg. 5:27 is double, evoking simultaneously death and eroticism, that Jael's image in Judges 4 and 5 partakes of the same liminal cross-culturally evidenced archetype, and that the sexual subduing of the defeated male warrior, the play "on sex and slaughter," is typical of epic battle language, linked in the imagination of those who portray and create warrior figures, in the lore of warriors themselves. Does this understanding of the double imagery of the death of Sisera lead to a special view of Jael as a woman? What might it reveal about the author and audiences of the material? Might it contribute to feminist interpretation of

Scripture or provide encouragement for feminist appropriators of biblical texts? Is the tale of Jael feminist literature in any sense? Why would this characterization of Jael appeal to an Israelite writer?[40]

M. Levine suggests that the writer is a woman, composing a polemic against rape.[41] It seems more likely that this archetype, like its specification in the Greek sphinx, manifests a man's fear of both death and his own sexuality, his insecurities, a male fantasy of Eros become Thanatos. The woman not only rejects but slaughters her lover. Sisera comes to Jael as a vulnerable supplicant, not as a victorious rapist. Whatever the deep cultural and psychological roots of the image of the woman "raptor," the tale as told nevertheless has important resonances both for feminist appropriators and all marginals. A woman who is in some sense the permanent marginal in Israelite patriarchal culture becomes a lens through which to appreciate and sympathize with poorly armed Israelite peasant revolters who face well-armed Canaanite soldiers of the establishment. It is of importance that an Israelite author of an early period[42] imagines the "womanization" of the enemy to be accomplished by a woman assassin. The author identifies with her even while employing an archetype dripping with phantoms of male fears and insecurities. She is turned against the enemy, thereby doubly strengthening the self-image and confidence of the writer himself. What the author fears most he turns outward against his enemy. Jael has identification power for the early Israelite audience, for in a sense Israel is Jael; she becomes an archetype or symbol for the marginal's victory over the establishment.[43]

The sexual nuance of Jael's portrait, this aspect of her archetype, is also significant as specified in this Israelite tale, for as feminist scholars tell us sex is politics; sex is a visceral means of asserting power. Hence the origins of the image of the defeated warrior as a seduced or raped woman. Having a woman do the womanizing, the man despoiled just as he is in a position of sexual seducer himself, makes for an especially powerful portrait of the victor.

The figure of Jael provides, moreover, a fascinating challenge to some of the views of "the feminine" and female psychology one finds in authors such as Neumann and McClelland cited above, an alternate model to challenge an outmoded psychoanalytical cosmology. Jael is a symbolization of self-assertion, a force of change, one who breaks free heroically from oppressive and suppressive forces. She is thus not to be identified with Neumann's Jungian unconscious, a conservative force holding back however aggressively change and development—

the power of the feminine in his terms—but with consciousness-development, ego, and change, the power of the masculine. She is moreover not the hero's helper but the hero herself.

A scholar and educator such as David McClelland helped to create in the 1950s and 60s a worldview in suggesting, in his study of harlequin as lover/death, for example, that

> Whether in giving birth to a baby, nursing it, looking after a husband, or participating in the sexual act itself, a woman can be thought of as yielding or giving or surrendering herself in order to gain satisfaction.

Virtually suggesting that the unattached, "liberated" career woman risks schizophrenia, he writes:

> That is, the demon lover is in a sense the projection of her need to yield in order to fulfill herself. So he exerts a powerful attractive force. Yet at the same time he appears dangerous because he represents a sexuality that may be considered wrong or more seriously a surrender of consciousness or the self that may appear to threaten the central core of her being. In normal women the conflict is fairly readily resolved; they fall in love and learn more or less successfully how to fulfill themselves by only seeming to die in order to nurture and to create—less rather than more successfully in twentieth-century America where women too often try to pattern their lives after the male model which is quite different.[44]

One suspects that McClelland's treatment of harlequin symbolism evidences a man's effort to deal with some of his own ambivalences concerning women, his desire to appeal and to control. The woman is perceived as wishing, on some level, to be subdued and despoiled. The Jael tale read by modern women provides an alternate symbolism. One is not suggesting that women become men-slayers in some simple-minded reading, but rather that the tale is rich in images of directed action, self-assertion, and consciousness on the part of the underdog. The archetype expressing on many levels male anxieties can thus become a powerfully charged model for all marginals, in particular women.

NOTES

1. In his study of the Song of Songs, Marvin Pope suggests that love is associated with death in literature and ritual because people need to assert the power of love over death. I would suggest rather that a text such as Song 8:6 more literally asserts that on some level love is death and death love. Pope's analysis of images of love and death, while erudite

and bibliographically extensive, reduces, rationalizes, and somehow misses the power of this metaphoric equation. (*Song of Songs* [Garden City, New York: Doubleday, 1977], 228–29.)

2. Emily Vermeule, *Aspects of Death in Early Greek Art and Poetry,* Sather Classical Lectures, vol. 46 (Berkeley: University of California, 1979), 101–2; 145 ff., 157–58; 163–64, 171–73.

3. David C. McClelland, *The Roots of Consciousness* (Princeton, N.J.: Van Nostrand, 1964), 182–216.

4. E.g. Anat. See the recent treatment of this scene from the tale of Baal and Anat (*CTA* 3.B.13–14) by Robert M. Good, "Metaphorical Gleanings from Ugarit," *JJS* 33 (1982): 55–59.

5. E.g. Anat, Paghat. See Michael D. Coogan, *Stories From Ancient Canaan* (Philadelphia: Westminster, 1978), 46–47; 111–12.

6. E.g. Ishtar (*Gilgamesh Epic,* ANET[3]), 83–85; 505; Circe, (*Odyssey,* 10:203 ff.)

7. Sigmund Freud, *Civilization and Its Discontents,* ed. and trans. James Strachey (New York: W.W. Norton, 1962).

8. Erich Neumann, *The Great Mother: An Analysis of the Archetype,* trans. Ralph Manheim, Bollingen Series, vol. 47 (Princeton: Princeton University, 1964).

9. Jung himself writes as follows: "Just as every individual derives from masculine and feminine genes, and the sex is determined by the predominance of the corresponding genes, so in the psyche it is only the conscious mind, in a man, that has the masculine sign, while the unconscious is by nature feminine. The reverse is true in the case of a woman." *The Archetypes and the Collective Unconscious,* Bollingen Series, vol. 20 (New York: Pantheon, 1959), 175.

10. Delbert R. Hillers, "The Bow of Aqhat: The Meaning of A Mythological Theme," in *Orient and Occident; Essays Presented to Cyrus H. Gordon on the Occasion of his Sixty-fifth Birthday,* ed. Harry A. Hoffner, ADAT 22 (Neukirchen-Vluyn: Neukirchener, 1973), 71–80.

11. Hillers, "The Bow," 73–74.

12. Hillers, "The Bow," 73–78.

13. Hillers, "The Bow," 78.

14. On the anima-sister see Erich Neumann, *The Origins and History of Consciousness,* trans. R. F. Hull, Bollingen Series, vol. 42 (Princeton: Princeton University, 1954), 201–4.

15. Neumann, *Great Mother,* 148.

16. Neumann, *Great Mother,* 172, 194, 202–3.

17. Ronald Hendel, *The Epic of the Patriarch: The Jacob Cycle and the Narrative Traditions of Canaan and Israel,* HSM 42 (Atlanta: Scholars, 1987), 73.

18. J. Glenn Taylor, "The Song of Deborah and Two Canaanite Goddesses," *JSOT* 23 (1982): 99–108.

19. Robert Alter, "From Line to Story in Biblical Verse," *Poetics Today* 4 (1983): 615–37, 129–37; Robert Alter, *The Art of Biblical Poetry* (New York: Basic, 1985), 43–49.

20. Like Alter, Mieke Bal draws distinctions between portraits of Jael in Judges 4 and Judges 5. She argues that the prose account is "masculine" and authored by a man where the poetic account is "feminine" and, at least implicitly, authored by a woman, though the quality of the voice and not some specific identification of the author is her interest (Mieke Bal, *Murder and Difference: Gender, Genre, and Scholarship on Sisera's Death* [Bloomington: Indiana University, 1988]). Bal discusses the Jael tale again, presenting major threads of argument found in the book, in "Tricky Thematics," *Semeia* 42 (1988): 133–55, 145–46.

21. Alter, "From Line to Story," 633.

22. Alter, "From Line to Story," 635.

23. Mordecai Levine, "The Polemic Against Rape in the Song of Deborah," *Beth Mikra* 25 (1979): 83–84 (Hebrew).

24. Alter, "From Line to Story," 635.

25. Alter, "From Line to Story," 630.

26. Barnabas Lindars, "Deborah's Song: Women in the Old Testament," *Bulletin of the John Rylands University Library of Manchester* 65 (1983): 158–75, 171.

27. Michael D. Coogan, "A Structural and Literary Analysis of the Song of Deborah," *CBQ* 40 (1978): 146–66, 151.

28. Robert G. Boling, *Judges*, AB (Garden City, N.Y.: Doubleday, 1975), 104.

29. Alberto Soggin, *Judges,* OTL (Philadelphia: Westminster, 1981), 83.

30. Like the Rabbinic traditions he cites, Yair Zakovitch sagely recognizes the sexual nuances of language such as "between her legs," "lay" and "kneeled" but tends to overliteralize the scene in his exegesis, "Sisseras Tod," *ZAW* 93 (1981): 364–74.

31. Pope, *Song,* 231.

32. In some instances in the Masoretic text, the object of *škb* has been vocalized to suggest a direct object of a transitive verb as in the English slang "to lay her." See Gen. 34:2; Lev. 15:24; 2 Sam. 13:14.

33. The word *šādûd* that I translate "despoiled" is not found in most of the Greek manuscript tradition. In the Greek or Septuagintal tradition, Jer. 4:30 begins "And you, what are you doing." *Šādûd,* a predicate adjective, is moreover in masculine form whereas the subject "you" is feminine. For these reasons, some modern commentators omit *šādûd,* suggesting that the word was not originally found in the Hebrew text of Jer. 4:30 [e.g. John Bright, *Jeremiah,* AB (Garden City, N.Y.: Doubleday), 31; William Holladay, *Jeremiah 1: A Commentary on the Book of the Prophet Jeremiah,* chaps. 1–25, Hermeneia (Philadelphia: Fortress, 1986), 144–45, who provides a most circuitous and speculative explanation for the word's presence in the

Masoretic Hebrew text]. On the other hand, J. A. Thompson recently accepts the reading *śādûd,* translating "despoiled" [*The Book of Jeremiah* (Grand Rapids: Eerdmans, 1980), 231] and most older commentators also accept the Masoretic text translating *śādûd* with the wonderfully Victorian phrase "when thou art spoiled" or "spoiled one" thereby fully conveying the sexual nuance of the term. [See John Skinner, *Prophecy and Religion: Studies in the Life of Jeremiah* (Cambridge, England: Cambridge University, 1940), 37; S. R. Driver, *The Book of the Prophet Jeremiah* (New York: Charles Scribner's Sons, 1907), 26; A. W. Streane, *The Book of the Prophet Jeremiah, Together with Lamentations* (Cambridge, England: Cambridge University, 1805), 43]. This text-critical problem raises important and fundamental methodological questions. What constitutes an original text? Is it not equally worthwhile and more reasonable to discuss what constitutes a valid text? The Masoretic version of Jer. 4:30 makes excellent sense and contributes to the imagery of Israel the harlot. What of matters of prosody? Omitting *šādûd* allows one to divide the verse into three segments of equal length: And you, what are you doing/In dressing in scarlet/In decking yourself in golden ornaments. On the other hand, my arrangement of the text allows for a prosodic structure whereby long and short lines alternate to create a limping, lament meter as the prophet mourns over the fallen people. This pattern continues in v. 31.

For these reasons, I accept the Masoretic reading. The lack of gender agreement may be explained by an author's veering between his female metaphor and male subject. As noted recently by Michael L. Barré, certain "inconsistencies in gender and even number are not uncommon in biblical Hebrew." Barré is particularly interested in references to geographic areas, treated as feminine in biblical Hebrew versus references to the people of that area, treated as masculine ["The Meaning of *lʾ ʾšybnw* in Amos 1:3–2:6," *JBL* 105 (1986): 611–31, esp. 614 and 616].

34. For others' comments on the style of v. 27 see J. Blenkinsopp, "Ballad Style and Psalm Style in the Song of Deborah: A Discussion," *Bib* 42 (1961): 61–76, esp. 74; Alan J. Hauser, "Judges 5: Parataxis in Hebrew Poetry," *JBL* 99 (1980): 23–41, esp. 34–38.

35. Vermeule, *Aspects of Death* (cited in n. 2).

36. Vermeule, *Aspects of Death,* 101.

37. Vermeule, *Aspects of Death,* 102, 157.

38. Vermeule, *Aspects of Death,* 157.

39. Vermeule, *Aspects of Death,* 171.

40. For a presentation of material from Tamil folk tradition that makes for fascinating comparison with the biblical narrative explored here, see David D. Shulman, "Battle as Metaphor in Tamil Folk and Classical Traditions," in *Another Harmony,* eds. Stuart H. Blackburn and A. K. Ramanujan (Berkeley: University of California), 105–30. Shulman explores images of eroticism and death in battle in the *Catakaṇṭarāvaṇaṉ Katai* (see 122–23), noting that the "folk source," as opposed to the classical sources, "prefer(s) to identify violence with the woman, passivity with the male . . ." (120–21). He asks

whether the violent portrait of the goddess Sītā "represent(s) a masculine fear of female sexuality" or "*female* fantasies of power . . ." (121).

41. Mordecai Levine, "A Polemic." In an interesting and methodologically fresh essay that probes the possibilities of reconstructing a history of Israelite women, Jo Ann Hackett describes Judges 5 as "a very female piece of literature." ["In the Days of Jael: Reclaiming the History of Women in Ancient Israel," in *Immaculate and Powerful: The Female in Sacred Image and Social Reality,* eds. C. W. Atkinson, C. H. Buchanan, and M. R. Miles, (Boston: Beacon, 1985), 15–38, esp. 32–33. Cf. Mieke Bal cited in n. 20 above.]

42. It is agreed among scholars that Judges 5 is an example of early Hebrew poetry dating to the twelfth or eleventh centuries B.C.E. I am in general agreement with Norman Gottwald's portrayal of this period as a time of revolt by rural "have-nots" against the urban upper classes, the "haves," in a Canaanite version of feudalism. For a full presentation of his view of early Israelite history see *The Tribes of Yahweh: A Sociology of the Religion of Liberated Israel 1250–1050 B.C.* (Maryknoll, N.Y.: Orbis, 1979).

43. Jo Ann Hackett's description of the period of the Judges as a time of "social dysfunction" ("In the Days," 25) and her examination of issues of status, power, and authority are relevant in this context (see "In the Days," 23–33).

44. McClelland, *The Roots of Consciousness,* 192.

5 FROM THE CHILD IS BORN THE WOMAN: THE STORY OF JEPHTHAH'S DAUGHTER*

PEGGY L. DAY

Embedded in the cycle of stories that cluster around the legendary[1] figure of Jephthah (Judg. 11:1—12:7) is a terse reference to an annual festival celebrated by the "daughters of Israel" in commemoration of Jephthah's daughter, who was offered up to Yahweh by her father as a holocaust sacrifice (*ʿōlâ*) in payment of a vow (Judg. 11:29–40).[2] As the story is told in the text, the daughter's death is a crucial scene in the unfolding of Jephthah's character, posing as it does a potential moral dilemma: should he break his vow, or should he keep it and sacrifice his daughter? Although clearly devastated[3] when his daughter comes forth to meet him with timbrels and dancing, he does not ponder long: his vow to Yahweh takes precedence over his daughter's life (11:34–35). He does, however, grant her a stay of execution, and it is during the interval between the sealing of her fate and her ritual slaughter that she is said to perform certain actions that were repeated[4] annually in memory of her. This paper is primarily concerned with determining the nature of the annual festival held in commemoration of the person who, from the text's point of view, is significant in that she is Jephthah's virgin daughter (11:39, *not* 11:37; 38—see below).[5] In terms of the ritual remembrance, however, I will argue that her virginity is not the key issue. Rather, it is the social recognition of her transition to physical maturity[6] that is commemorated through the annual performance of a women's life-cycle ritual, or rite of passage.[7] More precisely, the story of Jephthah's daughter functioned as an etiology of this annual rite. The participants most

* Several people read drafts of this paper and offered helpful advice. I especially would like to thank Jo Ann Hackett, Brian Peckham, and Ronald Shepherd for their comments and suggestions.

likely would have understood the rite to be the repetition/commemoration of an actual first-time event, but from a scholarly point of view it is more correct to describe the story as an etiology or foundation legend, and to speak of Jephthah's daughter as a culture heroine.

In order to understand the nature of the annual observance, we must first establish what the foundation legend portrays Jephthah's daughter as doing during her two-month reprieve. The RSV translates (11:37): "And she said to her father, 'Let this thing be done for me; let me alone two months, that I may go and wander[8] on the mountains, and bewail my virginity, I and my [female] companions.'" The issue here is how to understand the phrase *wĕʾebkeh ʿal-bĕtûlay,* which the RSV translates "[that I may] bewail my virginity." First, let us focus on *bĕtûlay,* RSV's "my virginity." There is growing recognition amongst biblical scholars that *bĕtûlîm*[9] typically does not mean virginity, but rather designates an age group.[10] Likewise, the related term *bĕtûlâ* does not mean virgin, but rather denotes a female who has reached a certain stage in her life. It is somewhat akin to the English term "adolescent," although *bĕtûlâ* refers specifically to females. Three passages offer particularly convincing evidence. In Genesis 24, when Abraham's servant goes in search of a bride for Isaac, he encounters Rebekah at a spring. The narrator describes Rebekah as "a very attractive girl, a *bĕtûlâ* whom no man had known" (Gen. 24:16). If *bĕtûlâ* means "virgin," then why did the narrator add the phrase "whom no man had known"? Likewise, in reference to the 400 young women who were not put to death after the conquest of Jabesh-Gilead, the narrator describes them with the term *bĕtûlâ,* once again immediately specifying that they had not "known a man" (Judg. 21:12).[11] In both instances either the qualification is redundant, or *bĕtûlâ* does not mean virgin. Finally, Joel 1:8 reads: "Lament like a *bĕtûlâ* girded in sackcloth, for the husband [*baʿal*] of her youth."[12] It seems, therefore, reasonable to surmise that *bĕtûlâ* does not mean virgin. Thus *bĕtûlîm,* which in Judg. 11:37 means the state or condition of being a *bĕtûlâ,* should not be translated "virginity." Rather, it refers to a particular stage in the female life cycle and, like the word "adolescence," is best understood as a social recognition of puberty. More precisely, I would define a *bĕtûlâ* as a female who had reached puberty and was therefore potentially fertile, but who had not yet given birth to her first child.[13] When we are told in v. 39 that Jephthah's daughter had not known a man, it is our first indication that she was a virgin, and it is noted *not* in connection with her retreat to the hill country but rather as a condition pertaining at the time she was sacrificed. In other words, it is her status as a *bětûlâ,* not her virginity, that is the focus of attention when she and her companions go off to the hills. We should expect, therefore, that the ritual observance her story explains would have had the same focus.

The second problem that needs to be addressed centers on the semantically slippery preposition *ʿal.* The RSV translation implies that she is bewailing *because of* her virginity [*sic*],[14] but this is not at all clear from the Hebrew. In a recent study of precisely this problem, Karlheinz Keukens[15] has argued that *bětûlay* is not the *cause* of Jephthah's daughter's lament, but rather specifies when the lament takes place. In other words, Jephthah's daughter requests and is granted permission to perform a *bětûlîm* lament. This is what she and her female companions go off to the hill country to do, thereby "instituting" a custom that is construed as an annual repetition of their actions. What I would reconstruct, therefore, is an annual ceremony at which young women were socially recognized as having left childhood behind and entered *bětûlîm,* physical maturity.[16] This ceremony included a ritual lament which, in the vernacular of rites of passage, acknowledged the "death" of one stage in life in preparation for entry into a new stage.[17] In order to make this reconstruction more plausible let us look at two other dying maidens and the customs instituted to commemorate their deaths.

IPHIGENEIA

A number of biblical scholars have suggested parallels between Jephthah's daughter and Iphigeneia,[18] a Greek legendary heroine.[19] She is first mentioned in the *Cypria* (7th–6th centuries B.C.E.), a poem that tells of the preliminaries to and initial part of the Trojan war.[20] The goddess Artemis, angry with Agamemnon for killing a deer,[21] sends storms to prevent the Greek fleet from sailing out of Aulis bay for Troy. The seer Calchas determines the reason for the goddess's ire and recommends the sacrifice of Iphigeneia, who is brought to Aulis on the pretext of marrying Achilles. At the moment of sacrifice Artemis substitutes a deer and spirits Iphigeneia off to Taurica. This, however, is far from the only version of Iphigeneia's story.[22]

Considered together, Euripides' (5th c. B.C.E.) two plays *Iphigeneia at Aulis* and *Iphigeneia in Tauris* are interesting indeed. While it must be borne in mind that Euripides animates his characters in a manner that is ofttimes foreign to the epic world from which he draws them, he nevertheless transmits some useful information. In *Iphigeneia at Aulis* he does not mention why Artemis required Agamemnon to sacrifice his daughter, but he does preserve the tradition that she was brought to Aulis on the pretext of becoming Achilles' bride (lines 99–100). In other words, Iphigeneia is a nubile young woman. In *Iphigeneia in Tauris* (line 18 ff.) he does not attribute Artemis' anger to the killing of a deer, but rather to the fact that Agamemnon had vowed to sacrifice to her the loveliest thing the year gave birth to, and had not yet made good his vow. The loveliest thing born that year was Iphigeneia.[23] At the end of the play, Athena tells Iphigeneia what she must do once she returns home from her Tauric captivity (l. 1463 ff.). Iphigeneia is to serve in the Artemis sanctuary at Brauron, and when she dies she is to be buried there, and the clothing of women who die in childbirth is to be dedicated to her.

In the Artemis sanctuary at Brauron (on the east coast of Attica near Athens), the following rite took place. Young girls—between the ages of five and ten according to the only tradition that specifies age[24]—performed what was called the *arkteia,* a ritual seclusion during which the girls were identified as *arktoi,* "she-bears."[25] Performance of the *arkteia* was necessary before an Athenian girl was permitted to marry: "the Athenians [ ] made decree that no maiden should be given in marriage to a man unless she first 'act the bear' in honor of the goddess."[26] There are various legends (including multiforms of a single legend) that explain the *arkteia,* both as it was practiced at Brauron as well as at Munychia.[27] According to one stream of tradition,[28] a bear living at Brauron and sacred to Artemis had been killed, and so the goddess sent a plague. Apollo was consulted, and he instructed that the *arkteia* was to be performed in payment for the slain bear. To the sanctuary at Munychia the following specific legend was attached:[29]

> A certain Embaros played a subtle trick in prayer. For he set up the sanctuary of Munychian Artemis. And a bear appeared in it, and was slain by the Athenians, and so a plague arose. For this the god proclaimed release if someone should sacrifice his daughter to Artemis. And Embarus [*sic*] promised that he would do this on condition that his family should have the priesthood for life [ie. in perpetuity]. Decking out his daughter, he hid her in the inner recess, and adorning a goat in clothing, sacrificed it as if it were his daughter.

Note how similar in structure the Embaros legend (slightly supplemented by information from the "generic" bear legend) is to the *Kypria* version of the sacrifice of Iphigeneia: an animal (bear/deer) is slain (by Athenians/Agamemnon), Artemis is angered, Artemis sends ill fortune (plague/storms), the cause is determined (by consulting Apollo/

Calchas) and the sacrifice of an unmarried young woman demanded (Embaros' daughter/Agamemnon's daughter). And in both cases an animal is substituted for the young woman. It is with these parallels in mind that we turn to a tradition attached to Brauron:[30]

> But others say that what happened to Iphigenia happened in Brauron, not in Aulis. Euphorion: "Sea-girt Brauron, cenotaph of Iphigenia". And it is thought that Agamemnon sacrificed Iphigenia in Brauron, not in Aulis, and the bear was given in her stead, not a deer. And that is why they perform a *mysterion* for her.[31]

Iphigeneia, brought to Aulis on the pretext of marriage, has been "moved" to Brauron[32] where her story clearly functions as an etiology for a female puberty rite performed by Athenian girls as a prerequisite for marriage.

KORE

Whereas Iphigeneia, like Jephthah's daughter, is a legendary heroine, Kore/Persephone is clearly a goddess. In Greek myth, she was swept off to the underworld by Hades while she and her companions the Okeanids were in a meadow picking flowers.[33] Biblical scholars who suggest parallels between Kore and Jephthah's daughter typically either give the goddess a passing nod and nothing more[34] or acknowledge her simply as a "dead or ousted spirit of [agricultural] fertility"[35] or "vegetation goddess."[36] Whereas it would be impossible to categorically deny any relationship between Kore (and her mother, Demeter, who goes in search of her) and agricultural fertility, this does not imply that a strictly agricultural interpretation is the only meaningful dimension of the myth of Kore's descent.[37] The intimate relationship between human, female fertility and agricultural productivity has been noted, for example, by Audrey Richards:[38]

> It is difficult to be certain how far human fertility is associated with agricultural fertility in [the *chisungu* female puberty] rites. I was never specifically told that the garden mimes were done to make the gardens yield, but merely to 'teach the girls to garden', but it would certainly be hard to distinguish very clearly between the productivity of the girls and the productivity of the seeds they sow in [puberty] rites which involve the constant handling of seeds of different kinds.

In what follows, I will be exploring the possibility that the myth of Kore's descent into the underworld symbolized not only a particular phase of the agricultural cycle, but also served as the mythic expression of a women's initiatory rite of passage.

In a work entitled *Couroi et Courètes,* Henri Jeanmaire[39] established that the term Kore (Greek *kourē/korē*), typically used as a byname for Persephone, means "young girl of initiatory age." Proceeding from this observation, he argued that the myth of Kore's abduction into the underworld reflected an archaic Greek women's initiation. His position has been endorsed by Bruce Lincoln who, in a recent study,[40] has examined the *Homeric Hymn to Demeter* from this perspective in detail. He notes that, in addition to the meaning of her name, Kore is clearly depicted as "a beautiful, full-breasted, teenage girl"[41] when she is snatched from the world of the living and whisked off to the world of the dead. Rather than interpret Kore's sojourn in the nether regions as the mythic expression of seasonal agricultural sterility, Lincoln understands her time in the underworld as a mythic expression of the liminal or transitional phase of a rite of passage.[42] In support of this, and by way of explaining why the goddess has the double name Kore/Persephone, Lincoln notes that she is called Kore, "the maiden," prior to her stay with Hades in the nether regions but by a new name, Persephone, once Hermes has been dispatched to bring her back to earth.[43] Again, both the generic/status designation of initiates in transition and the renaming[44] once initiation is complete are wholly typical of rites of passage.

It is beyond the scope of this essay to discuss the numerous rituals and celebrations that were tied to the myth of Kore's descent into the underworld and Demeter's search for her.[45] I will focus on one festival, Thesmophoria, which was exclusively a women's festival and was the most widely celebrated festival of the Greek world.[46] Information about this festival must be garnered from numerous, disparate, and often contradictory sources (men were barred from participating and the particulars kept secret, so it is no wonder that there is conflicting information), but it seems clear that it was most often celebrated as an annual three-day festival. According to the main witness, a scholium to Lucian's *Dialogi meretricii,*[47] this festival was tied specifically to Kore's descent into the netherworld. The first day of the Athenian festival was called *anodos,* "the way up," either because the participants processed up the hill upon which the festival took place, or perhaps as an elliptical allusion to ascents and descents made in connection with throwing live pigs down a chasm. The scholium tells of Kore's descent in order to explain this aspect of the festival: when Kore was abducted, the pigs of a certain swineherd were also swallowed up in the chasm. The second day of the festival (*nesteia,* "fasting") was spent in fasting and lamentation, identified specifically by some sources as sorrow for Kore's descent.[48] The women "imitate the ancient way of life," dressing simply, reclining on wattled beds and, in one location, even prohibiting the use of fire.[49] On the third day (*kalligeneia,* a name signifying fair-born offspring) a great banquet was held.

Given the sketchy and sometimes contradictory information we have about the Thesmophoria, it is no wonder that classicists differ in their assessments of it. In that the rotting remains of the pigs that were fetched up from the chasm were mixed with seed that was subsequently planted, it is clear that there was an aspect of agricultural fertility involved in the festival. But why were the rotting remains of pigs believed to be efficacious for the fecundity of the crops? I suspect that the answer lies in their ritual identification with Kore who, by virtue of her sojourn in the underworld, was transformed into a fertile woman. It is important to note in this regard that the Greek word used of the swineherd's pigs in the scholium, *choiros,* "young pig," was a common slang term for female genitalia.[50] Thus it is the nubile goddess's potential fecundity that is mixed with the seeds, presumably to the mutual advantage of both the crop and the physically mature female. The *choiros* enlivened the seed, but the seed also was implanted in the fertile *choiros.*

Our examination of the myth of Kore's descent and the yearly Thesmophoria festival has not yielded as conclusive results as the data tying the story of Iphigeneia to a female puberty rite. For Iphigeneia the evidence is explicit; for Kore/Persephone, the interpretation is admittedly conjectural. What is clear is that the myth of Kore's descent can be read as describing a rite of passage, and that her death was annually commemorated by an exclusively women's festival that included a day of ritual lamentation and was concerned with female fertility. It is a matter of speculation whether the festival should be interpreted strictly as a female puberty rite.[51] Perhaps the story of Kore's descent originally reflected a female puberty rite but was later reinterpreted in the context of the Thesmophoria as pertaining to fertility within the bounds of marriage.[52]

SYNTHESIS

What can Kore and Iphigeneia teach us about the story of Jephthah's daughter? It would be a mistake to draw facile conclusions that ignore cultural distinctions, but the cross-cultural stability of both the structure and symbolism of life-cycle rituals provides some common ground for comparison. On a superficial level, the three maidens differ: Kore, a goddess, is abducted and returns; an animal is substituted for Iphigeneia;[53] and Jephthah's daughter is killed by her father. Kore, a divine maiden and therefore immortal, has the luxury of being able to return from the dead, although it is important to remember that she emerges not as the generic Kore but as the transformed and individualized Persephone. In the language of myth the initiand's experience of "dying" and being "reborn" can be expressed symbolically as the death and return of a single deity who, paradoxically, is both one goddess and also two. This goddess dies as Kore and returns as Persephone just as the initiand, at first a generic maiden, emerges as a named, individual woman. In this respect Kore dies just as surely as Jephthah's daughter does, and just as anonymously, for both are every girl-child. Iphigeneia also dies, but in the guise of a different idiom. She dies each time a goat is sacrificed to Artemis Brauronia, just as the girls who "act the bear" die as children and are transformed into marriageable young women.[54] With Iphigeneia we move from the language of myth and into the language of sacrificial ritual. Iphigeneia and the goat are one, just as Kore is one with the pigs that are cast into the chasm at the Thesmophoria.[55] Jephthah's daughter must die under her father's knife because she is neither a divine and therefore immortal maiden capable of rebirth nor was an animal sacrifice performed as part of the annual festival held in her honor.[56] Kore, Iphigeneia, and Jephthah's daughter all "tell the story" of leaving immaturity behind, but they do so in different languages.

As Edwin Ardener noted in reference to his work among the Bakweri,[57] men and women in a given culture generate, interpret, and appropriate myths and symbols in gender-distinct ways. Kore's story, it seems to me, can be read both as a female rite of passage and as a myth of agricultural cycles. Perhaps the former aspect was accentuated in the exclusively female context of the Thesmophoria. Iphigeneia's story, in contrast, seems to have been attached secondarily to a female puberty rite. That is, in terms of chronological priority Iphigeneia's story seems to have been more primitively linked with the issue of prebattle sacrifice and not women's life-cycle ritual,[58] although it is important to note that Iphigeneia's story became attached to the Brauronian rite because it exhibited the same story pattern as the bear legend, which was the more primitive foundation legend. This suggests that something inherent in the pattern itself made Iphigeneia's story an appropriate counterpart to the Brauronian rite. In any event we have a clear example of how Athenian women appropriated and contextualized a story in terms of their own life experience. In the case of the story of Jephthah's daughter, we do not have enough evidence to judge whether it was the original foundation legend of the annual rite or whether it, like Iphigeneia's story, was appropriated and made relevant to women's experience. What we can say, I think, is that both stories had gender-distinct meanings when contextualized within women's life-cycle rituals, and it is striking that in both cases the paradigm involved explicit self-sacrifice.

When I first began working on the story of Jephthah's daughter I anticipated focusing on the connection between male violence and virgin sacrifice that this story shares with a number of cultures around the world. As important and illuminating as this exploration no doubt would be, I began to realize that to focus on this aspect of the story would be to focus on the male psyche.[59] I chose instead to make the women's festival the pivotal interest of my inquiry, and the rewards have been rich. Among the broader implications of this study is the need to move beyond purely descriptive (and often derogatory) terminology such as "fertility cult" and ask what, specifically, fertility ritual *is,* what its symbolic dimensions are, and how it functions in the lives of women. Further, we need to reassess what ancient Near Eastern myths of "dying and rising" deities are all about,[60] and discover whether and how it makes a difference when the deity in question is female rather than male.

As we have seen, Israelite women told the story of Jephthah's daughter in the context of a rite of passage from immaturity to adolescence. In her landmark work, *In a Different Voice,* Carol Gilligan[61] has traced women's moral development through an adolescent stage of total self-sacrifice to mature recognition that they must take their own well-being as well as others' well-being into account when making moral decisions. When Jephthah's daughter learns of her father's vow, she totally disregards her own welfare and tells her father to "do to me according to what has gone forth from your mouth" (11:36). If women today wish to appropriate the story of Jephthah's daughter and contextualize it in their own lives, they would do well to hear Gilligan's voice as it resonates with the words of Jephthah's daughter who, as archetype of female adolescence, resolved a moral dilemma by completely ignoring her own well-being. Now as then Jephthah's daughter should be understood to represent the adolescent phase of female development, and it is important to realize that adolescent morality must be abandoned along the road to full maturity.

NOTES

1. Irrespective of the general position one takes on the historicity of the so-called period of the judges, it is clear that the story of Jephthah's vow and its dire consequences has at its core a widespread folk motif. See Stith Thompson, *Motif Index of Folk-Literature* (Indiana: Indiana University, 1958) S 241 Homecomer's Vow: Child unwittingly promised (see also S 242–47); W. Baumgartner, "Jephtas Gelübde, Jud 11, 30–40," *AfR* 18 (1915): 240–49; T. H. Gaster, *Myth, Legend and Custom in the Old Testament* (New York: Harper and Row, 1969), 430–33, 534–35.

2. Cf. Simon B. Parker, "The Vow in Ugaritic and Israelite Narrative Literature," *UF* 11 (1979): 693–700.

3. Hebrew *krʿ* (11:35). This is an ironic choice of vocabulary because *krʿ* commonly is used of warriors felled in battle (Ps. 18:40 // 2 Sam. 22:40; Ps. 20:9; 72:9; 78:31; cf. Judg. 5:27; Isa. 46:1–2; 65:12). Thus Jephthah, who has returned from battle a victor, is nevertheless felled like a defeated warrior by his own daughter.

4. The crux here is *lĕtannôt* (v. 40), which describes what the daughters of Israel do each year for Jephthah's daughter. I agree with those scholars (e.g. C. F. Burney, *The Book of Judges* [London: Rivingtons, 1920], 129; A. Soggin, *Judges* [Philadelphia: Westminster, 1981], 87) who derive the word from *tānâ*, "recount, repeat." As Passover, for example, was construed as an annual commemoration of the first Passover and was observed by ritually "repeating" the events that tradition ascribed to the first Passover, so the festival commemorating Jephthah's daughter would include repetition of the actions that tradition ascribed to her.

5. Although the biblical text relates a legend *about* a women's ritual, we need to bear in mind that, in all likelihood, the tale is told in a male recension. In an article entitled "Belief and the Problem of Women" (J. S. La Fontaine [ed.], *The Interpretation of Ritual: Essays in Honour of A. I. Richards* [London: Tavistock, 1972], 135–58) anthropologist Edwin Ardener notes that men and women in a given culture generate, interpret, and appropriate myths and symbols in distinct ways. The problem with much ethnographic data, Ardener points out, is that male informants have been the fieldworker's source for the interpretation of the beliefs of *both* males and females ("Belief," 139–40). Analyses of cultures generated in this way discuss women as well as men and therefore seem, on the surface, to give a complete description of the culture in question. But when information is collected in this fashion, as Ardener states, women are "effectively missing in the total analysis or, more precisely, they are missing in the same way as were the Nuer's cows, who were observed but also did not speak" ("Belief," 140). The biblical

text as "informant" is susceptible to the same criticism that Ardener makes with respect to the interpretation of ethnographic data.

6. By physical maturity I mean menarche, a woman's first menstruation. The relationship between this physical event and ritual/social recognition of it is complex, and varies from culture to culture. When social recognition temporally corresponds to physical reality the referent of the ritual is clear, and can be confidently termed a menarcheal rite. But when social recognition of female sexual maturity is not temporally tied to this physical event, terminology becomes a problem. I will use the expression "female puberty rite" to describe pre- or post-menarcheal ceremonies that mark a female's readiness to enter social adulthood. Once this transition has been made, a woman is (socially) ready for marriage.

7. The foundational work on life-cycle ritual is Arnold van Gennep's *Les Rites de Passage* (trans. Monika Vizedom and Gabrielle Caffee, *The Rites of Passage* [Chicago: University of Chicago, 1960]). Noting cross-cultural similarities in the structure and symbolism of rituals performed at critical transition points in the human life-cycle (birth, puberty, marriage, childbirth, and death), van Gennep provided a framework for describing and comparing life-cycle rituals. Since van Gennep's time, several schools of thought in a variety of academic disciplines have appropriated the basic notion of a rite of passage. With specific regard to life-cycle rituals associated with the female reproductive cycle, see esp. Monika Vizedom (*Rites and Relationships: Rites of Passage and Contemporary Anthropology* [London: Sage, 1976], esp. 25–63), Karen and Jeffery Paige (*The Politics of Reproductive Ritual* [Berkeley: University of California, 1981], esp. 1–42), Audrey I. Richards (*Chisungu: A Girls' Initiation Ceremony Among the Bemba of Northern Rhodesia* [London: Faber and Faber, 1956]), and Bruce Lincoln (*Emerging from the Chrysalis: Studies in Rituals of Women's Initiation* [Cambridge, Mass.: Harvard University, 1981]). In order to establish the plausibility of understanding Judg. 11:40 as a reference to a female puberty rite, I consulted this literature to discover whether any correlations existed between the practice of such rites and other cultural factors (such as matrilocal vs. patrilocal residence patterns, lineage reckoning, economic resource base, etc.). Although correlations have been suggested with, for example, residence patterns, fraternal interest group strength, and the presence of all-female work groups, there seems to be no single correlative factor that can definitively "predict" whether women in ancient Israel would or would not have practiced such a rite. Therefore the hypothesis that they did remains a live option. Cross-cultural data do suggest, however, that such a rite would not have been the innovation of a state society. Cf. Judith K. Brown, "A Cross-Cultural Study of Female Initiation Rites," *American Anthropologist* 65 (1963): 837–53; K. and J. Paige, *Politics*, esp. 22 and n. 53, 94–95; Frank W. Young, *Initiation Ceremonies: A Cross-Cultural Study of Status Dramatization* (Indianapolis: Bobbs-Merill, 1965).

8. RSV derives MT's *wĕyāradtî,* transparently pointed as a form of the root *yārad* "to go down," from the root *rwd* "to wander." This emendation is unnecessary; MT is intelligible both syntactically and semantically (contra H. Orlinsky, "Critical Notes on Genesis 39:14, 17, Jud 11:37," *JBL* 61 [1942]: 93–94; G. R. Driver, "L'interprétation du texte masorétique," *ETL* 26 [1950]: 347). Read "that I may go down [hendiadys] to the hill country."

9. In biblical Hebrew, personal pronouns (e.g. "my") can be suffixed to the nouns they modify. Judg. 11:37's *bĕtûlay* is *bĕtûlîm* plus a personal pronominal suffix.

10. B. Landsberger, "Jungfräulichkeit: ein Beitrag zum Thema Beilager und Eheschliessung," in *Symbolae Iuridicae et Historicae Martino David Dedicatae,* ed., J. A. Ankum et al. (Leiden: Brill, 1968), 57–58; M. Tsevat, *"bĕthûlāh; bĕthûlîm," TDOT* 338–43; Gordon J. Wenham, *"bĕtûlāh* 'A Girl of Marriageable Age,'" *VT* 22 (1972): 326–48; Karlheinz Keukens, "Richter 11, 37 f.: Rite de Passage und Übersetzungsprobleme," *BN* 19 (1982): 42, n.6; Clemens Locher, *Die Ehre einer Frau in Israel* (Orbis Biblicus et Orientalis 70; Göttingen: Vandenhoeck und Ruprecht, 1986), 121–92. In the strictly legal material *bĕtûlîm* can mean virginity, but this is a specialized meaning.

11. Wenham, *"bĕtûlāh,"* 340–41.

12. Cf. Tsevat, *"bĕthûlāh,"* 341.

13. Joel 1:8 (cited above) demonstrates that a married woman still could be called a *bĕtûlâ.* Further, as Wenham notes (*"bĕtûlāh,"* 343–44), in Esth. 2 the women whom King Ahasuerus had slept with during his search for a new queen are still, after having spent a night with the king, referred to as *bĕtûlôt.* Thus marriage and intercourse do not terminate young women's inclusion in the category of *bĕtûlîm.* There is no direct evidence to prove that a young woman was no longer a *bĕtûlâ* after she had given birth to her first child, but there is some suggestive cognate evidence. Note, for example, the intriguing Aramaic incantation text, cited by Wenham (326–27), which speaks of a *btwlt*ʾ who is in labor but does not give birth. Note also the stock epithet at Ugarit of the goddess Anat, *btlt* ʿ*nt,* Magical Papyrus. Harris describes her as a goddess who conceives but does not bear. Cf. Tsevat, *"bĕthûlîm,"* 339–40; J. C. de Moor, "Studies in the New Alphabetic Texts from Ras Shamra 1," *UF* 1 (1969): 182; R. Stadelmann, *Syrisch-palästinensische Gottheiten in Ägypten* (Leiden: Brill, 1967), 108–9.

14. That is, RSV portrays her as lamenting because she is going to die a virgin. Gustav Boström has proposed that Jephthah's daughter wails because she is about to *lose* her virginity (*Proverbiastudien* [Lund: Gleerup, 1935], 117–19. Cf. Hans Walter Wolff, *Hosea* [Philadelphia: Fortress, 1974], 13; Leonhard Rost, "Erwägungen zu Hosea 4:13 f.," *Festschrift Alfred Bertholet* [Tübingen: J.C.B. Mohr, 1950], esp. 455–57). He characterizes the annual observance as a sex cult, modeled on Canaanite practices, in which Israelite women were dedicated to the deity (presumably Baal) by an act of ritual defloration. This interpretation was challenged by Wilhelm Rudolph

("Präparierte Jungfrauen?" *ZAW* 34 [1963]: 69) who correctly noted that Boström's interpretation contradicts the text itself, which clearly states (Rudolph says three times, I would say once) that Jephthah's daughter died a virgin. For a general discussion of the actual evidence for ancient Near Eastern "sex cults," see Robert Oden (*The Bible Without Theology* [San Francisco: Harper and Row, 1987], 131–53). Additionally, I would note that terminology such as "sex cult" and "fertility rite" is often used in scholarly literature with a decidedly derogatory connotation, implying something that is evolutionarily prior to or culturally alien to Israelite religion. (For a sensitive critique of the Frazerian model that this implies, see Gary A. Anderson, *Sacrifices and Offerings in Ancient Israel: Studies in Their Social and Political Importance*, HSM 41 [Atlanta: Scholars, 1987], 4–14.) Insofar as "sex cults" and "fertility rites" are associated with female reproduction, I suspect that this is an example of the marginalization of women's sexuality by categorizing it as "prior" or "other."

15. Keukens, "Richter 11, 37 f.," 41–42.

16. An annual ceremony celebrating the initial menses of selected girls is performed, for example, by the Mescalero Apaches. Cf. Claire R. Farrer, "Singing for Life: The Mescalero Apache Girls' Puberty Ceremony," *Betwixt and Between: Patterns of Masculine and Feminine Initiation,* eds. Louise C. Mahdi et al. (La Salle: Open Court, 1987), 239–63.

17. As van Gennep demonstrated, ritual death is a typical feature of rites of passage. Richards (*Chisungu,* 20) specifically notes that ritual lament and/or ritual burial are typical features of puberty rites.

18. This essay will not treat the parallels between Jephthah's rash vow and its consequences and the vows of Idomeneus (Servius' commentary on Vergil's *Aeneid,* 3.121; H. Albertus Lion, *Commentarii in Virgilium Servanian* [Göttingen: Vandenhoeck und Ruprecht, 1826], 196) and Maeander (*de fluviis* ix; English trans. in *The Complete Works of Plutarch* [New York: Crowell, 1909] vol. 5, 739–40) nor will it treat the sacrifice of Polyxena.

19. The problem of categorizing Iphigeneia is actually more complex: Hesychius, for example, identifies her with the goddess Artemis. However she is best known as the daughter of the legendary worthy, Agamemnon.

20. Cf. *The Oxford Classical Dictionary* (Oxford: Clarendon, 1970), 338–39. The plot of the *Cypria* is preserved in an epitome of the fifth century C.E. philosopher Proclus (*Chrestomathia*; Thomas W. Allen, *Homeri Opera* [Oxford: Oxford University, 1912] vol. 5, 93–109. The relevant text is p. 104, lines 12–20.).

21. Artemis is, among other things, the goddess of the hunt.

22. See esp. Albert Henrichs, "Human Sacrifice in Greek Religion: Three Case Studies," *Le sacrifice dans l'antiquité* (Entretiens sur l'antiquité classique 27; Geneva: 1981), 198–208, 236–42. David Marcus (*Jephthah and His Vow* [Lubbock, Tex.: Texas Tech, 1986], 42–43) discusses many of the traditions about Iphigeneia, but not those that link her to Brauron and Munychia (see

below). He concludes that Iphigeneia contributes little to our understanding of the biblical text. I hope to demonstrate that he is incorrect.

23. The father's rash vow and its relation to success in battle are obvious parallels to the story of Jephthah and his daughter.

24. Scholium in the Leyden MS of Aristophanes' *Lysistrata,* l. 645; *Suda* s. v. *arktos.* Cf. Hugh Lloyd-Jones, "Artemis and Iphigeneia," *Journal of Hellenic Studies* 103 (1983): 92–93 and n. 32. Paula Perlman ("Plato *Laws* 833C–834D and the Bears of Brauron," *GRBS* 24 [1983]: 115–24) argues that girls between the ages of ten and fourteen or fifteen were *arktoi.* Robin Osborne (*Demos: The Discovery of Classical Attika* [Cambridge: Cambridge University, 1985], 165) does not challenge the age range stated in the scholium and the *Suda.* Rather, Osborne notes that in other cultures puberty rituals may anticipate menarche.

25. Angelo Brelich, "Symbol of a Symbol," in *Myths and Symbols: Studies in Honor of Mircea Eliade,* eds. J. M. Kitagawa and C. H. Long (Chicago: University of Chicago, 1969), 201, but see Henrichs, "Human Sacrifice," 207 n. 1.

26. Scholium in the Ravennas MS of Aristophanes' *Lysistrata,* l. 645. (Trans. by William G. Rutherford, *Scholia Aristophanica* [New York: MacMillan, 1896], 203). Cf. S. E. Cole, "The Social Function of Rituals of Maturation: The Koureion and the Arkteia," *ZPE* 55 (1984): 238–44; Perlman, "Bears of Brauron," 116 and n. 6.

27. Cf. Angelo Brelich, *Paides et Parthenoi* (Rome: Istituto per gli Studi Micenei ed Egeo-Anitolici, 1969) vol. 1, esp. 247 ff.; Brelich, "Symbol," 201–7; William Sale, "The Temple-Legends of the Arkteia," *Rheinisches Museum für Philologie* 118 (1975): 265–84; Henrichs, "Human Sacrifice," 198–208; Lloyd-Jones, "Artemis," 91–98.

28. This is the sequence reconstructed by Sale ("Temple-Legends," 272).

29. Pausanias Lexicon, in Eustathius *Iliad* 2.273. The Greek text is given by Brelich (*Paides,* vol. 1, 248); English translation by Sale ("Temple-Legends," 276).

30. Scholium to the Leyden MS of Aristophanes' *Lysistrata,* l. 645. The Greek text is given by Sale ("Temple-Legends," 266); English translation following Sale ("Temple-Legends," 273).

31. For other traditions locating Iphigeneia at Brauron, see Henrichs ("Human Sacrifice," 200, n. 1).

32. Sale ("Temple-Legends," 283–84) suggests that the legend moved from Brauron to Aulis rather than the reverse. Henrichs ("Human Sacrifice," 200, n. 1) thinks that the Iphigeneia legend was secondarily localized at Brauron. Henrichs has the better of the argument.

33. I am following here the *Homeric Hymn to Demeter* (lines 1–23), which is the earliest extant rendition of Kore's abduction. For the Greek text, see N. J. Richardson, *The Homeric Hymn to Demeter* (Oxford: Clarendon, 1974).

34. Most recently, Robert Alter (Robert Alter and Frank Kermode, eds., *The Literary Guide to the Bible* [Cambridge, Mass.: Belknap, 1987], 17).

35. Gaster, *MLCOT,* 431.

36. Burney, *Judges,* 334.

37. For example, J. Prytz Johansen ("The Thesmophoria as a Women's Festival," *Temenos* 11 [1975]: 80) notes that the Thesmophoria, a Demeter/Kore festival celebrated in most locations at the time of fall sowing, was on Delos and at Thebes celebrated two months earlier. This leads him to conclude that the connection between the Thesmophoria and the agricultural calendar was of secondary importance. Walter Burkert (*Greek Religion* [Cambridge, Mass.: Harvard University, 1985], 245; *Homo Necans* [Berkeley: University of California, 1983], 260–62) makes this same point independently, and draws the same conclusion.

For an extensive collection of the ancient sources for the Thesmophoria, see Allaire Chandor Brumfield (*The Attic Festivals of Demeter and their Relation to the Agricultural Year* [New York: Arno, 1981], 70–103). Brumfield's analysis of the Thesmophoria, steeped as it is in a Frazerian model of magic and fertility, is disappointing.

38. Richards, *Chisungu,* 125.

39. Henri Jeanmaire, *Couroi et Courètes: Essai sur l'éducation spartiate et sur les rites d'adolescence dans l'antiquité hellénique* (Lille: Bibliothèque Universitaire, 1939), 26–43, 268–82, 298–305. Jeanmaire's work has been critically appropriated by Angelo Brelich (*Paides et Parthenoi*; "Symbol," 195–207).

40. Bruce Lincoln, *Emerging From the Chrysalis,* 71–90. Walter Burkert (*Structure and History in Greek Mythology and Ritual* [Berkeley: University of California, 1979], 57) goes so far as to say that the "girl's tragedy" pattern in general reflects initiation rituals.

41. Lincoln, *Emerging,* 74.

42. Lincoln, *Emerging,* 77. In spite of Kore's (unwilling) defloration by Hades, Lincoln reads the story as the mythic expression of a puberty rite and not a marriage rite. His interpretation is possible. Among the Tiyyar caste of southwestern India (*Emerging,* 7–16), for example, there is a female puberty rite which features symbolic defloration. Audrey Richards (*Chisungu,* 124) also notes that female puberty rites among the Bemba of northern Rhodesia include actions which her female informants described as "reproducing the sex act." K. and J. Paige (*Politics,* 105–6) offer an example of a menarcheal rite in which a member of the woman's own moiety is the first to have intercourse with her, thus establishing a degree of claim on her future offspring. These potential parallels would have to be examined in light of archaic Greek social structure in order to determine their applicability.

43. Lincoln, *Emerging,* 79. The argument rests on expunging two passages in which the goddess Hekate appears. Lincoln notes that these passages have long been considered secondary. Lincoln also asserts ("The Rape of Persephone: A Greek Scenario of Women's Initiation," *HTR* 72 [1979]: 229–30) that, with one exception, the goddess is *always* called Persephone after Hermes has been dispatched to bring her back to earth. (He explains this exception [*Hymn,* l. 337] as a reference to the time when the goddess resumes

her role as initiand.) On this point Lincoln is incorrect: the goddess is referred to as *kourē* in l. 493. Thus we can say that the goddess acquires a proper name (Persephone) upon emerging from the liminal state, but we cannot say that she is no longer referred to by the generic term Kore.

44. Note the renaming of Abram (Gen. 17:5), Sarai (Gen. 17:15) and Jacob (Gen. 32:28 [J source]; 35:10 [P source]) at points of transition from one status to another.

45. Burney (*Judges,* 332) mentions an intriguing reference to the worship of Kore at Shechem, which his source (Epiphanius) connects with the commemoration of Jephthah's daughter's death. I have been unable to locate this reference.

46. Burkert, *Greek Religion,* 242.

47. See Brumfield, *Attic Festivals,* 73–79; Prytz, "Thesmophoria," 78–82. Brumfield traces the source of this scholium to the first century B.C.E.

48. Brumfield, *Attic Festivals,* 83 and n. 55.

49. Burkert, *Greek Religion,* 244, 443 n. 29; Prytz, "Thesmophoria," 86. The return to a primitive lifestyle is one of the ways that rites of passage symbolize that the initiands are naive with respect to the knowledge that they will need to function in their soon-to-be-acquired new status.

50. Burkert, *Homo Necans,* 259; Mark Golden, "Male Chauvinists and Pigs," *Classical Views* 32, n.s. 7 (1988), 1–12.

51. Prytz ("Thesmophoria," *passim*) argues that the Thesmophoria should be interpreted this way.

52. Golden, "Pigs," 6–7.

53. This is not true for all the tellings of Iphigeneia's story. In Aeschylus' *Agamemnon,* for example, Iphigeneia dies on the altar, but as Henrichs ("Human Sacrifice," 198–99) notes, this is probably an innovation that allows Aeschylus to explore the moral dimension of Agamemnon's act. I think it inappropriate to apply the same reasoning to the biblical story precisely because the biblical text does not moralize Jephthah's decision.

54. So also Lloyd-Jones, "Artemis," 97.

55. Burkert (*Homo Necans,* 65) also senses these identifications: "the maiden [is] represented by a goat for Artemis and a pig for Demeter. The myths, however, call them Iphigeneia and Kore and, at least in some rituals (initiation and mystery rites), the substitution is made explicit."

56. The latter point is, of course, speculation on my part. I am combining the "logic" of sacrificial language, the fact that the festival was celebrated exclusively by women, and the observation that women in Israelite culture (as far as we know) were not permitted to preside over animal sacrifices. Cf. Nancy Jay, "Sacrifice as Remedy for Having Been Born of Woman," in *Immaculate and Powerful: The Female in Sacred Image and Social Reality,* eds. Clarissa W. Atkinson et al. (Boston: Beacon, 1985), 283–309.

57. Ardener, "Belief," 135–58; see n. 5, above.

58. Cf. Burkert, *Homo Necans,* 65–67; Henrichs, "Human Sacrifice," 200 n. 1.

59. It is intriguing to note that the story of Jephthah's "fatal victory" conforms to the typically male fantasy pattern of physical and emotional excitement and pride, followed by failure and despair. For a detailed description of this pattern, see Robert May (*Sex and Fantasy: Patterns of Male and Female Development* [New York: W. W. Norton and Company, 1980]). Although May's study has rich implications for understanding the biblical presentation of Jephthah's story, one brief example must here suffice. May notes (63) that "the defensive strategy most associated with the male fantasy pattern is projection. This strategy is based on externalizing, on finding someone else to blame and hold responsible." It is striking that Jephthah blames his daughter for the misfortune that in fact proceeds from his own ill-formulated vow (v. 36; cf. Phyllis Trible, *Texts of Terror* [Philadelphia: Fortress, 1984], 101–2).

60. The scholarly literature concerning Adonis, Baal, Tammuz, Eshmun, and Melqart as dying (and rising) gods cannot be reviewed here. It has recently been suggested by Noel Robertson ("The Ritual Background of the Dying God in Cyprus and Syro-Palestine," *HTR* 75 [1982]: 339–40) and Brian Peckham ("Phoenicia and the Religion of Israel: The Epigraphic Evidence," in *Ancient Israelite Religion: Essays in Honor of Frank Moore Cross*, eds. P. D. Miller et al. [Philadelphia: Fortress, 1987], 84) that Jephthah's daughter's lament is tied to mourning for a male deity, either Adonis (Robertson) or Eshmun (Peckham). John Gray (*The Legacy of Canaan* (Leiden: Brill, 1957], 53) remarks that the story's lament in the hill country finds a parallel in Anat's search for the dead Baal. The logic of these conclusions escapes me. It is Jephthah's daughter who dies and the annual lament is construed as the reenactment of her own lament prior to her own death. I see no good reason to suppose that Jephthah's daughter has gone off to the hills to mourn Adonis'/Eshmun's/Baal's death as a prelude to her own demise.

61. Carol Gilligan, *In a Different Voice* (Cambridge, Mass.: Harvard University, 1982).

6 "TO PLAY THE HARLOT": AN INQUIRY INTO AN OLD TESTAMENT METAPHOR

PHYLLIS BIRD

This chapter explores a number of problems related to the translation and interpretation of the Hebrew root *znh,* with particular attention to its metaphorical or figurative use.[1] It is prompted by problems in translation and definition, difficulties in determining the boundary between literal and figurative uses, and interest in the use of a metaphor drawn, apparently, from female behavior to characterize the behavior of collective Israel.

The translation "play the harlot" is RSV's conventional rendering of the Hebrew verb *zānâ,* in both literal and figurative uses, replacing the familiar but archaic "go awhoring" or "commit whoredom" of KJV. Unlike the "whoring" language that may describe either male or female activity ("to have unlawful sexual intercourse *as* or *with* a whore"),[2] the "denominative" rendering of RSV defines the behavior by reference to a female model. Both translations, however, share an orientation toward the professional prostitute. Is this a peculiarity of English idiom or does it represent the Hebrew understanding? A primary question for investigation must be the relationship of verbal uses to the noun *zônâ* ("prostitute").

Another question concerns the meaning of the verb when used with a masculine subject.[3] Most of the examples represent clearly metaphorical uses, describing pursuit of other gods (Judg. 2:17; 8:33; Deut. 31:11) or participation in illicit cultic activity (Lev. 20:5; 17:7; Judg. 8:27). In Num. 25:1, however, the usual cultic and metaphorical interpretations are strained, and the translation of RSV appears ludicrous: "While Israel dwelt at Shittim the people (*hā'ām*) began to play the harlot (*wayyāḥel . . . liznôt*) with the daughters of Moab." Is the usage here figurative or literal, or does it represent some other type of extended use?[4]

A further question is raised by the common identification of prostitution and "sacred or cultic prostitution." The assumption of such an institution as a pervasive and constitutive feature of Canaanite religions is fundamental to most interpretations of the root *znh* and discussion of "fertility cult religion."[5] Although the institution is construed in different ways, the term by which it is designated is never called into question. Yet the concept expressed by combining words for "sacred" (or "cultic") and "prostitution" is not found in the Hebrew Bible or in any ancient Semitic language.

From biblical Hebrew and Akkadian sources we know only of "prostitutes" (Heb. *zônâ*; Akk. *ḫarīmtu*) and "sacred/consecrated women" (Heb. *qĕdēšâ*; Akk. *qadištu*) along with other classes of female cult functionaries (*ēn/ēntu, nadītu, ugbabtu, ištarītu, kulmašītu*).[6] While prostitutes *may* have functioned at times in the cultic sphere (in which case the circumstances require careful attention) and while hierodules[7] *may* have had functions or duties involving sexual activity (here too the circumstances require careful attention), the terms used in the indigenous languages to describe these two classes never connect the sacred sphere with prostitution or prostitution with the cult.[8] It is only through association that the interpretation arises, and it is only in the Hebrew Bible that the association is made in a deliberate manner. It would appear then that the identification is the result of a specifically biblical and, I shall argue, polemical interpretation.[9]

In the limited scope of this essay it is impossible to give attention to all of the interlocking issues that affect interpretation of this root and its unique metaphorical employment in the Hebrew Bible. I shall begin with a summary treatment of the primary meaning(s) of the root and then move to a detailed examination of selected texts in the book of Hosea, which appear to represent the earliest metaphorical usage.

znh/zônâ

The basic meaning of the root as expressed in the verb *zānâ* is "to engage in sexual relations outside of or apart from marriage,"[10] activity that is normally understood as illicit; hence the primary definition of BDB: "commit fornication."[11] In relation to *nʾp* "commit adultery," with which it is often associated and may at times coincide, *znh* is the more general or inclusive term. Cognate usage (Aramaic, Ethiopic, and Arabic) exhibits a similar broad meaning, especially evident in Arabic *zanā* "to commit adultery, fornicate, whore" (cf. *zinan* and *zināʾ*,

"adultery, fornication"; *zānin* "fornicator, adulterer"; *zāniya* "whore, harlot, adulteress").[12]

As a general term for extramarital sexual intercourse, *znh* is limited in its primary usage to female subjects, since it is only for women that marriage is the primary determinant of legal status and obligation. While male sexual activity is judged by the status of the female partner and is prohibited, or penalized, only when it violates the recognized marital rights of another male, female sexual activity is judged according to the woman's marital status. In Israel's moral code, a woman's sexuality was understood to belong to her husband alone, for whom it must be reserved in anticipation of marriage as well as in the marriage bond. Violation of a husband's sexual rights, the most serious of sexual offenses, is signified by the term *n'p* "adultery"; all other instances of sexual intercourse apart from marriage are designated by the term *znh.*[13] These include premarital sex by a daughter, understood as an offense against her father or family (Heb. "father's house"), whose honor requires her chastity (Deut. 22:13–21; Lev. 21:9; cf. Gen. 34:31); or sex by a levirate-obligated widow (Gen. 38:6–11, 24–26), understood as an offense against her father-in-law or her deceased husband's family.[14]

It also includes the activity of the professional prostitute, who has no husband nor sexual obligation to any other male. Herein lies a critical distinction. Whereas the promiscuity of a daughter or levirate-obligated widow offends the male to whom each is subject and is penalized accordingly, the harlot's activity violates no man's rights or honor, and consequently is free from the sanctions imposed on the casual fornicator. Strictly speaking, her activity is not illicit—and neither is her role.[15]

The distinction between the two classes of activity (fornication and prostitution) described by the common root *znh* is strikingly illustrated by the account of Judah's reaction to Tamar in two episodes of the narrative in Genesis 38. In the first, he embraces a woman whom he identifies as a *zônâ* (v. 15, RSV: "he thought her to be a harlot"); in the second he condemns to death a woman whose activity is identified by the verb *zānâ* (v. 24, RSV: "your daughter-in-law has played the harlot [*zānětâ*]"). The irony of the situation, on which the story turns, is that the two women are one, and so too is their action. But it is construed differently according to the perceived circumstances, more particularly, according to the socio-legal status of the woman involved. In the first instance, *znh* describes the woman's profession ("he thought her to be a harlot") and consequently her status—as an ostracized but tolerated purveyor of sexual favors for men. In the second, *znh* describes the activity of a woman whose socio-legal status ("your daughter-in-law" *kallāteka*) makes such activity a crime.

Hebrew linguistic usage links the fornicator and the prostitute, but it also distinguishes them, by syntactic and contextual means. A proper understanding of the root *znh* and its usage in the Hebrew Bible requires careful and discriminating attention to linguistic, literary, and sociological factors that determine meaning.

The Hebrew term for "prostitute," *zônâ*, is the *qal* feminine participle of the verb *zānâ*, used as a noun of profession either alone ([*haz*]*zônâ* "[the] prostitute") or in apposition to *ʾiššâ* "woman" (*ʾiššâ zônâ* "a prostitute woman").[16] Thus in Hebrew conception the prostitute is "essentially" a professional or habitual fornicator, a promiscuous or unchaste woman, whose role and profession are defined by her sexual activity with men to whom she is not married. The noun represents a special case of the activity denoted by the *qal* verb. Despite this apparent relationship of dependence, however, virtually all discussions of the root reverse the order of influence, pointing to prostitution as the determining content of the verbal usage and thereby perpetuating the fixation on the professional model exhibited in the common English translations "play the harlot" and "go awhoring."[17] Is such a shift justified, and under what conditions?

The semantic relationship between the verbal and nominal uses of the root is, in fact, complex, affected in part at least by the figurative usage that dominates in the Hebrew Bible and invites interchange. Once the participle has become the identifying term for the prostitute, this specialized usage may exercise a secondary or "reverse" influence on the verb. The verb may be understood to describe the exercise of the profession (Amos 7:17), or it may acquire connotations and associations that were originally peculiar to the noun. Nevertheless, the basic meaning of the verb as describing fornication or illicit extramarital relations should be the starting point for interpreting any given use.

Another factor contributing to the problems of determining the meaning of the root is inadequate sociological analysis of the phenomenon of prostitution. The figure designated by the Hebrew participle *zônâ* represents a recognized institution, known throughout the ancient Near East and most urban cultures, whose relatively constant features can be described and analyzed quite apart from the terminology used for it in any given language or culture.[18] Thus while Hebrew linguistic usage gives important clues to Israel's understanding of prostitution, it does not suffice to describe the nature of the institution or how it functioned. It is the historically functioning institution, however, with all of its associations, that supplies the content of the term *zônâ,* not the etymology. What is needed is a sociologically adequate account of the institution as it functioned in ancient Israel. This is especially urgent in view of the widespread assumption of an analogous or allied institution in the sacred sphere likewise identified by the term "prostitution."

In lieu of that needed account a few words of analysis must suffice. Prostitution shares with fornication, as defined in Israel, a fundamentally female profile,[19] despite the fact that both activities require active male participation and may involve male initiation (cf. Gen. 38:15–16). This asymmetry of conception and description is a characteristic feature of patriarchal societies, reflecting a general pattern of asymmetry in gender-related roles, values, and obligations (a phenomenon recognized in a more limited way by the notion of the "double standard"). The anomaly of the prostitute as a tolerated specialist in an activity prohibited to every other woman is a particular feature of patriarchal society, representing an accommodation to the conflicting desires of men for exclusive control of their wives' sexuality (and hence offspring[20]) and, at the same time, for sexual access to other women. The greater the inaccessibility of women in the society as a result of restrictions on the wife and unmarried nubile woman, the greater the need for an institutionally legitimized "other woman." The prostitute is that "other woman," tolerated but stigmatized, desired but ostracized. As I have attempted to show elsewhere, attitudes toward prostitution are characterized by ambivalence in every society, and the biblical evidence does not support the notion of a sharp distinction between Israelite and Canaanite society with respect to the prostitute's legal or social status.[21]

In my analysis, neither the verb *zānâ* nor the noun *zônâ* in their primary uses refers to cultic activity or have cultic connotations. Where then does the cultic interpretation arise, and under what conditions? Does it represent Israelite understanding or is it an interpreter's imposition? I shall limit attention to three linked texts in the book of Hosea, which represent, I believe, the primary literary and religio-historical context for the development of the figurative usage. The discussion must remain partial and tentative, since the key texts contain multiple interlocking problems of interpretation, some unresolved and others incapable of summary treatment. I have chosen, nevertheless, to begin with these texts, because I believe they are critical and because they illustrate a number of different interpretive problems.

THE BIRTH OF A METAPHOR: *ZNH* IN THE BOOK OF HOSEA

The opening words of the book present a sign-action that introduces the governing metaphor of chapters 1–3 and the theme of the collected oracles, articulated by use of the root *znh* (1:2).[22] Hosea is commanded to get a "woman/wife of promiscuity" (*ʾēšet zĕnûnîm*) and "offspring/children of promiscuity" (*yaldê zĕnûnîm*), "because the land is utterly promiscuous (turning) away from Yahweh" (*kî-zānōh tizneh hāʾāreṣ mēʾaḥărê yhwh*). The prophet is to represent by his marriage and family life Yahweh's relationship to Israel as a relationship subverted by Israel's promiscuous behavior. The use of *znh* in the interpretive *kî* ("for, because") clause is clearly figurative, with the land (grammatically feminine) replacing the usual female subject. Although the underlying metaphor is that of marriage, the use of *znh* rather than *nʾp* serves to emphasize promiscuity rather than infidelity, "wantonness" rather than violation of marriage contract or covenant. The connotations of repeated, habitual, or characteristic behavior are reinforced by the emphatic verbal augment (*zānōh*) and by repetition of the noun *zĕnûnîm* ("promiscuity, fornication") to characterize both the wife and the children.

The woman is not described as a *zônâ*, although most commentators speak inaccurately of Hosea's marriage to a harlot.[23] Rather, as an *ʾēšet zĕnûnîm* she is characterized as a woman of loose sexual morals, whose promiscuous nature is exhibited in her "fornications" (*zĕnûnîm*). The use of the abstract plural noun points to habitual behavior and inclination rather than profession (cf. *rûaḥ zĕnûnîm* "spirit of promiscuity" 4:12; 5:4). It is also open to extended or figurative meanings. In fact, the pairing of "woman of promiscuity" with "children of promiscuity" would appear to point in that direction, since, as we have seen, fornication normally describes a woman's activity. What sense can it make applied to the children?

Although *zĕnûnîm* can be understood to refer to the woman in both expressions and thus to characterize the children as the product of her promiscuous activity ("children [born] of promiscuity"), the mimicking construction of the paired terms and the linkage without an intervening verb suggest that the author intended to claim for the children the same nature as their mother. The message of the sign-action, enunciated in the following *kî* clause and elaborated in chapter 2, is that the land "fornicates"—and so do its inhabitants (children). The identification and interchange between mother and children, land and people is clear in chapter 2, where the mother's pursuit of her lovers is equated with cultic activities of the general population—and especially males. Thus mother and children should not be sharply differentiated.

What then does *zĕnûnîm* mean when applied to the children? I suggest that term be read in its incongruous "literal" (but abstract) sense. The function of the sign-act is to shock, and intimate, and confound—and more particularly to point forward to the explanation that follows. As in other prophetic sign-actions, the sign depends on the interpretive word for its meaning and is chosen and/or formulated in the light of the intended message. The message in this case is that the land is unfaithful to Yahweh—like a promiscuous wife and promiscuous children. The characterization of the wife by *zĕnûnîm* makes sense as literal description (even if it raises question of plausibility), but the duplicate characterization of the children must be heard as strange and enigmatic, raising a question about the meaning of both uses. That, I think, is exactly what it was meant to do, opening the way to the explanation that follows. But the explanation is as enigmatic as the action it interprets. What does it mean to say that the land "fornicates"?

The meaning of the charge is revealed only in chapter 2, to which it points and on which it depends.[24] The implication, however, is clear: the land (people) has relations with other lovers in place of (*mē'aḥărê*, lit. "from after/behind") Yahweh. The logical supposition is that the "affairs" are with other gods, although 1:2 does not identify the object(s) of Israel's affections. It points, rather, to the aggrieved husband, with a construction that is unique to Hosea. The sequence *zānâ* + *min* / *mē* "(away) from" occurs only in Hosea, and Ps. 73:27, and appears to be dictated by the marriage metaphor to which Hosea has adapted his usage. Normally *zānâ* does not carry the notion of infidelity, which is supplied by the context and made explicit here by Hosea's inventive construction. In each of the three occurrences of the sequence in Hosea (1:2; 4:12; 9:1) the *min* is compounded with another preposition that serves to connect the statement to a following expression. In the case of *mē'aḥărê* the expression that explains the usage is found in 2:5 (cf. 13),[25] where the charge of fornication (*zānĕtâ 'immām* "their mother *znh*-ed") is interpreted by the quotation, "For she said, 'I will go *after* ('*aḥărê*) my lovers.'" The preposition "after" belongs to the idiom *hālak 'aḥărê* "walk after," "follow." Hosea has appropriated it to describe, in a privative construction (*zānâ min*), the relationship to the one abandoned.

The charge of fornication that opens the book is elaborated in an extended allegory in 2:2–13 (Heb. 4–15), which develops the figure of the promiscuous bride and points to the activity underlying the metaphor. The opening accusation employs the mother-children metaphor and *zānâ*/*zĕnûnîm* language of 1:2, and likewise identifies mother and land (2:3; cf. v. 12). In 5b the summary charge of promiscuity (5a) is substantiated with a quotation from the accused:

> For she said, "I will go after my lovers,
> who give me my bread and my water,
> my wool and my flax, my oil and my drink."

The picture presented in these words is that of a woman who seeks lovers for their gifts, called specifically "hire" (*ʾetnâ*)[26] in v. 12. Here the metaphor points to the figure of the professional prostitute, who is distinguished from the casual fornicator by her mercenary motive and multiple partners (pl. "lovers"). But she is also depicted as a wife (vv. 2, 7, 13) and mother (vv. 2, 4, 5) who has "behaved shamefully" (*hōbîšâ* // *zānĕtâ* "committed fornication," v. 5a), and it is her status as wife that is reflected in the punishment envisioned in vv. 3 and 10.[27] It appears that the author has drawn upon the full range of images and attitudes associated with the root *znh* to create his portrait of wayward Israel. It also suggests that the distinction between fornication and prostitution was essentially a legal one and that popular opinion regarded the behavior as essentially the same.

But what is represented by the metaphor, and to what extent are the terms of the figure dictated by the activity it describes? It is clear from the nature of the gifts mentioned in v. 5 that they are, directly or indirectly, the products of the land (cf. vv. 8, 9, 12) that depend on the life-sustaining gift of rain. Israel thinks they come from her lovers, whom she pursues (vv. 5, 7), adorning herself to win their favor (v. 13); but they are in fact the gifts of her husband Yahweh (v. 8), who will take them away, exposing her nakedness (vv. 9, 10, 12; cf. v. 3). The allegory is transparent: Israel has turned to the Canaanite rain god Baal (pejoratively represented as plural lovers) when her covenant lord, Yahweh, is the true God of fertility; the means of her lovemaking is the cult (vv. 8, 11, 13). The allegory is consistent, and daring in its appropriation of the basic fertility myth of the earth mother wed to the rain god.

The fundamental issue, in Hosea's view, is still the same as in the days of Elijah, viz., Who is the true god of fertility, Baal or Yahweh?—but now there is no contest. The battle of rival deities for national homage and state support has been won. What Hosea attacks is a Yahweh cult perverted by practices derived from the old (Baal) religion of the land, so that, in effect, it is really Baal that is worshiped ("courted") in these practices, not Yahweh.[28] The plural reference to the object of Israel's promiscuous devotion ("lovers," vv. 5, 7, 10, 12, 13; "the baals," v. 13; cf. v. 17) is, I suggest, an intentional device for "belittling" Baal, denying him a proper name and the status of a true rival. It also serves to identify the deity with the local cult places, and reinforces the impression of feverish cultic/sexual activity suggested by reference to multiple feasts (vv. 11, 13).

Despite the innuendo of chapter 2, the suggestion of cultic sex remains just that. The sexual language belongs exclusively to the allegory, while the cultic activity to which it points is represented in terms elsewhere descriptive of normative Yahweh worship: pilgrim feast (*ḥag*), new moon, and sabbath—every appointed feast (*kōl mŏʿēd*) (v. 11).[29] It is only in chapter 4 that sexual language is employed in a non-metaphorical way in conjunction with cultic language—and the key term is *znh.*

Hosea 4:11–14 is a judgment oracle framed by short proverbial sentences (vv. 11 and 14b).[30] The indictment begins in v. 12 with a condemnation of oracular practices, followed by an explanatory *kî* clause employing the root *znh,* which functions as a leitmotif in the pericope, uniquely combining literal and metaphorical uses:

> My people[31] inquires of his (= its) "tree"
> and his "rod" gives him answer,
> For a *spirit of fornication* (*rûḥ zĕnûnîm*)
> has led (them) astray,
> and *they have fornicated* (*wayyiznû*)
> from under (*mittaḥat*) their God.

The charge of seeking oracular guidance by illicit means is couched in language that suggests both idolatry/apostasy ("tree" and "rod" as cult objects associated with other gods or illicit cult)[32] and sexual activity ("tree" and "rod" as phallic symbols). The sexual innuendo of the opening bicolon is reinforced by the use of *znh* in the following sentence. The language is strongly reminiscent of 1:2 in its combined use of *zānâ* and *zĕnûnîm* and in the syntax of the verb (with *min* + a preposition of position, here *taḥat* "under"). As in 1:2, the language functions metaphorically to characterize the nation as promiscuous in its inclination (*rûaḥ zĕnûnîm*) and activity (*wayyiznû*). Here, however, the appeal to a female interpretive model cannot be explained by the grammatical gender of the subject. There is no personification of the land as mother; instead the people themselves (*ʿammî*) are the subject, represented throughout the pericope by male-defined activity as well as masculine gender. NJV reflects this shift to a masculine subject by employing male-oriented or gender-neutral terminology ("a lecherous impulse," "they have strayed"). Yet the model for the usage continues to be the promiscuous bride, as reference to the wronged partner implies—employing a preposition (*taḥat* "under") that is even more sexually suggestive.[33]

The indictment of cultic practice continues in vv. 13–$14a_{\beta}$ in a quatrain whose first and final lines form an inclusio marked by parallel syntax, rhyming Hebrew verb forms, and identical opening and closing verbs.[34]

1. ($13a_{\beta}$) On the mountain-tops they "perform sacrifices,"
   and on the hills they "make offerings,"
2. ($13a_{\beta}$) Under oak and poplar
   and terebinth—because its shade is good.
3. (13b) That is why their[35] daughters fornicate
   and their daughters-in-law commit adultery;
4. ($14a_{\beta}$)[36] For they themselves "divide" with the prostitutes
   and "perform sacrifices" with the hierodules.

The first two lines describe cultic activity in literal, but suggestive terms. The verbs, which resume the present tense (impf.) of the opening indictment, represent the primary terms for cultic action, *zbḥ* "to sacrifice" and *qṭr* "to burn incense" or "present offerings,"[37] but both are given an unusual vocalization (*piel*) used elsewhere only of illicit cultic activity.[38] Introductory prepositional phrases place emphasis on the locus of the activity ("*on* the mountaintops" and "*on* the hills"), making location a key to the interpretation. This emphasis is underlined in the second line by a list of tree names introduced by a new preposition, without an additional verb. The preposition *taḥat* "under" creates a complementary pair with the *ʿal* ("upon") of the preceding line, but also picks up the *taḥat* of the *mittaḥat* ("from under") in v. 12: the people have *znh*-ed *from under* their God by "offering" *under* trees—because their shade is "good"![39]

The accented terms of location (*on* the heights and *under* shady trees) suggest what this "offering" really involves. As in the opening indictment, the message of sexual activity is carried by innuendo, without the use of explicitly sexual language; and as in v. 12, it is followed by an interpretive word employing the verb *zānâ*—only this time the usage is literal. Line 3 (v. 13b) describes the consequences of the activity condemned in lines 1 and 2: "That is why their (your) daughters fornicate and their (your) daughters-in-law commit adultery."[40] The structure of the argument is clear: what the men do has consequences in their daughters' behavior. But what kind of consequences? That is the central interpretive problem of the pericope.

It is commonly understood to mean that the women engage in some form of "cultic prostitution" and that this activity represents the female side of the male activity alluded to in 13a, and spelled out in 14a$_{\beta}$. Both context and syntax require a literal reading, but does this include a specialized cultic meaning? The following considerations, point, I believe, to a non-cultic interpretation, at least as the "first reading."

1. The pericope as a whole envisions the worshiping community as a body of males, although in the author's mind they represent collective Israel ("my people," v. 12). The description of the daughters' behavior is not one of the series of charges against Yahweh's "people." It is, rather, an argument directed at the men themselves, aiming to bring home to them the consequences of their actions.
2. The function of the statement, as indicated by the initial *ʿal-kēn* ("therefore," "for this reason"), is to draw a connection between two sets of circumstances that had not previously been linked (cf. 4:3). The revelatory force of the statement is in the correlation, not in the description of the activity itself, which must be clearly abhorrent. If the young women had been engaging in sexual activity at the sites of the men's "worship," the connection would be obvious and there would be no need for the *ʿal-kēn.*
3. The intention of the *ʿal-kēn* clause is best realized when the verbs are understood in their "plain sense," as describing the loose sexual conduct of those women for whom the men addressed bear responsibility. Fornication and adultery will be immediately recognized as the most serious of women's offenses; attributed to female dependents (daughters and daughters-in-law, not wives), these sexual improprieties also constitute an attack upon the men's honor.[41] The statement assumes a concern for the women's sexual morals; its message consists in linking their sexual activity

to the men's cultic activity, a link that is dramatically substantiated in the climactic final statement ($14a_{\beta}$).

To summarize, the men are accused of cultic impropriety, the women of sexual impropriety. (The women's offense is obvious; the men's is "under cover.") It may be sexual activity that defiles the men's worship, but it is worship that is the central concern of the pericope, as the verbs show. The men's worst offense is to dishonor God by their perverted worship. The women's worst offense is to dishonor their fathers and fathers-in-law by their sexual conduct. The men dishonor their Lord (metaphorical use of *zānâ,* v. 12b); the women dishonor their lords (literal use of *zānâ*, v. 13b). This differential assessment of male and female behavior, as well as the overall male orientation of the pericope, illustrates the asymmetry of roles, activities, and values noted earlier as a characteristic of patriarchal societies. A further example is found in the concluding line.

Line 4 (v. $14a_{\beta}$) of the reconstructed quatrain is linked to the preceding line (v. 13b) by repetition of the root *znh* (*tiznênâ* "fornicate," *hazzônôt* "prostitutes"), which carries the decisive meaning in both lines, and by a focus on paired classes of women. It is tied to line 1 by parallel construction and repetition of the initial verb to form an inclusio. Line 4 resumes (with emphatic *hēm* "they themselves") the 3mp subject of the first two lines, continuing the description of the men's activity and extending the series of prepositional phrases that define and condemn their action by reference to the circumstances in which it is performed. Here, however, for the first time, an explicitly sexual term (*zônôt*) appears, revealing what lay behind the earlier veiled references; the "sacrifices" *on* the mountaintops and hills and *under* the trees were performed *with* (*ʿim*) prostitutes and hierodules. The final statement sharpens the charges by focusing on a single determining feature of the activity that correlates the men's behavior with that of the women in the preceding line.

The correlation achieved through the use of *znh* does not equate the two pairs of women, nor describe the same activity; rather it points to an underlying connection between the activities of the fathers and the daughters. Each line makes a single, and distinct, statement: line 3, the men's female dependents are promiscuous; line 4, the men perform their "worship" with promiscuous women.

It is usually argued that the pairing of *zônôt* and *qĕdēšôt* means either that the *zônôt* are "sacred prostitutes," at least here, or that the *qĕdēšôt* are (simply) prostitutes.[42] Neither argument fits the requirements of the passage. The classes must be distinct in order to be identified, and the *qĕdēšôt* must be understood as having an essentially cultic identity, as indicated by the etymology of the term and by the use of *zbḥ* ("sacrifice") to describe the activity performed with them. They represent a cultic role, but one associated in Israelite (prophetic) thought with "Canaanite" worship, not Yahweh worship. Thus the placement of the term *qĕdēšôt* in final position serves as the climactic revelation that these cult sites and cultic activities really belong to Baal, not Yahweh.[43]

The meaning of the paired terms, however, is given in this context by the initial *zônôt.* Through this pairing and ordering the reader is meant to understand that *qĕdēšôt* are equivalent to prostitutes. But this directed reading is clearly polemical; it tells us what the prophet thought about the *qĕdēšôt,* but it does not give us any reliable information about the function or activities of these women, except that they must have been a recognized presence at the rural sanctuaries in Hosea's day. There may also be shock value in mentioning the *zônôt* first. While *qĕdēšôt* belong in a cultic context, though not a Yahwistic cult, *zônôt* do not. They belong in public squares and inns and along the highways (Josh. 2:1; Gen. 38:15; Jer. 3:2; Isa. 23:16; Prov. 7:10–12), not at sanctuaries. Naming them as the company with whom the men conduct their worship tells us that this is perverted worship; naming *qĕdēšôt* as the men's companions says that it is "Canaanite"/ Baal worship.

Zônôt are defined by their sexual activity, *qĕdēšôt* by their cultic association. It is impossible to determine the nature of their cultic service from the biblical sources, which are too fragmentary and polemical. It is clear, however, from the limited OT references that the Israelite authors understood their role to include some form of sexual activity, which they identified with prostitution. Through juxtaposition with *zônâ* the term *qĕdēšâ* acquired the sense of "sacred prostitute." Neither the assumption of sexual activity, however, nor its equation with prostitution can be taken at face value. Since Israel appears to have recognized no legitimate role for women as cult functionaries during the period in which *qĕdēšôt* are attested,[44] it would be easy for Israelites to assume that the presence of women at a sanctuary involved sexual activity. It is possible then that the charge of "sacred prostitution" has no base in cultic sex, but is rather a false inference.[45] It is also possible to understand the charge as a polemical misrepresentation of a cultic role that did involve some form of sexual activity, but was not understood by the practitioners as prostitution; the identification of the hierodule's role with the prostitute's would represent a distorted, outsider's view of the institution. A final possibility is that the isolated biblical references to *qĕdēšôt* represent a perverted remnant of an earlier Israelite or Canaanite cult, perpetuated in a perverted Israelite cult.[46] That is suggested by the presence of *zônôt.*

The text offers no justification for viewing the *zônôt* as cultic functionaries. It does suggest that prostitutes found the rural sanctuaries an attractive place to do business, quite possibly by agreement with the priests. The verb (*prd* "divide, separate") offers little help in determining the role of the *zônôt* at the sanctuary, since it has been conformed to the series of polemical *piels* and occurs nowhere else in this vocalization or in connection with *zônôt.* Does it designate a cultic action as the other verbs of the series?[47] The usage appears to be deliberately veiled and avoids the common verbs of sexual encounter.

The *zônôt* and *qĕdēšôt* of the rural sanctuaries must be viewed as a small, specialized class and therefore not descriptive of the general female population, whose younger generation is represented by the daughters and brides of v. 13b. They are not the daughters, or wives, of the men addressed by the oracle.[48] The argument of the concluding lines, which compares male to female activity, is not based on the identity of the actions or of the actors (strictly speaking, it is not a condemnation of the "double standard"). Rather it uses a case of transparent guilt in the secular sphere (*zānâ* of the daughters) to engage the male subjects and then exposes their involvement in similar activity in the sacred sphere (association with *zônôt*), insisting that the men's behavior is equally reprehensible, *or more so,* since it defiles worship with sexual activity.[49] In the final analysis such "worship" amounts to a rejection of Yahweh for other love objects (metaphorical *znh,* v. 12b). The fact that Hosea does not use the verb *zānâ* to describe the men's activity in line 4, despite his attempt to compare male and female behavior, confirms the interpretation of its use in v. 12 as metaphorical.

To summarize, in the primary texts of Hosea the root *znh* has the same basic meaning exhibited elsewhere in historical-legal usage, namely "to engage in illicit/extramarital sexual activity, to fornicate"; and as a professional noun (*zônâ*), "a prostitute." The subject is always female[50] and the activity has, in itself, no cultic connotations. Alongside this basic meaning and corresponding to it in its primary images is a metaphorical usage created by Hosea to characterize and indict Israel's worship. In its original(?) form, Israel (represented as the land, mother of the inhabitants, but interchanging with the inhabitants themselves, always conceived as male) is depicted as a promiscuous wife who abandons her husband for lovers, behaving like a common prostitute in pursuit of hire. The activity represented by the metaphor is cultic activity, which the metaphor reveals to be in effect service of "the baals" rather than Yahweh. It exhibits the character of "nature worship" in its aims, location, and means, including activity of a sexual nature, which Hosea represents as "simply" fornication.

The metaphorical use of *znh* invokes two familiar and linguistically identified images of dishonor in Israelite culture, the common prostitute and the promiscuous daughter or wife. As a sexual metaphor, it points to the sexual nature of the activity it represents. Its female orientation does not single out women for condemnation; it is used rather as a rhetorical device to expose men's sin. By appealing to the common stereotypes and interests of a primarily male audience, Hosea turns their accusation against them. It is easy for patriarchal society to see the guilt of a "fallen women"; Hosea says, "You (male Israel) are that woman!"

NOTES

1. This chapter presents preliminary and abbreviated arguments from a larger study in progress, titled provisionally "Harlot and Hierodule in Israelite Anthropology and Theology." In many cases the length and format of the present essay do not permit full argumentation or documentation of critical points, for which the reader is referred to the forthcoming work.

The only major study of the root is the unpublished Ph.D. dissertation of O. E. Collins, "The Stem *ZNH* and Prostitution in the Hebrew Bible" (Brandeis, 1977; University Microfilms International 77–13364), which, in my view, has serious flaws in literary-linguistic and sociological analysis. A superior, though less exhaustive, treatment is given by M. Hooks in chapter 3 of his dissertation, "Sacred Prostitution in Israel and the Ancient Near East" (Hebrew Union College, 1985) 65–151. The best summary treatment is that of S. Erlandsson, "*zānāh,*" *TDOT* 4 (1980): 99–104; cf. J. Kühlewein, "*znh,* huren," *THAT* 1 (1978): 518–20. See also articles on prostitution or "sacred prostitution" and commentaries, especially F. Hauck and S. Schultz, "*pórnē, pórnos, porneía, porneúō, ekporneúō,*" *TDNT* 6 (1968): 579–95; W. Kornfeld, "L'adultère dans l'Orient antique," *RB* 57 (1950): 92–109; and J. P. Asmussen, "Bemerkungen zur Sakralen Prostitution in Israel," *ST* 11 (1958): 167–92.

2. *Webster's Seventh New Collegiate Dictionary* (Springfield, Mass.: G. & C. Merriam, 1972).

3. The examples cited below are all of the *qal* (basic) stem. The *hiphil* (8x, all masc.) functions in most cases as a causative of the *qal*; on its use in Hosea see below.

4. Collins saw the problem of determining literal and figurative uses as one of the primary methodological problems in previous treatments of the root ("The Stem *ZNH*," 13–17).

5. See Hooks, "Sacred Prostitution," for a comprehensive review (survey of theories, 1–4) and critique of this assumption.

6. The functions of the women designated by these terms (which have limited geographical and chronological distribution) are still poorly understood. See J. Renger, "Untersuchungen zum Priestertum in der altbabylonischen Zeit," *ZA* 58 (1967): 114–87; R. Harris, "The NADĪTU Woman," in *Studies Presented to Leo Openheim* (Chicago: University of Chicago, 1964); and Hooks, "Sacred Prostitution," 10–23.

7. I use the Greek term, meaning "temple slave," as a convenient and arbitrary class term for all nonpriestly cultic personnel, since the languages in question lack a single designation.

8. Cf. Collins, "The Stem *ZNH*," 33–34; Hooks, "Sacred Prostitution," 10–45, 152–85.

9. The idea may also have arisen independently in classical sources. It has certainly been nourished by the sensationalist accounts of Herodotus (*Histories* I, 199) and Lucian (*De Dea Syria* §16) describing the strange religious and sexual customs of the Babylonians and Phoenicians. Neither, however, uses the expression "sacred prostitution" in his descriptions of practices which he attributes to the general female population, rather than to professional prostitutes or hierodules. See Hooks, "Sacred Prostitution," 32–36, 40–41.

10. So also Erlandsson, "*zānāh*," 100; followed by Hooks, "Sacred Prostitution," 70.

11. BDB also gives as a second basic meaning "be a harlot." In its classification of uses, however, it lists as 1. "*be or act as a harlot*," offering the alternative "commit fornication" only for Num. 25:1, specified as a "man's act." Further categories are 2. "fig. *of improper intercourse with foreign nations*," 3. "*of intercourse with other deities*, considered as harlotry, sts. involving actual prostitution," and 4. "*zwnh* of moral defection" (only Isa. 1:21). The *pual* and *hiphil* uses are all defined in terms of "fornication," further classified as "sexual" or "religious." Cf. *HALAT*, 263–64.

12. Hans Wehr, *A Dictionary of Modern Written Arabic*, ed. J. Milton Cowan (Ithaca, N.Y.: Cornell University, 1961). See further Collins, "The Stem *ZNH*," 4–12; Hooks, "Sacred Prostitution," 67–69.

13. *znh* is not used for incest or other prohibited relationships, such as homosexual relations or bestiality. It focuses on the absence of a marriage bond between otherwise acceptable partners.

14. Although Tamar is living in her father's house as a widow (Gen. 38:11), she is identified as Judah's daughter-in-law in the critical scene when she is accused of "playing the harlot" (v. 24). For a fuller discussion of this case, see my article, "The Harlot as Heroine: Narrative Art and Social Presupposition in Three Old Testament Texts," *Semeia* 46 (1989): 119–39.

15. On the legal and social status of the prostitute, see below and Bird, "The Harlot as Heroine"; cf. S. Niditch, "The Wronged Woman Righted: An Analysis of Genesis 38," *HTR* 72 (1979): 147.

16. Cf. Benjamin Kedar-Kopfstein, "Semantic Aspects of the Pattern *gôṭēl*," *Hebrew Annual Review* 1 (1977): 158, 164–65.

17. A major problem with Collins's study ("The Stem *ZNH*") is his understanding of the root in its "primary, literal sense" as referring to "actual prostitution" (13). As a result, he can only ask what *kind* of prostitution (secular or sacred) it designates and whether it is literal or figurative. Cf. Hooks, "Sacred Prostitution," 70. F. I. Anderson and D. N. Freedman (*Hosea*, AB 24 [Garden City, N.Y.: Doubleday], 1980, 160) appear to be alone in challenging the common English interpretations.

18. See Bird, "The Harlot as Heroine," 3–4; J. H. Gagnon, "Prostitution," *The International Encyclopedia of the Social Sciences*, vol. 12, ed. D. L. Sills (New York: Macmillan and Free Press, 1968), 592–98; P. H. Gebhard, "Prostitution," *The New Encyclopedia Britannica*, vol. 15, 15th ed. (Chicago: University of Chicago, 1980), 75–81; and V. and B. Bullough, *Women and Prostitution: A Social History* (Buffalo: Prometheus, 1987).

19. The prostitute has no male counterpart; male prostitution, which was homosexual, was a limited phenomenon and is poorly attested in our sources. There is no masculine noun corresponding to *zônâ*, which is paired with *keleb* "dog" in Deut. 23:19.

20. Collins emphasizes male concern for legitimacy of offspring as the primary motive in identifying activity by *znh* ("The Stem *ZNH*," 263).

21. Bird, "The Harlot as Heroine," 121–22, 127, 132–33.

22. For basic literary and historical analysis, see Anderson and Freedman, *Hosea*; J. L. Mays, *Hosea*, OTL (Philadelphia: Westminster, 1969); and H. W. Wolff, *Hosea: A Commentary on the Book of the Prophet Hosea*, Hermeneia (Philadelphia: Fortress, 1974).

23. Cf. JB "marry a whore, and get children with a whore"; NAB "a harlot wife and harlot's children." In contrast, Wolff argues that the term describes activity in the popular sex cult of the day and thus characterizes the woman as an "average, 'modern' Israelite woman" (14–15).

24. Cf. commentaries and G. Yee, *Composition and Tradition in the Book of Hosea: A Redactional Investigation*, SBLDS 102 (Atlanta: Scholars, 1987).

25. Heb. 2:7, 15. To avoid cumbersome double notation, only the RSV numbering is given for verse references in chapter 2.

26. Apparently a variant of *ʾetnān* (9:1; Deut. 23:19; Mic. 1:7; etc.), "a harlot's wages."

27. Wolff, *Hosea*, 34; cf. J. Huehnergard, "Biblical Notes on Some New Akkadian Texts from Emar (Syria)," *CBQ* 47 (1985): 433–34.

28. The emphasis is on cultic practice rather than on rival/foreign gods. Hosea never directly identifies the "lovers" with "the baals." The expression "other gods" (*ʾĕlōhîm ʾăḥērîm*) occurs only in 3:1, with *pōnîm ʾel-* ("turning

toward") as in Deut. 31:18, 20. I regard 3:1–5 as a redactional composition that does not reflect Hosea's own usage here. Cf. commentaries.

29. The clue to the condemnation is not in the names of the feasts, which represent a catalogue of Israel's traditional and mandated days of offering, but in the qualifying personal pronouns ("*her* pilgrim feast," etc.) and the cover term, *mĕśôśāh* "her rejoicing." The feasts commanded by Yahweh have become occasions for Israel's pursuit of her own pleasure or gain; and so Yahweh condemns them as "(feast) days of the baals" (v. 13).

30. For literary and textual analysis see commentaries and my forthcoming work. I take the people (*ʿammî,* v. 11) to be the subject throughout and view *zĕnût* of v. 11a as secondary and belonging to v. 10.

31. Reading with MT, followed by RSV and Mays, *Hosea,* 72; cf. NJV; Wolff, *Hosea,* 72; and Anderson and Freedman, *Hosea,* 343, 364–65 (who read "my people" with the preceding verse). My translation is literal where necessary to bring out features of the Hebrew lost in a more idiomatic rendering.

32. The terms suggest the asherah pillars and standing stones (*maṣṣēbôt*) associated with open air sanctuaries in numerous texts (e.g., Deut. 16:21; Judg. 6:25); for idols, see Jer. 2:27; 10:8.

33. It might be argued that the metaphor of the promiscuous wife is lost altogether here, with the root becoming simply a figurative term for illicit cult and/or cultic sex. Or one might view this usage as drawing on a broader root-meaning, describing male as well as female involvement in extramarital sex. Attempts to "defeminize" the usage are made difficult, however, by *mittaḥat* and by the possessive pronoun ("*their* God"; cf. Num. 5:19, 20, 29). The remaining occurrence of *zānâ min/mē* in Hos. 9:1 (*kî zānētâ mēʿal ʾĕlōhêkâ* "for you have fornicated from upon your God") clearly has a female model in mind although the verb is masculine, as here, addressing collective Israel. The accusation of fornication is followed immediately in 9:1 by the amplification, "you loved (a harlot's) hire (*ʿetnān*) upon (*ʿal*) all grain-threshing floors," recalling the figure of the prostitute and repeating other key terms (*ʾhb* "love" and *dāgān* "grain") of chapter 2. We must conclude then that collective Israel is personified as female in each of these uses of *znh* and accused of "acting like a promiscuous woman/prostitute."

34. My reconstruction of the quatrain omits 14aα as a later addition. The notion of punishment, even when negated, is out of place here, and the inclusion of this line obscures the symmetry and interconnections of the original oracle. The force of the argument is not substantially altered by the deletion. See commentaries.

35. MT (Hebrew) has 2mp suffixes ("your") on both nouns, which may be original, occasioned by a shift in the argument at this point to draw the consequences of the indictment for the listeners, addressed now directly (cf. Mays, *Hosea,* 73). The shift to 2nd person may also have been introduced when the secondary "no punishment" statement was added. Wolff (85) and Anderson and Freedman (369) see different groups addressed by lines 3 and 4. I have translated as 3rd person to enable English readers to

connect the male subjects, whom I believe to be the same throughout, whether addressed directly or indirectly.

36. See n. 34.

37. The paired terms constitute a *merismus* intended to cover all forms and occasions of cultic activity. Cf. Wolff, *Hosea,* 86.

38. I have used quotation marks in translating all four of the *piel* verbs in the first and final lines as an attempt to duplicate the Hebrew use of a system of vocalization that suggests something else is intended by these terms than they usually convey. None of these verbs is normally used in this stem. Cf. Wolff, *Hosea,* 35. This polemical use of the *piel* is characteristic of Hosea, who provides the earliest examples of the usage and may well be its originator.

39. Cf. 14:7–8 (Heb. 8–9), where Yahweh is likened to an evergreen cypress (the largest of trees), and his protecting "shade" (RSV "shadow") is described by the same term used here (*ṣēl*).

40. "Daughters" (*bānôt*) and "daughters-in-law" (*kallôt,* lit. "brides," here = "son's brides") are paired for purposes of poetic parallelism. They are to be understood as a single class, viz. sexually mature, young, female dependents. Cf. Anderson and Freedman, *Hosea,* 369; Wolff, *Hosea,* 86–87.

41. Deut. 22:21; Lev. 21:9; cf. Gen. 34:31.

42. So M. Gruber ("Hebrew *qĕdēšāh* and her Canaanite and Akkadian Cognates," *UF* 18 [1986]: 133–48), who argues that the etymology points to a basic meaning of "set apart," in this case "for degradation," in other Hebrew uses and in Akkadian "for exaltation" (133, 148). Hooks ("Sacred Prostitution," 187) arrives at a similar conclusion, drawing on the notion of "taboo."

43. Cf. the placement of "days of the baals" in the final verse of 2:2–13 to reveal the identity of the previously mentioned "lovers" (vv. 5, 7, 10, 12) and feast days (v. 11).

44. See my essay, "The Place of Women in the Israelite Cultus," in *Ancient Israelite Religion: Essays in Honor of Frank M. Cross,* ed. P. D. Hanson, P. D. Miller, S. D. McBride (Philadelphia: Fortress, 1987), 405–8.

45. This is the burden of Hooks's argument, for Israel and for the entire ancient Near East ("Sacred Prostitution," 203–7).

46. What Hosea describes is an *Israelite* fertility cult, not a Canaanite cult. Survivals, and/or revivals, of older, pre-Yahwistic practices (among them the role of the *qĕdēšôt*) must be assumed, but it is impossible to learn from the biblical sources what role these may have played in the earlier cult or how the practices were understood by the practitioners.

47. The term is usually understood to mean something like "go aside" (so RSV; NJV; Wolff, *Hosea,* 72; Mays, *Hosea,* 762), with the idea of joining (sacred) prostitutes in groves adjacent to the sanctuaries. Anderson and Freedman (370) suggest, however, that it may refer to the dismembering of the sacrificial victim. Might it suggest a division of the priestly portion with the prostitute?

48. The professional women should probably be understood as recruited from the general Israelite population, but they are treated here as "other women." On the father's role in causing or permitting a daughter's promiscuity, whether casual or commercial, see Lev. 19:29 and commentary by Collins, "Sacred Prostitution," 103–5.

49. Cf. the argument employed in the judicial parables, 2 Sam. 12:1–7 and 14:2–20.

50. In addition to the texts treated, cf. 3:3 *tiznî* (*qal* with feminine subject and literal meaning). Three instances of the *hiphil* occur in the book (4:10,18; 5:3), all involving some textual problems. A provisional survey of these occurrences suggests that the *hiphil* is meant to represent the male activity in fornication, much as the male activity in giving birth to a child (*yld qal* with female subject) is normally represented by the *hiphil,* although in metaphorical usage the *qal* can have a male subject (e.g., Deut. 32:18, of God).

7 VERSE AND REVERSE: THE TRANSFORMATION OF THE WOMAN, ISRAEL, IN HOSEA 1–3

MARY JOAN WINN LEITH

When one thinks of myths of creation in the Hebrew Bible, two related stories spring immediately to mind: God's creation by the word in Genesis 1, and the account, scattered throughout the Bible, of the divine warrior Yahweh's victorious battle against the sea monster/dragon of chaos.[1] There is a third creation myth in the Bible, however: the creation of Israel, the people of God, though this myth appears as history in epic narrative form. The earliest description of Israel's formative experience at the Reed Sea (Exod. 15) is essentially a historicized presentation of Yahweh's primordial battle,[2] and Exodus 15 clearly demonstrates that the events of the exodus, wilderness wandering, and possession of the promised land are much more Israel's creation myth than the *tōhû wābōhû* of Genesis 1.[3] This, I believe, is the implicit understanding of the prophet Hosea. However, Hosea, in chapters 1–3, has also imaginatively modified the myth, for the purposes of his own prophetic rhetoric, so that Israel metaphorically becomes a woman who must suffer the cosmic consequences of her wickedness but who ultimately enjoys the equally cosmic blessings of redemption and recreation. Her transformation from the former to the latter can be charted as a mythic journey that conforms closely to the pattern of a rite of passage.

True to his calling as a watcher of the covenant, the prophet Hosea condemns his contemporaries—fellow Israelites and the political and religious establishments of the northern kingdom—for a multitude of covenantal sins, the worst of which is Israel's attribution of its fertile abundance to the Canaanite storm and fertility god, Ba'al Hadad (2:8).[4] Israel must suffer the imminent punishment of the covenant curses, though Hosea also promises redemption beyond the doom.

Like the other classical prophets, Hosea for the most part eschews the use of overtly mythic imagery. Mainstream biblical scholarship asserts that the classical prophets "were . . . responsible for historicizing Israel's religion, for integrating the cosmic vision into history, for causing myth to retreat before a more 'secularized,' 'humanistic' worldview."[5] It made perfect sense for Hosea to reject divine warrior imagery; such imagery would only perpetuate Israel's sinful confusion of Yahweh with Yahweh's arch-rival, Baʿal. Nonetheless Hosea displays in less overt ways a grounding in mythic thought, and, in particular, in the themes of a creation myth. This mythological pattern and conceptual framework undergirds Hosea's understanding not only of the woman Israel's sinful behavior and God's imminent punishment, but also of God's restoration of the people.

Not surprisingly, Hosea puts special emphasis on the thematically resonant triad of exodus, wilderness wandering, and possession of the promised land, and so doing, he taps into the mythical as well as historical dimensions of Israel's creation.[6] For example, God threatens to return the sinful woman Israel to the wilderness where God originally created her, to:

> . . . strip her naked
> make her as the day she was born,
> and make her like a wilderness. (Hos. 2:3)[7]

God is reversing time (itself an essential product of cosmogony) as well as the pattern of Israel's creation.[8] In acknowledging the mythic nature of these creative events, rich in the themes of chaos and order, sterility and fertility, death and birth, we may better understand the profound depth of Hosea's ongoing dialogue with Israel's mythic worldview.

Hosea's message has three "movements": accusation, punishment, and restoration, and he maintains his feminine metaphor throughout them. I intend to show, first, that in his accusations, Hosea reverses the images of Israel's creation to deprive God's people of their very identity, separating them from all they consider theirs. God's punishment is then described by the prophet in terms of a banishment to the wilderness, a wilderness initially sterile and fraught with the terrors of chaos, but ultimately transformed into the wilderness in which God originally found (or created) the beloved child, Israel. Finally, Hosea describes the reconciliation between Yahweh and Israel as a new creation, a new covenant, and a marriage celebration in which

God and the bride return to the now fruitful *naḥălâ,* the land of Israel's divine inheritance. This tripartite conceptualization conforms to the pattern of what anthropologists have long recognized as a rite of passage,[9] an issue that I will discuss presently.

Let us turn, first, to a closer examination of Hosea 1–3 where creation myth, national history, and ritual converge on several levels in the story of Hosea, his wife, and children.[10] The "first movement," the accusation, appears at the start of each chapter. In Hos. 1:2, Yahweh tells the prophet:

> Go, take to yourself a wife of harlotry and have children of harlotry, for the land commits great harlotry by forsaking the Lord.

Obediently, Hosea marries Gomer. The text never calls Gomer a *zônâ* (prostitute);[11] she is a "wife (or woman) of harlotry," *ʾēšet zĕnûnîm,* a nebulous term, unique to Hosea, which does not connote professional prostitution.[12] The third chapter says that Hosea bought a woman "beloved of a paramour . . . , an adulteress" (3:1), for "fifteen shekels of silver and a lethech of barley" (3:2).

Hosea's wife, the focus of all three chapters, has troubled scholars because the first and third chapters of Hosea contain conflicting data about her. The woman of harlotry and the adulteress have committed related but not identical misdeeds. I view the contradictions as variants of oral tradition.[13] As multiforms the two accounts do not depend on each other but they most likely reflect oral performances of a story that had quickly become a part of Israel's traditional repertoire of tales about Hosea.[14] I leave the argument over whether Hosea 1–3 preserves the actual biographical "facts" of Hosea's life to others. What is important is that both accounts preserve the essential image of a wife deemed unfit by virtue [sin?] of sexual misconduct.

Why has Hosea portrayed his sinful land as the epitome of a wicked woman? I believe it has as much to do with the community's mythic sense of identity as it has to do with any possible actual participation by Israelite men and women in the supposed sacred prostitution of the Baʿal cultus. Throughout Hosea 1–3, Hosea, like Amos before him, employs a literary technique that may be called reversal. He depicts a through-the-looking-glass world to emphasize Israel's perversion of its covenantal relationship with God.

It is important here to keep in mind that though he uses imagery derived from female sexuality, Hosea is addressing his prophecies to his fellow citizens and Israel's elite, but not to Israelite women.[15] In patriarchal Israel, women were not full partners in the covenant. So Hosea, on one level, is calling the Israelites "women." This is not a frivolous accusation. The prophet plays on male fears of woman as "other." It is even conceivable that Hosea is alluding to a covenant curse. Lists of curses in ancient Near Eastern treaties occasionally include a threat to turn the signatory's men into women. The treaty between Ashurnirari V of Assyria and Mati'ilu of Arpad includes the threat:

> If Mati'ilu sins against this treaty with Ashurnirari . . . may Mati'ilu become a prostitute, his soldiers women, may they receive [a gift] in the square of their cities (i.e., publicly) like any prostitute. . . .[16]

Hosea takes advantage of the mythic and cultural symbols at his command to mark off the distinction between the Israel he sees and the Israel Israel thinks it is. This is the motivation for Hosea's recourse to what may have already become a traditional accusation in the covenant lawsuit, that faithless Israel has played the harlot.[17] Hosea never says his wife is a ritual prostitute. Nevertheless, Yahweh seems to be accusing the wife Israel of promiscuity and/or prostitution in the presence of Baʿal worship:

> "And I will punish her for the feast days of the Baʿals
> when she burned incense to them
> and decked herself with her ring and her jewelry
> and went after her lovers
> and forgot me," says the LORD. (Hos. 2:13)

Recently, after examining the sources regularly cited for the existence of sacred prostitution, Robert Oden concluded that the currently available evidence is not sufficient to prove that such an institution existed in ancient Syria-Palestine or Mesopotamia.[18] Oden cites Fredrik Barth's studies of the symbolism of ethnic boundary marking,[19] which showed that ethnic groups define themselves in terms of categorical opposition between *themselves* and *others*. One important set of distinguishing categories includes "the standards of morality and excellency by which performance is judged,"[20] especially including sexual and eating habits. ". . . [E]thnic boundaries are marked less by any 'objective' criteria than they are by the kinds of conduct and standards to which a group says it holds firm and from which the group charges its neighbors depart."[21] Oden suggests that, "Sacred prostitution *as accusation* played an important role in defining Israel and Israelite religion as something distinctive."[22]

When the Israelites accused their traditional enemies—indeed, their cultural opposites—the Canaanites, of sexual improprieties in the practice of the Baʿal cult, the Israelites were saying more about their perception of themselves and their own Yahwistic cult than about the Canaanites. They defined their ideals of morality and ritual correctness in terms of opposition to supposed, but not necessarily real, Canaanite sexual indecencies. The thematic pairing of the Baʿal cult with prostitution comes out of Israel's religio-cultural traditions, and it is a good example of an ethnic boundary marker at work. Hosea, however, manipulates the marker so that *Israel* becomes a participant in the detestable sexual rituals ascribed by the Israelites to their Canaanite neighbors. The sexual rituals Hosea accuses the woman of carrying out in chapter 2 can be viewed as a metaphorical description of the perversion of Yahweh's cult.[23] As in his characterization of Israel as a woman, Hosea here is saying that Israel has become precisely what it defines itself as *not* being. The language he uses to make this point reverses the very terms on which Israel had "presented to its members and the wider world a full articulation of its deepest values and beliefs. . . ."[24] Israel no longer has a valid claim to be the people of Yahweh.

Hosea has additional ways of negating Israel's identity, for example, in his children's names, particularly "Not my people," whose naming is accompanied by God's declaration, "I am not your *ʾehyeh*" (1:9); or when, in 3:4, God says Israel must "dwell many days without king or prince, without sacrifice or pillar, without ephod or teraphim." A people without any leaders or any cult is no people. Though not part of Hosea 1–3, Hosea accurately reads the situation:

> My God will cast them off . . .
> they shall be wanderers among the nations. (Hos. 9:17)

and:

> Israel is swallowed up;
> already they are among the nations. . . . (Hos. 8:8)

When Hosea imagines this Israel reduced to a mere cipher among the nations, he ironically reminds his listeners that "the nations" were the ones God and Israel drove out of the promised land.[25] Israel's possession of the promised land was the specific manifestation of God's part in the covenant. In Israel's symbolic vocabulary, wandering among the nations and wandering in the wilderness are equal signifiers of chaos. In addition, Hos. 8:8 contains more than a metaphor. I cannot help thinking that the verb "swallowed" (*blʿ*) must have reminded listeners of Exod. 15:12, when "the earth swallowed [pharaoh and his army]." "Earth" (*ʾereṣ*) in that song signified the underworld god of death.[26] Being "among the nations" is being dead. Hosea's symbolic lexicon thus includes three equivalent images: being "among the nations," exile in the wilderness, and death. Stripped of its identity, Israel is set adrift in chaos.

Now, in this "second movement," Hosea's limber poetry can accommodate simultaneous pictures: the promised land reduced to a sterile wasteland:

> And I will lay waste her vines and
> her fig trees . . .
> I will make them a forest,
> and the beasts of the field
> shall devour them. (Hos. 2:12; cf. 2:3,9)[27]

and the woman Israel stripped naked "as in the day she was born," made "like a wilderness" (2:3). We see the woman lost and assaulted by the perils of the wilderness the land has become: thirst (2:3), thorns (2:6), disorientation (2:6). Mythically speaking, barrenness and wilderness here are *functionally* the same as the chaos that regularly threatens created order in ancient Near Eastern myths. Elsewhere Hosea is even more explicit about Israel's fate. In 13:1 Ephraim "incurred guilt through Baʿal and died." In God's punishment, Israel's election and creation by God are reversed and the forces of chaos prevail, at least for now.

In the Hebrew Bible, the wilderness has two faces: it can be threatening or benign. As the inhospitable land of thorns and drought, it is chaos; it is the country into which the scapegoat is driven (Lev. 16:15–22), where beasts of the field may devour you (Hos. 2:12). Furthermore, it was a place of constant rebellion by ungrateful Israelites (cf. particularly Psalm 78). The Priestly tradition explains the forty years' wandering as God's punishment (Num. 14:26–38). But God also found Israel in the wilderness (Hos. 9:10), cared for Israel there, and made the covenant there, "It was I who knew you in the wilderness" (Hos. 13:5). Hosea 2:3 suggests Israel was born in the wilderness.

The first movement of Hosea's message accused the woman Israel of covenant violation (1:2; 2:2,5; 3:1). In the second, Hosea tore away her identity as God's own (1:4–8; 2:3,6,9,12; 3:4). He thus exiled the woman Israel spatially to the chaos/wilderness and temporally back to Israel's primordial days when she did not yet know God and was essentially unborn. A great poet can surprise the audience by mixing the familiar with the unexpected. Hosea does this in the climactic third movement. Having perverted cherished Israelite ideals to create a vision of utter alienation, he confounds expectation. In both 1:10–11[28] and 2:14–23, he reverses his images with the promise of a new beginning. In 2:14–15, God, the (true) lover says:

> Therefore, behold, I will allure her
> and bring her back into the wilderness,
> and speak tenderly to her
> and there I will give her her vineyards,
> and make the Valley of Achor
> a door of hope.
> And there she shall answer as in the days
> of her youth. . . . [29]

Hosea suddenly transforms the "chaotic" wilderness into the "ordered" wilderness of God's election.[30] Israel's only hope for regenerative salvation lies in the punishment itself. The woman must go back to the beginning time, to Mircea Eliade's *illo tempore* of cosmogony;[31] she must be found again and reborn in a new creation.

Yahweh and Israel, no longer the "wife of harlotry" or the nonexistent entity among the peoples, find each other as in the beginning and are reconciled:

> "And in that day," says the LORD,
> "You will call me, 'my husband'
> and no longer will you call me, 'my
> Ba'al.'" (Hos. 2:16)

The rejected form of address, *Baʿal,* implies not only a different deity, but also a different, more dominating relationship. *Baʿal* literally means "lord." The word for "man," *"ʾîš"* means "husband," just as the word for "wife," *"ʾiššâ"* means "woman." God's new title, "husband," signals a new beginning, a new betrothal, and a (re)new(ed) covenant, whose inauguration sounds strikingly like a (re)creation of the world:[32]

> And I will make for you a covenant on that day with the beasts of the field, the birds of the air, and the creeping things of the ground; and I will abolish the bow, the sword, and war from the land; . . . And in that day, says the Lord, I will answer the heavens and they shall answer the earth and the earth shall answer the grain, the wine, and the oil, and they shall answer Jezreel. . . .[33] (Hos. 2:18; 21–22)

Earlier I stated that in this three-stage pattern I detected similarities to a rite of passage, a ritual attached to the crucial transitional stages of human life such as birth, puberty, marriage, and death. Most importantly, rites of passage regulate the person's relation to, and identity in, the community at large. Because family is such an important motif in Hosea 1–3, Hosea cannot help but mention events that were actual rites of passage in Israel: marriage, birth, and the naming of children.[34] However, I do not wish to focus on the particular events in Hosea that may constitute rites of passage in Israelite society. Rather, I am intrigued by the ramifications of the presence of such a symbolically rich *pattern* in the general plotline of Hosea 1–3.

Rites of passage generally involve a series of rituals in three steps: rites of separation, transition rites, and rites of incorporation.[35] It should be immediately apparent that these can be compared to the three "movements" of Hosea 1–3. The accusation stressed the woman Israel's estrangement and separation from Yahweh;[36] Hosea goes so far as to depict a nullification of Israel's identity. In the second "movement," estrangement led to exile in the threatening wilderness (or her actually becoming the wilderness); but the wilderness is a charged place where transformations can happen so that the second "movement" flows into the third. God and Israel are reconciled as husband and wife, and the recreated natural world joins the wedding festivities.

Hosea 1–3 contains more than just the tripartite division of a "generic" rite of passage. In many cultures, the symbolism of death and rebirth is particularly apparent in the outstanding rite of passage, the initiation of boys and girls into the adult community. "The distinctive mark of initiation is the temporary seclusion of the initiands [*sic*] from everyday life to a marginal existence. . . . [A] dimension of death and new life is introduced."[37] The experience of the participant in such a rite of passage is almost inevitably validated by being understood as a return to the sacred time and/or place of an important myth (or myths) of society.[38] The rituals effect "a complete change in the novice's ontological status."[39] "[T]he novice dies to his profane, nonregenerate life to be reborn to a new, sanctified existence . . . , to a mode of being that makes learning, *knowledge,* possible. . . ."[40] The initiant returns to society "newborn or resuscitated," endowed with sacred knowledge.[41]

All these assumptions, it seems to me, are present in Hosea, especially the richly poetic Hosea 2. In addition, there are certain resonant details that fit in well with the symbolism of initiation. The woman is stripped "naked as in the day she was born" (2:3). The image of a gate in and/or out of the place of initiation[42] appears when the desolate Valley of Achor becomes a "door of hope" (2:15). Hosea and Gomer's children are condemned in 2:4 along with their mother, but they drop out of the action until the very end of chapter 2 (22–23). When Yahweh gives all three of them new, positive names, Yahweh is performing a standard ritual in an initiation rite.[43] Similarly, Yahweh also reveals a new name, "husband," perhaps an echo of the revelation in the wilderness of the divine name, Yahweh. Even the sexual metaphor for Yahweh's new relationship with the woman Israel fits here; the initiant gains sexual as well as sacred knowledge.[44] God declares to the woman in Hos. 2:20, "I will betroth you to me in faithfulness; and you shall know the LORD." As many commentators have pointed out, the language is deliberately ambiguous, since the "knowing" here can be covenantal or sexual.

I doubt that Hosea deliberately set out to describe Israel's experience in Hosea 1–3 as a rite of passage. I do believe, however, that because Hosea's "story" focuses on the subjects (though not the rites themselves) of marriage, birth, and naming, the prophet, consciously or unconsciously, constructed its telling in a way that echoed a ritual pattern. Furthermore, the ritual pattern itself was so elemental in Israelite life experience that it lent itself easily to Hosea's prophecy. He seems to feel instinctively that his prophetic story of Israel's experience is a story of the death, rebirth, and renewal of the Israelite community.

If we acknowledge that Hosea 1–3 contains such a pattern of a rite of passage or more specifically, the pattern of an initiation rite, how then does this affect our appreciation of Hosea 1–3? The answer to this question may be found in the purpose of the initiation rite itself. "The mystery of initiation gradually reveals to the novice the true dimensions of existence . . . by introducing him to the sacred. . . ."[45] An initiation transports the initiate from one level of existence in the community to a higher one, and the idea of growth in knowledge and maturity cannot be detached from the symbolism of the rebirth. When Hosea exults in the joyous betrothal and marriage in chapter 2, he is celebrating a transformation of Israel's spiritual capacities; her ordeal has fit the woman for a new, enhanced relationship with God. Where before in the woman's eyes "God" meant "Lord" (*Baʿal*), now "God" means "husband," and Israel's reconciliation with Yahweh begins on surprisingly intimate terms ("allure," "speak tenderly"),[46] congruent with the sexual wordplay around Yahweh's renewed covenant/ marriage with Israel that ends the marriage section of the passage.

The transgression that initially prompted Hosea's attack on Israel in Hosea 1–3 was Israel's infidelity (harlotry) in worshipping Baʿal and not Yahweh. I find it significant that in 2:18, directly before Yahweh makes the marriage vow, he abolishes "the bow, the sword, and war from the land." Yahweh seems to be saying that the attributes of the divine warrior[47] that he shared with Baʿal no longer apply to his relationship with Israel.[48] I began this discussion by mentioning the divine warrior's battle of creation. Hosea seems intent on dismissing precisely the sort of mythic battle motifs that are so clearly present in Exodus 15, while at the same time preserving the "creation language" manifest in his description of the sterile earth's transformation into blossoming fertility, an event that traditionally followed the divine warrior's victory over chaos.[49] The prophet is making a carefully crafted theological statement about Yahweh in an attempt to reshape Israel's heretofore cavalier attitude toward Yahweh.

I also suggested above that one motivation for Hosea's portrayal of Israel as a woman was to augment his negation of Israel's identity. Yet at the end of the tale, Israel is still a woman; no sex change has occurred to restore Israel's manhood. However, I believe that just as Hosea has managed all along to confound expectation, he now changes the rules, so to speak. He keeps the image of the woman, but in a different context. The "wife of harlotry" belonged to the semantic wordfield of the covenant curses. By the time the woman has undergone her punishment, there is an entirely new context in which to view the woman, centered on ideals of social legitimacy and moral rectitude. It is now acceptable for Israel, if only metaphorically, to be a woman.[50]

NOTES

1. Cf. Ps. 74:12–17; Ps. 89:5–13; Job 41:1–8.

2. Frank Cross, *Canaanite Myth and Hebrew Epic* (Cambridge: Harvard University, 1973), 112–44.

3. While the Hebrew Bible employs epic narrative to tell this creation story and treats the events as national history, the events must also be recognized as essentially mythic. They conform to a working definition of myth as "an integral part of the ways in which . . . society presents to its members and the wider world a full articulation of its deepest values and

beliefs. . . ." Robert A. Oden, *The Bible without Theology: The Theological Tradition and Alternatives to It* (San Francisco: Harper and Row, 1987), 40.

4. Israel's sins: on the political level, Israel has accepted kings without divine approval (8:4), and, fearing the power of Egypt and Assyria who lurk with evil intent beyond its borders, Israel has made foreign alliances (5:13). On the religious level, the corruption of the cult establishment has infected the population as a whole (4:4–10); in the cult itself, Israelites go through the motions of ritual oblivious of any spiritual commitment (6:6).

5. P. D. Hanson, *The Dawn of Apocalyptic* (Philadelphia: Fortress Press, 1975), 17. It has been almost axiomatic in introductory courses to the Hebrew Bible that a "unique view of history" evolved in ancient Israel. This understanding of Israelite religion (with its decidedly bibliocentric subtext) evolved out of nineteenth-century German historiography and has since flourished—roots, fruit, and all—a beloved, seldom-examined scholarly heirloom. (For a useful summary of the history of this approach, see Oden, *Bible without Theology*) Particularly since the 1970s, however, biblical scholarship has welcomed myth like a lost child back into its household. This is partly because it became impossible to ignore the striking similarities between the literatures of Israel and of its neighbors. In addition, as Oden stresses (45–46), new modes of historical inquiry, new definitions of myth that reject the Grimm brothers' stricture that a myth must be about the gods, and new ways of thinking about mythology have altered the old categories of biblical literature. Without abandoning a sense that the Israelites "read" Yahweh's presence in their history, scholars today acknowledge myth as an essential underpinning of the Bible.

6. Wilderness language: 2:3; 2:12b; 2:14; 9:10; 12:9; 13:4–5. Return to the land of Egypt: 2:15, 7:16; 8:13; 9:3; 9:17; 12:5. Yahweh as parent: 2:3; 2:15; 11:1; 11:3; 11:8.

7. *RSV* numbering.

8. Hosea's imagery here is suggestively fluid. Israel is portrayed as a woman partly on the basis of the feminine gender of the word for "land," *ʾēreṣ*. In Hosea's speech, this word stands almost always for the promised land that is Israel, just as "the people" is also Israel. Both the land and the woman endure God's punishment.

9. The classic work on the subject is Arnold van Gennep's *Les Rites de Passage* (trans. Monika Vizedom and Gabrielle Caffee, *The Rites of Passage* [Chicago: University of Chicago, 1960]).

10. Hosea 1–3 is not all one performance unit, but, as the editor[s] recognized, there is a notable coherence of theme that must reflect the thinking of the prophet himself. Each chapter (*RSV* numeration) contains a similar three-part plot, though it is expressed in different words and with different emphases. Taken all together, the chapters amplify and comment on each other. In particular, Hosea 2 takes up the motif of the children from the preceding chapter and develops it in a moving climax. Hosea 3 is the shortest and most schematic. Since I am interested in patterns, themes,

and motifs, I will point them out in whichever chapter they appear most helpful to my discussion.

11. Phyllis Bird presents the nuances of the various biblical terms for prostitute, harlot, etc., in "'To Play the Harlot': An Inquiry into an Old Testament Metaphor," elsewhere in this volume.

12. Gomer, which means something like "accomplished" in the sense of "fulfilled," is mentioned by name only once (1:3). Elsewhere she is called a "mother."

13. In focusing here on oral tradition, I do not wish to imply a rejection of the important related principles of form criticism. I believe the methodologies amplify one another.

14. Cf. Albert Lord, *The Singer of Tales* (New York: Atheneum, 1973), 99–123. "Any single performance that we may choose of a song in [a] group of interrelated families must be understood in terms of its brothers and sisters and even its cousins of several removes. While recognizing the fact that the singer knows the whole song before he starts to sing (not textually, of course, but thematically), nevertheless, at some time when he reaches key points in the performance of a song he finds that he is drawn in one direction or another by the similarities with related groups at those points. . . . In a variety of ways a song in tradition is separate, yet inseparable from other songs [123]." Or to paraphrase a line from Gregory Nagy (*The Best of the Achaeans: Concepts of the Hero in Archaic Greek Poetry* [Baltimore: Johns Hopkins, 1979], 43), "There may theoretically be as many variations on [the theme of Hosea's marriage] as there are compositions. Any theme is but a multiform, and not one of the multiforms may be considered a functional 'Urform.'"

15. Cf. Phyllis Bird, "The Place of Women in the Israelite Cultus," in *Ancient Israelite Religion: Essays in Honor of Frank M. Cross,* eds. P. D. Hanson, P. D. Miller, and S. D. McBride (Philadelphia: Fortress, 1987), 397–419. It should be noted that unlike other prophets—Amos (4:1) and Isaiah (3:16), for example—who directly accuse Israelite women for their sins, Hosea blames the men of Israel for the sexual improprieties of the women. In Hosea 4:14, God may even be excusing the Israelite women from any punishment for purported sexual crimes. (This depends on reading *l'* with the MT as "not." Conversely, it might be asseverative [Francis I. Anderson and David Noel Freedman, *Hosea,* AB (Garden City, N.Y.: Doubleday, 1980), 369]. Women, it would appear, do not even exercise autonomy over their sins!

16. *ANET,* 533, late second millennium (trans. Erica Reiner). Cf. also *ANET,* 540 (trans. D. J. Wiseman), a vassal treaty of Esarhaddon, with a curse that reads, "May [the gods] spin you like a spindle whorl, may they use you like women in the sight of your enemy."

17. In the Hebrew Bible, the Deuteronomist and prophets influenced by Dtr use this metaphor most often. Its use by Hosea, an eighth-century northern prophet whose speech has Deuteronomistic overtones, is among the earliest examples. In Num. 25:1, P begins the Baal Peor incident:

". . . Israel dwelt in Shittim . . . [and] the people played the harlot with the daughters of Moab." (Note that "the people" here are actually only the men.) Hosea 8:10, and perhaps 5:2, refers to this incident. In Numbers the expression is not exclusively metaphorical. Does the priestly source reflect an old tradition of this story that Hosea also knew?

18. Oden, *Bible without Theology,* 153 and chap. 5.

19. Fredrik Barth, ed., *Ethnic Groups and Boundaries: The Social Organization of Culture Difference* (Boston: Little, Brown, 1969). Oden (132–5) summarizes this data.

20. Barth, "Introduction," *Ethnic Groups,* 14 (Oden, 133).

21. Oden, *Bible without Theology,* 133.

22. Oden, *Bible without Theology,* 153.

23. Cf. Bird in "'To Play the Harlot'."

24. Oden, *Bible without Theology,* 40.

25. Cf. Ps. 78:55.

26. F. M. Cross and D. N. Freedman, "The Song of Miriam," *JNES* 14 (1955): 247, n. 39.

27. Space does not permit a discussion of Hosea's subtle play on the idea of "the land," which is in close parallel with the motif of the woman.

28. RSV, Hos. 2:1–2 in the Hebrew. I retain this passage and concur with Freedman and Anderson (199) that Hosea "often sets the most opposite ideas side by side in striking contrast."

29. The "Valley of Achor" and the "door of hope" are images which in and of themselves, irrespective of their biblical allusiveness (Josh. 7:20–26), suggest (symbolize?) the womb and birth canal.

30. Vineyards symbolize not only fertility and the promised land (cf. Num. 13:23), but also the important concept of created order; the terraced vineyards of Israel required generations of labor-intensive nurturing to be truly fruitful. Cf. Lawrence E. Stager, "The Archaeology of the Family in Ancient Israel," *BASOR* 260 (1985): 5–6.

31. Mircea Eliade, *The Sacred and the Profane: The Nature of Religion* (New York: Harcourt Brace, 1959), 70.

32. Others have noted here the similarity to the recreation of the earth after the flood in the priestly version of the story. Cf. Tikva Frymer-Kensky, "Pollution, Purification, and Purgation in Biblical Israel," in *The Word of the Lord Shall Go Forth,* eds. C. L. Meyers and M. O'Connor (Winona Lake, Ind.: Eisenbrauns, 1983), 410.

33. Hosea 2:21–22 conforms to a pattern in folk literature (like "The House that Jack Built") that also appears in a Mesopotamian exorcism spell employing similar, ordered imagery to restore the afflicted person to her or himself. Cf. Erica Reiner, *Your thwarts in pieces Your mooring rope cut: Poems from Babylonia and Assyria, Michigan Studies in the Humanities,* 5 (University of Michigan, 1985), 94–100.

34. These rituals are discussed in the ever-helpful volume of Roland de Vaux, *Ancient Israel,* vol. 1, *Social Institutions* (New York: McGraw-Hill, 1965).

35. Van Gennep, *Passage,* 11 (and *passim*).

36. Another anthropological approach to this pattern in Hosea is taken by Tikva Frymer-Kensky in "Pollution" (see above n. 32). She discusses Israel's purity laws and attempts to show that Hosea's prophecy reflects the belief that the woman/land Israel has been polluted by sin and is in need of ritual purification.

37. Walter Burkert, *Greek Religion* (Cambridge, Mass.: Harvard University, 1985), 260. The description is not confined to Greek ritual. Cf. also Mircea Eliade, *Birth and Rebirth: The Religious Meanings of Initiation in Human Culture* (New York: Harper and Row, 1958).

38. Eliade, *The Sacred,* 187.

39. Ibid., 187.

40. Ibid., 188.

41. Ibid., 188.

42. Ibid., 179–84.

43. Consider the biblical figures who receive new names upon entering in a covenant with God, beginning with Abram/Abraham and Sarai/Sarah (Gen. 17:5,15).

44. Eliade, *The Sacred,* 188.

45. Ibid., 191.

46. In Hos. 2:14, the verb translated "allure" (*pty*) has overtones of seduction, as in Exod. 22:16, "If a man seduces a virgin who is not betrothed . . ." "Speak tenderly" (lit. "speak to her heart") applies to courtship and wooing (cf. Ruth 2:13). Anderson and Freedman, *Hosea,* 271–2.

47. For examples of ancient mythic associations of the divine warrior Yahweh with the bow, sword, and war, cf. Gen. 9:13; Judg. 7:20; and Exod. 15:3, respectively.

48. The juxtaposition here calls to mind 1 Kings 19:11–13, Elijah's vision of God on Mt. Horeb, which stresses Yahweh's difference from Baʿal.

49. This may be one of the early steps in the process that culminated in the priestly account of creation by the word. Hosea makes a striking claim for the power of divinely inspired words in 6:5.

50. At the same time, Hosea is no closet feminist; though he rejects the idea of God as elevated lord, he derives his model of God as husband and Israel as wife from marriage in patriarchal Israel: the husband was the dominant partner. Cf. Carol Meyers, "Procreation, Production, and Protection: Male-Female Balance in Early Israel," *JAAR* 51 (1983): 569–93.

8 "AND THE WOMEN KNEAD DOUGH": THE WORSHIP OF THE QUEEN OF HEAVEN IN SIXTH-CENTURY JUDAH

SUSAN ACKERMAN

The typical historian of ancient Israelite religion, especially the historian of the first-millennium cult, relies heavily, if not exclusively, on the Bible. This is unavoidable, since the Bible is in essence the only written source (and indeed the only significant source of any kind) that describes the religion of first-millennium Israel and Judah. Yet it has become increasingly obvious to historians of Israelite religion that the Bible's descriptions of the first-millennium cult are highly selective. The biblical materials, which come predominantly from the hands of priests and prophets, present priestly and prophetic religion as normative and orthodox in ancient Israel. Nonpriestly and nonprophetic religious beliefs and practices are condemned as heterodox and deviant. A more nuanced reconstruction of the religion of ancient Israel, however, would suggest that despite the biblical witness neither the priestly nor prophetic cult was normative in the religion of the first millennium. Rather, a diversity of beliefs and practices thrived and were accepted by the ancients as legitimate forms of religious expression.

Uncovering this diverse character of ancient Israelite religion requires a special methodology. First, we must train ourselves to supplement continually the biblical picture of Israelite religion by referring to other sources. Archaeological remains from Israel, especially iconographic and epigraphic materials, are crucial, as is comparative data from the ancient Near East and from elsewhere in the Mediterranean world. This evidence, however, often is sparse and not easily interpreted. Thus, more important methodologically is that we learn to treat our major source, the Bible, differently. We must examine the biblical presentations of the orthodox with an eye to the heterodox, seeking, for example, to look without prejudice at those cultic practices that the biblical writers so harshly condemn. Only when we acknowledge the polemical nature of many biblical texts can we see underlying their words evidence of the multifaceted nature of ancient Israelite religion.

It is this second methodological point in particular that helps illuminate an often overlooked aspect of ancient Israelite religion: women's religion. The all-male biblical writers treat this issue with silence or hostility; still, a careful reading of the biblical texts suggests that the women of Judah and Israel had a rich religious tradition.[1] The women of early sixth-century Judah, for example, devoted themselves to the worship of a goddess called the Queen of Heaven (Jer. 7:16–20; 44:15–19, 25). Indeed, although the prophet Jeremiah makes the women of Judah and Jerusalem the object of his special scorn due to their devotion to the Queen of Heaven (Jer. 44:25), the women are steadfast in their worship of the goddess: baking cakes "in her image" as offerings (Jer. 7:18; 44:19) and pouring out libations and burning incense to her (Jer. 44:15, 19). This devotion in the face of persecution indicates that the worship of the Queen of Heaven was an important part of women's religious expression in the sixth century. Here, by establishing the identity of the goddess called in the Bible the Queen of Heaven,[2] I propose to explore why the women of Judah found this goddess's cult so appealing.

Scholars, unfortunately, have reached no consensus on the identity of the Queen of Heaven. The great east Semitic goddess Ištar,[3] Ištar's west Semitic counterpart, Astarte,[4] the west Semitic goddess Anat,[5] and even the Canaanite goddess Šapšu[6] have been suggested. Other scholars maintain that it is impossible, given the available data, to determine to which of the Semitic goddesses the Queen of Heaven corresponds.[7] Finally, there are some who believe that the Queen of Heaven is not one deity, but rather a syncretistic goddess who combines the characteristics of east Semitic Ištar and west Semitic Astarte.[8]

My own sympathies lie with this latter position, which sees in the Queen of Heaven characteristics of both west Semitic Astarte and east Semitic Ištar. The Queen of Heaven as described in the Bible certainly shares with Astarte many features, first, the title of Queen or some related epithet. In texts from the Egyptian New Kingdom (1570–1085 B.C.E.) Astarte is called "Lady of Heaven."[9] More notably, in the first millennium Astarte bears the title Queen. On the obverse face of the Kition tariff inscription, which lists the monthly expenditures for the temple of Astarte at Kition, Astarte is referred to as "the holy Queen" and "the Queen."[10] The Phoenician hierophant Sakkunyaton also refers to Astarte's queenly role in first-millennium religion. He describes her as the co-regent of King Zeus Demarous (Canaanite Baʿl Haddu) and remarks that she wears on her head a bull's head as an emblem of "kingship" (*basileias*).[11]

The biblical Queen of Heaven also shares with Astarte an association with the heavens. Astarte's astral features, already indicated in the second millennium by the Egyptian title "Lady of Heaven," are numerous in first-millennium religion. In both the Eshmunazor and the Bodashtart inscriptions from Phoenicia Astarte's sacred precinct in Sidon is called "the highest heavens."[12] Elsewhere in the Mediterranean world Astarte's association with the heavens is suggested by her identification with Greek Aphrodite, the goddess of Venus, the Morning and Evening Star. This identification of Astarte with Aphrodite is made clear by Sakkunyaton, who writes, "the Phoenicians say that Astarte is Aphrodite,"[13] and also by a fourth-century Greek/Phoenician bilingual that translates the Phoenician name "Abdʿaštart the Ashkelonite" as "Aphrodisios the Ashkelonite."[14] Notably, moreover, the Astarte or Aphrodite worshiped by Abdʿaštart and other Ashkelonites was Aphrodite of the Heavens (*Aphroditē ourania*); Herodotus (1.105)[15] and Pausanius (1.14.7) remark on the cult of Aphrodite of the Heavens in Ashkelon. This correspondence of Astarte with Greek Aphrodite of the Heavens is confirmed by a second-century inscription from Delos dedicated to "Palestinian Astarte, that is, Aphrodite of the Heavens."[16]

Another datum showing Astarte's association with the heavens comes from Pyrgi, a site on the west coast of Italy about thirty miles west-northwest of Rome. The bilingual inscription found at Pyrgi is dedicated in its Phoenician version to Astarte and in its Etruscan form to the goddess Uni. J. Fitzmyer notes that Etruscan Uni is Roman Juno, and, significantly, that Uni is "closely associated" with "Juno of the Heavens" (*Juno caelestis*) in Roman Africa.[17] More evidence, later in date, comes from Herodian, who reports that the Phoenicians call Aphrodite of the Heavens (= Astarte) "Queen of the Stars" (*astroarchē*).[18] Moreover, Apuleius calls Caelestis Venus of Paphos "Queen of Heaven" (*regina caeli*).[19] Latin *Caelestis Venus* is a simple translation of Greek *Aphroditē ourania,* Aphrodite of the Heavens, whom we have identified with Palestinian Astarte.

In addition to the fact that Astarte in her epithets can be associated with the heavens, it is important to note that Astarte has other astral aspects.[20] In her iconography Astarte is symbolized by a star. Like Greek Aphrodite and Ištar, her Mesopotamian counterpart, Astarte is identified with Venus, the Morning and Evening Star. Sakkunyaton also remarks on Astarte's astral features: "When traveling around the world, she [Astarte] discovered a star which had fallen from the sky. She took it and consecrated it in Tyre, the holy island."[21]

A third characteristic Astarte shares with the biblical Queen of Heaven is her close association with fertility. The fertility aspects of the Queen of Heaven are made clear in Jer. 44:17, where the people of Judah claim that when they worshiped the Queen of Heaven, "we had plenty of food and we prospered." Conversely, "since we stopped worshiping the Queen of Heaven and stopped pouring out libations to her, we have lacked everything and been consumed . . . by famine" (44:18). At the same time, the Queen of Heaven seems to have a secondary association with war: according to her followers as quoted in Jeremiah, her proper worship guaranteed that the people "saw no evil" (44:17), but when her cult was abandoned, "we were consumed by the sword" (44:18). Astarte, too, has in addition to attributes of fertility associations with war.

The most striking evidence for Astarte's role as a guarantor of fertility is found in the Hebrew Bible, where the noun *ʿaštārôt,* a form of the divine name Astarte (*ʿaštart*), means "increase, progeny." Astarte's association with fertility is also demonstrated by her characterization as a goddess of sexual love at Ugarit, the thriving Levantine metropolis of the late second millennium. There Astarte plays the role of divine courtesan. This is particularly clear in one text, where El, the high god of the Ugaritic pantheon, sits enthroned at a royal banquet, flanked by Astarte, his lover, and Baʿl Haddu, his regent.[22] This depiction of Astarte as a goddess of sexual love continues into the mid- to late first millennium, as her identification with Greek Aphrodite, the Greek goddess of love, indicates. It is also known from Egypt, where Astarte, along with the goddess Anat, is called one of "the great goddesses who conceive but do not bear."[23]

Astarte's associations with war are in general not as well known as her character as a fertility goddess. An Egyptian New Kingdom stele of Merneptah from Memphis depicts the goddess with shield and spear,[24] and other Egyptian representations of Astarte show her on horseback carrying weapons of war.[25] Pharaoh Thutmose IV (Eighteenth Dynasty) is described as being mighty in the chariot like Astarte.[26] Along with Anat, Astarte is called a shield to Pharaoh Ramesses III[27] and a part of a thirteenth-century king's war chariot.[28] In the second millennium she carries the epithet "Lady of Combat";[29] similarly an Egyptian text from the Ptolemaic period (late first millennium) describes her as "Astarte, Mistress of Horses, Lady of the Chariot."[30] In the Canaanite realm Astarte acts as a war goddess in concert with Horon in Ugaritic mythology.[31] In biblical tradition the armor of the dead Saul is taken by the Philistines to the temple of Astarte (1 Sam. 31:10), which may also indicate the goddess's associations with war.

A fourth reason for identifying Astarte with the biblical Queen of Heaven is that the cult of Astarte has as a crucial element the offering of cakes, a ritual that also plays an important role in the worship of the Queen of Heaven (Jer. 7:18; 44:19). The Kition Tariff inscription mentioned above is again noteworthy, for line 10 of that inscription mentions "the two bakers who baked the basket of cakes for the Queen";[32] the Queen, I have argued, must be Astarte.[33] In addition, W. Culican has drawn attention to a Hellenistic votive model found off the Phoenician coast.[34] The model shows six figures positioned around a domed object. Culican identifies four identical seated females as votaresses. Another female figure stands and is pregnant; Culican believes her to be the fertility goddess, Astarte. This identification cannot be certain, but Astarte's well-attested popularity in the Phoenician and Punic realm in the late first millennium (see below), coupled with her known fertility attributes, make Culican's hypothesis attractive. Culican identifies the sixth figure on the model, a male, as a priest of the goddess. The domed object around which the six figures cluster is interpreted as a beehive oven. Culican proposes the scene is a cake-baking ritual in honor of Astarte. This is a speculative, but, in light of the Kition Tariff inscription and Jer. 7:18 and 44:19, an appealing suggestion.

A fifth and final factor that suggests that the biblical Queen of Heaven is Astarte is the popularity of the goddess Astarte in the west Semitic cult of the first millennium. Hundreds of Phoenician and Punic personal names incorporate the divine element *ʿštrt*, Astarte.[35] The goddess's name also appears in many Phoenician and Punic inscriptions, both from the Phoenician mainland and from the Mediterranean world and North Africa. The inscription of Paalaštart from Memphis (KAI 48), in addition to other first-millennium Egyptian material cited above, attests to the popularity of Astarte in Egypt. In Israel the Deuteronomistic historians accuse the people of worshiping Astarte in Judg. 2:13; 10:6; 1 Sam. 7:4; 12:10; 1 Kgs. 11:5, 33; and 2 Kgs. 23:13.[36] Also in Sakkunyaton Astarte is an important goddess, a wife of Kronos[37] and, as we have noted, a co-regent with Zeus

Demarous/Baʿl Haddu.[38] Astarte is thus a worthy candidate for the Queen of Heaven.

But certain elements of the worship of the Queen of Heaven remain unexplained if we interpret the cult of the Queen of Heaven only as a cult of west Semitic Astarte. For example, the word used in Jer. 7:18 and 44:19 for the cakes baked for the Queen, *kawwānîm,* is used nowhere in the extrabiblical materials that pertain to Astarte. Similarly, the biblical reference to baking cakes "in her image" (Jer. 44:19) cannot be understood by reference to the worship of west Semitic Astarte. Third, west Semitic evidence attests to no special role for women in the cult of Astarte. However, as we will see, these elements in the cult of the Queen of Heaven can be explained if we examine the cult of the east Semitic goddess, Ištar.

Certainly Ištar is a goddess who appropriately bears the title "Queen of Heaven." Indeed, the ancient Sumerian name of Ištar, Inanna, was thought by the subsequent inhabitants of Mesopotamia, the Akkadians, to mean "Queen of Heaven" (reading *[N]IN.AN.NA[K]*), and thus the name Inanna is routinely rendered in Akkadian texts as "Queen of Heaven" (*šarrat šamê*) or "Lady of Heaven" (*bēlet šamê*).[39] Ištar is also called by related epithets: "Queen of Heaven and the Stars," "Queen of Heaven and Earth," "Lady of Heaven and Earth," "Sovereign of Heaven and Earth," and "Ruler of Heaven and Earth."[40] In the West, too, Ištar is known as "Lady of Heaven." In an Egyptian New Kingdom inscription from Memphis Ištar of Nineveh (called by the ancient scribe Hurrian Astarte[41]) is given this title.[42] Ištar has other astral features in addition to her epithets.[43] In Mesopotamia, for example, Ištar is equated with Sumerian *DIL.BAT,* the Sumerian name of the planet Venus.

Also Ištar is a fertility goddess, as the Mesopotamian stories of Dumuzi/Tammuz and Inanna/Ištar show. These stories tell of the young fertility god, Tammuz, a symbol of prosperity and yield, and his courting and wooing of the maiden Ištar, who represents the communal storehouse in which harvested foodstuffs were kept. Tammuz is successful in his courtship, and the young fertility god and goddess marry. With their sexual union they guarantee fruitfulness in the land and bounty in the storehouse. This is symbolized in the myth by the fact that Tammuz, as his wedding gift to Ištar, brings to Ištar produce to be placed in her storehouse.[44] The identification of Ištar with the grain storehouse in these myths and elsewhere demonstrates her role in guaranteeing continual prosperity and preventing famine, an attribute associated with the Queen of Heaven in Jer. 44:17–18.

Ištar also has associations with war. In the Epilogue to the Code of Hammurapi, Hammurapi calls Ištar "the lady of the battle and of the fight" (Col. 50 [Rs. 27], 92–93). Her powers on the battlefield are clearly indicated by the curse she is to inflict on Hammurapi's enemy (Col. 51 [Rs. 28], 2–23):

> May she shatter his weapon at the battle site. May she establish for him confusion (and) rioting. May she cause his warriors to fail. May she give the earth their blood to drink. May she pile up everywhere on the plain heaps of corpses from his army. May she not take pity. As for him, may she give him into the hands of his enemies. May she lead him, bound, to the land of his enemies!

The myth of Inanna and Ebeh, in which Inanna/Ištar assaults the mountain Ebeh, also attests to Ištar's warring nature.[45]

Lexicographers generally agree that *kawwānîm,* the word used for the cakes baked for the Queen of Heaven in Jer. 7:18 and 44:19, is a loan word from Akkadian *kamānu,* "cake."[46] In Akkadian texts *kamānu* cakes are often associated with the cult of Ištar. A hymn to Ištar reads as follows:

> O Ištar, merciful goddess, I have come to visit you,
> I have prepared for you an offering, pure milk, a pure cake baked in ashes (*kamān tumri*),
> I stood up for you a vessel for libations, hear me and act favorably toward me![47]

Another text describes a healing ritual associated with the Ištar cult, in which a cake baked in ashes (*kamān tumri*) is prepared in honor of the goddess.[48] Finally in the Gilgamesh epic, Gilgamesh describes how Tammuz brought ash cakes (*tumru*) to his lover Ištar (Gilg. 6.58-60). Although *kamānu* cakes are not specifically mentioned in the Gilgamesh passage, most commentators assume that the reference to *tumru* is a shorthand expression for the *kamān tumri,* "cake baked in ashes," the cake associated with the Ištar cult in our first two examples.[49]

Scholars who have commented on the biblical cult of the Queen of Heaven are generally puzzled by the phrase "cakes in her image" (*lĕha‘ăṣībāh*).[50] Those holding that the Queen of Heaven is Ištar often explain what "in her image" means by pointing to several clay molds found at Mari, a site in northwest Mesopotamia. These molds portray a nude female figure who holds her hands cupped under her breasts. Her hips are large and prominent.[51] It has been suggested that the molds represent Ištar, and that they were used to shape cakes baked in the image of the goddess. These cakes were then offered to Ištar as part of her sacrificial cult.[52] Although there are problems with this suggestion,[53] the proposal to relate the Mari molds to biblical *lĕhaʿăṣībāh* is intriguing.

Finally, we observe that women seem to have a special place in the Ištar cult. In Mesopotamian mythology, as we have noted, the largest complex of stories about Ištar deals with her courtship and marriage to the young fertility god Tammuz. Tammuz symbolizes in the myths the spring season of prosperity and yield, a season when dates and grain were harvested, calves and lambs were born, and milk ran during the spring milking season. But when the spring harvest season ended, the mythology perceived that the god Tammuz had died.[54] The death of Tammuz was an occasion of sorrow for his young bride, Ištar, and Akkadian mythology preserves many of her laments over her dead lover.[55] And as a woman, Ištar, laments the death of her lover in myth, it is women, devotees of Ištar, who lament Tammuz's passing in the rituals of the Mesopotamian Tammuz cult.[56] The place of women in the Mesopotamian Tammuz cult is vividly illustrated by Ezek. 8:14, where it is women who are specifically identified as those who sit at the gate of the Jerusalem temple's inner court mourning the death of the fertility god. I suggest that it is this special place of women in the cult of Tammuz that is reflected in the biblical materials about the Queen of Heaven.

At first glance, it may seem a long jump from the role of women in the mourning rites of the Tammuz cult to the role of women in baking cakes for the Queen of Heaven. But, in fact, the two are closely related. The *kamānu* cakes associated with the Ištar cult (the *kawwānîm* baked as offerings to the Queen of Heaven) are a staple food of Mesopotamian shepherds.[57] Tammuz is the prototypical and patron shepherd of Mesopotamia. Moreover, as we noted above, in the Gilgamesh epic Gilgamesh describes Tammuz as the one who heaps up ash cakes for his lover Ištar (Gilg. 6.58-60). The cult of Tammuz the shepherd is closely tied to the Ištar cult that involves the baking of offering cakes. The cultic participants who mourn the death of Tammuz are thus the worshipers who bake cakes for Ištar, the Queen of Heaven. And, as women play a crucial role in the ritual mourning over Tammuz, they also play an important role in the cult involving the baking of *kamānu* cakes.

I submit that the Queen of Heaven is a syncretistic deity whose character incorporates aspects of west Semitic Astarte and east

Semitic Ištar. This syncretism probably occurred early in Canaanite religious history, well before the sixth century. Certainly the people of Judah, in Jer. 44:17, and Jeremiah himself, in Jer. 44:21, describe the cult as one practiced by past generations. Moreover, we know that the cult of Ištar of Nineveh is attested in Egypt during the New Kingdom[58] and as far west as Spain by the eighth century B.C.E.[59] This would suggest that the cults of Astarte and Ištar were exposed to each other and began intermingling sometime during the last centuries of the second millennium. This syncretism then continued throughout the Iron Age. Indeed, the cult of the Queen of Heaven in the Iron Age prospered, attracting in particular the women of sixth-century Judah and Jerusalem.

But surprisingly, this women's cult did not prosper only in those spheres such as the home and the family where we might expect to find women's religion. To be sure, there is a strong domestic component to the cult, seen especially in Jer. 7:18, where "the children gather wood, the fathers kindle fire, and the women knead dough to make cakes for the Queen of Heaven." But if Jer. 44:17 and 21 are to be taken at all seriously, then the "kings and princes" of Judah are also among those who worshiped the Queen. And, if the worship of the Queen of Heaven was a part of the religion of the monarchy, the Queen's cult may also have been at home in what was essentially the monarch's private chapel, the temple. This is certainly suggested by Ezek. 8:14, where the women who participate in the related cult of wailing over the Queen's deceased lover, Tammuz, sit at the north gates of the temple's inner court. The presence of a temple dedicated to the Queen of Heaven in fifth-century Egypt, a century after Jeremiah, in Jeremiah 44, berates the Judahites who have fled to Egypt for worshiping the Queen of Heaven, is also suggestive.

J. A. Hackett has argued that women in ancient Israelite society had a higher status and more opportunities to hold public and powerful positions in times of social dysfunction.[60] Certainly the calamitous years of the late seventh and early sixth centuries, which witnessed the senseless death of King Josiah, the David *revividus,* in 609, the Babylonian exiles of 597 and 587, the final destruction of the temple by the Babylonians in 587, and the simultaneous end of Judahite political independence, qualify as a period of severe dysfunction. There is, admittedly, little evidence from this period for women wielding political power. But the biblical data about the Queen of Heaven do suggest that the women of late seventh- and early sixth-century Judah and Jerusalem exercised religious power.[61] They worshiped a goddess whose cult they found particularly appealing and went so far as to introduce the cult of that goddess into the temple compound itself.

Since it is winners who write history, the importance of this women's cult in the history of the religion of Israel has been obscured by our sources. The ultimate "winners" in the religion of early sixth-century Judah, the Deuteronomistic historians, the priest-prophet Ezekiel, and the prophet Jeremiah, were men. The biblical texts these men wrote malign non-Deuteronomistic, non-priestly, and non-prophetic religion, and in the case of the cult of the Queen of Heaven they malign the religion of women. But fortunately for us, the sources have not completely ignored some women's cults. The losers have not been totally lost. If historians of Israelite religion continue to push beyond biblical polemic, we should hear more and more the voices of the women of Israel witnessing to their religious convictions.

NOTES

1. See P. Bird's recent article ("The Place of Women in the Israelite Cultus," in *Ancient Israelite Religion: Essays in Honor of Frank Moore Cross,* eds., P. D. Miller Jr., P. D. Hanson, S. D. McBride [Philadelphia: Fortress, 1987], 397–419) for a good introduction to this subject.

2. The consonantal Hebrew text reads *lmlkt,* "to the Queen of" (Jer. 7:18; 44:17,18,19,25). But the MT vocalizes *limleket,* as if the word were *lmlʾkt,* "to the work of [heaven]," i.e., "to the heavenly host." Indeed, many Hebrew manuscripts read *lmlʾkt* (with an *ʾalep*), which is supported by the Targum and Peshitta and, apparently, by the G in Jer. 7:18 (*tę̄ stratįa*). But as is commonly recognized, the Masoretic pointing is an apologetic attempt to remove any hint that the people of Judah worshiped the Queen of Heaven. See R. P. Gordon, "Aleph Apologeticum," *JQR* 69 (1978–79): 112. The correct reading is *lĕmalkat,* "to the Queen of," supported by Symmachus, Theodotian, Aquila, the Vg, and the G of Jer. 44:17,18,19,25.

3. J. Bright, *Jeremiah,* AB 21 (Garden City, N.Y.: Doubleday, 1965), 56; M. Held, "Studies in Biblical Lexicography in the Light of Akkadian," *Eretz Israel* 16 (1982): 76–77 (Hebrew); M. H. Pope, *Song of Songs,* AB 7c (Garden City, N.Y.: Doubleday, 1977), 149 (but see n. 4); W. E. Rast, "Cakes for the Queen of Heaven," in *Scripture in History and Theology: Studies in Honor of J. Coert Rylaarsdam,* eds., A. L. Merrill and T. W. Overholt, PTMS 17 (Pittsburgh: Pickwick, 1977), 167–80; W. Rudolph, *Jeremia,* 3d ed. (Tübingen: J. C. B. Mohr, 1968), 55; M. Weinfeld, "The Worship of Molech and the Queen of Heaven and its Background," *UF* 4 (1972): 148–54; A. Weiser, *Das*

Buch des Propheten Jeremia, ATD 20, 21 (Göttingen: Vandenhoeck und Ruprecht, 1952), 70.

4. E. Bresciani and M. Kamil, *Le lettere aramaiche di Hermopoli,* Atti della Accademia Nazionale dei Lincei 8/12 (Roma: Accademia Nazionale dei Lincei, 1966), 400; R. du Mesnil du Buisson, *Etudes sur les dieux phéniciens hérités par l'Empire Romain* (Leiden: Brill, 1970), 126–27; W. Culican, "A Votive Model from the Sea," *PEQ* 108 (1976): 121–22; J. Fitzmyer, "The Phoenician Inscription from Pyrgi," *JAOS* 86 (1966): 287–88; W. Herrmann, "Aštart," *Mitteilungen des Instituts für Orientforschung* 15 (1969): 29, n. 67; W. L. Holladay, *Jeremiah 1,* Hermeneia (Philadelphia: Fortress, 1986), 254–55; M. H. Pope, "ʿAṯtart, ʿAštart, Astarte," in M. H. Pope and W. Röllig, "Syrien. Die Mythologie der Ugariter und Phonizer," *Wörterbuch der Mythologie,* vol. 1: *Götter und Mythen im vorderen Orient* (ed. H. W. Haussig; Stuttgart: Ernst Klett, 1965), 251 (but see n. 3); M. H. Silverman, *Religious Values in the Jewish Proper Names at Elephantine,* AOAT 217 (Kevelaer: Butzon & Bercker; Neukirchen-Vluyn: Neukirchener Verlag, 1985), 225, n. 6. In a newly published article, which appeared after I had completed my essay, S. M. Olyan also identifies the Queen as Astarte ("Some Observations Concerning the Identity of the Queen of Heaven," *UF* 19 [1987]: 161–74).

5. W. F. Albright, *Yahweh and the Gods of Canaan; A Historical Analysis of Two Contrasting Faiths* (Winona Lake, Ind.: Eisenbrauns, 1968), 130; M. Cogan, *Imperialism and Religion: Assyria, Judah and Israel in the Eighth and Seventh Centuries B.C.E.,* SBLMS 19 (Missoula, Mont.: Scholars, 1974), 85; A. S. Kapelrud, *The Violent Goddess; Anat in the Ras Shamra Texts* (Oslo: Universitetsforlaget, 1969), 13, 16; J. McKay, *Religion in Judah under the Assyrians, 739–609 B.C.,* SBT (Second Series) 26 (Naperville, Ill.: A. R. Allenson, 1973), 110–11, n. 19; B. Porten, *Archives from Elephantine; The Life of an Ancient Jewish Military Colony* (Berkeley and Los Angeles: University of California, 1968), 165, 177; A. Vincent, *La religion des Judéo-Araméens d'Eléphantine* (Paris: Geuthner, 1937), 635, 649–51.

6. M. Dahood, "La Regina del Cielo in Geremia," *RivB* 8 (1960): 166–68.

7. For example, J. Gray, "Queen of Heaven," *IDB* 3, 975a, b.

8. Note the comments of Fitzmyer, "Pyrgi," *JAOS* 86 (1966): 287; of Rast, "Cakes for the Queen of Heaven," *Scripture in History and Theology,* 170; and cf. Bright, *Jeremiah,* 56. M. H. Pope may also indirectly indicate his support of such a thesis, since he identifies the Queen of Heaven as Astarte in *Wörterbuch der Mythologie,* 251 (n. 4), but as Ištar in *Song,* 149 (n. 3).

9. Egyptian *nbt pt.* D. B. Redford ("New Light on the Asiatic Campaigning of Horemheb," *BASOR* 211 [1973]: 37) finds this epithet on a stone bowl of the Eighteenth Dynasty; the bowl is also discussed by M. Delcor ("La culte de la 'Reine du Ciel' selon Jer. 7, 18; 44, 17–19, 25 et ses survivances," *Von Kanaan bis Kerala,* AOAT 211 [Kevelaer: Butzon & Bercker; Neukirchen-Vluyn: Neukirchener Verlag, 1982], 114). For Nineteenth Dynasty inscriptions, see W. M. F. Petrie, *Memphis* 1 (London: School of Archaeology in Egypt and

Bernard Quaritch, 1909), 19, and M. G. Maspero, "Notes de Voyage," *Annales du service des antiquités de l'Egypte* 10 (1909): 131–32; Also Delcor, "La culte de la 'Reine du Ciel,'" *Von Kanaan bis Kerala,* 114; W. Helck, *Die Beziehungen Aegyptens zu Vorderasien im 3. und 2. Jahrtausend v. Chr.*, Ägyptologische Abhandlungen 5, 2d ed. (Wiesbaden: Otto Harrassowitz, 1971), 457–58; J. Leclant, "Astarté à cheval d'après les représentations égyptiennes," *Syria* 37 (1960): 10–13, and Fig. 1; R. Stadelmann, *Syrisch-Palästinensische Gottheiten in Ägypten,* Probleme der Ägyptologie 5 (Leiden: Brill, 1967), 104, 106.

10. See *CIS* 86 A; *KAI* 37 A, *mlkt qdšt* (line 7) and *mlkt* (line 10). (I am following the line numbers of *KAI* and most commentators; see further J. B. Peckham, "Notes on a Fifth-Century Phoenician Inscription from Kition, Cyprus (*CIS* 86)," *Or* 37 [1968]: 304, n. 2.) Note that although Astarte is not mentioned by name in lines 7 and 10, the title "queen" in an inscription concerned with the cult and temple of Astarte can refer to no other. This is acknowledged by almost all commentators. See as representative J. C. L. Gibson, *Textbook of Syrian Semitic Inscriptions* 3 (Oxford: Clarendon, 1982), 128; J. P. Healey, "The Kition Tariffs and the Phoenician Cursive Series," *BASOR* 216 (1974): 55; O. Masson and M. Sznycer, *Recherches sur les phéniciens à Chypre,* Hautes Etudes Orientales 2/3 (Genève et Paris: Librairie Droz, 1972), 44; Peckham, "Kition," *Or* 37 (1968): 312–13. The suggestion of H. Donner and W. Röllig (*KAI* 2, 55) that *mlkt* is a mistake for *mlʾkt,* "service," in line 7 (they do not comment on line 10) is surely not correct, as the scribe demonstrates in line 13 that he knows the proper spelling of *mlʾkt,* that is, with an *ʾalep* (see Masson and Sznycer, *Recherches,* 44).

11. Eusebius, *Praeparatio evangelica* 1.10.31. Also in connection with Astarte's royalty note the Tyrian "Throne of Astarte" (*KAI* 17) and the uninscribed "thrones" like it. See J. T. Milik, "Les papyrus araméens d'Hermoupolis et les cultes syro-phéniciens en Egypte perse," *Bib* 48 (1967): 572, and the bibliography listed there.

12. *šmm ʾdrm* in *KAI* 14 (Eshmunazor), 16 and 17; *šmm rmm* in *KAI* 15 (Bodashtart). On *KAI* 14 see further Gibson, *Syrian Semitic Inscriptions* 3, 112; Milik, "Les papyrus araméens," *Bib* 48 (1967): 561 and n. 2 on that page; J. Teixidor, *The Pagan God; Popular Religion in the Greco-Roman Near East* (Princeton: Princeton University, 1977), 39. On *KAI* 15 see F. M. Cross, *Canaanite Myth and Hebrew Epic; Essays in the History of the Religion of Israel* (Cambridge, Mass.: Harvard University, 1973), 142; Gibson, *Syrian Semitic Inscriptions* 3, 112; Milik, "Les papyrus araméens," *Bib* 48 (1967): 597–98; and, especially, O. Eissfeldt, "Schamemrumim 'Hoher Himmel,' ein Stadtteil von Gross-Sidon," *Ras Schamra und Sanchunjaton* (Halle: Max Niemeyer, 1939), 62–67 (No. 14).

13. Eusebius, *Praeparatio evangelica* 1.10.32; translation, H. W. Attridge and R. A. Oden, *Philo of Byblos, The Phoenician History; Introduction, Critical Text, Translation, and Notes,* CBQMS 9 (Washington, D. C.: Catholic Biblical Association of America, 1981), 55.

14. *KAI* 54. Phoenician *ʿbdʿštrt ʾšqlny;* Greek *Aphrodisiou Askalōnitēs.*

15. Note also 1.131 and 3.8.

16. *Astartę palaistinę, Aphroditę ouranią.* See P. Roussel and M. Launey, *Inscriptions de Délos* (Paris: Honoré Champion, 1937), #2305 (*editio princeps:* M. Clermont-Ganneau, "Une dédicace à ʿAštarté Palestinienne,' découverte à Délos," *CRAIBL* [1909]: 307–17). Also see Delos inscription #1719 in Roussel and Launey (*editio princeps:* A. Plassart, *Délos* 11 [Paris: E. de Boccard, 1928], 287), and the discussions of Delcor, "La culte de la 'Reine du Ciel,'" *Von Kanaan bis Kerala,* 117; R. A. S. Macalister, *The Philistines, their History and Civilization* (London: Oxford University, 1914), 94; McKay, *Religion in Judah,* 51.

17. Fitzmyer, "Pyrgi," *JAOS* 86 (1966): 288. The identification of Astarte with Juno, rather than with Etruscan *Turan,* Roman Venus, the usual equivalent of Greek Aphrodite, need not give pause, given the tremendous fluidity of the great Canaanite goddesses in the first millennium.

18. 5.6.4; pointed out by Delcor, "La culte de la 'Reine du Ciel,'" *Von Kanaan bis Kerala,* 115.

19. *Metamorphoses* 11.2; pointed out by Teixidor, *The Pagan God,* 36. *RES* 921, which reads *[ʿš]trt pp[s],* confirms that the cult of Palestinian Astarte was known at Paphos. See A. Dupont-Sommer, "Les Phéniciens à Chypre," *Report of the Department of Antiquities, Cyprus, 1974* (Nicosia: Department of Antiquities, Cyprus, and Zavallis Press, 1974), 93–94.

20. In addition to the data cited below, see J. J. M. Roberts, *The Earliest Semitic Pantheon* (Baltimore and London: Johns Hopkins University, 1972), 101, n. 285.

21. Eusebius, *Praeparatio evangelica* 1.10.31, trans., Attridge and Oden, *Philo of Byblos,* 55.

22. *Ugaritica* 5.2 (RS 24.252); see also *CTA* 14.3.146.

23. From the Papyrus Harris; see W. F. Albright, "The North Canaanite Epic of ʾAlʾêyân Baʿal and Môt," *JPOS* 12 (1932): 193; W. F. Albright, *Archaeology and the Religion of Israel* (Baltimore: Johns Hopkins University, 1942), 75; Helck, *Beziehungen,* 462; Leclant, "Astarté à cheval," *Syria* 37 (1960): 7; J. B. Pritchard, *Palestinian Figurines in Relation to Certain Goddesses Known throughout Literature,* AOS 24 (New Haven: American Oriental Society, 1943), 79. Also from Egypt, note the plaque of the composite goddess, Qudšu-Astarte-Anat, where the goddess holds a lotus and serpent, symbols of fertility (I. E. S. Edwards, "A Relief of Qudshu-Astarte-Anath in the Winchester College Collection," *JNES* 14 [1955]: 49–51).

24. Petrie, *Memphis* 1, 8, and Pl. 15, No. 37. See also Leclant, "Astarté à cheval," *Syria* 37 (1960): 10–13, and Fig. 1.

25. Leclant, "Astarté à cheval," *Syria* 37 (1960), *passim.* See also the "Lady Godiva" plaque found in D. Ussishkin's excavations at Lachish, which shows a goddess, Astarte, I would argue, standing astride a horse. See. D. Ussishkin, "Excavations at Tel Lachish—1973–1977. Preliminary Report," *Tel Aviv* 5 (1978): 21, and Pl. 8.

26. H. Carter and P. E. Newberry, *The Tomb of Thoutmosis IV,* Catalogue général des antiquités égyptiennes du Musée du Caire 15 (Westminster:

Archibald Constable and Co., 1904), 27 and Pl. 10; also *ANET*, 250a and n. 16.

27. W. F. Edgerton and J. A. Wilson, *Historical Records of Ramesses III*, Studies in Ancient Oriental Civilization 12 (Chicago: University of Chicago, 1936), 75; also *ANET*, 250a and n. 18.

28. W. R. Dawson and T. E. Peet, "The So-Called Poem on the King's Chariot," *JEA* 19 (1933): 169 (verso, lines 12–14); also *ANET*, 250a and n. 17.

29. Leclant, "Astarté à cheval," *Syria* 37 (1960): 25.

30. Leclant, "Astarté à cheval," *Syria* 37 (1960): 54–58, especially p. 57, and Pl. 4 (opposite p. 49); *ANET* 250a, n. 16.

31. *CTA* 2.1.7–8; 16.6.54–57. W. Herrmann has pointed out that the obverse of *PRU* 5.1 (19.39) also describes Astarte as a war goddess (Herrmann, "Aštart," *Mitteilungen des Instituts für Orientforschung* 15 [1969]: 7–16).

32. For the reading (*lʾpm || ʾšʾpʾyt ṭnʾ ḥlt*) and translation adopted here, see Peckham, "Kition," *Or* 37 (1968): 305–6. Peckham is followed by Gibson, *Syrian Semitic Inscriptions* 3, 124–25, and by Masson and Sznycer, *Recherches*, 26–27, 28–29. Healey ("Kition," *BASOR* 216 [1974]: 54) offers an alternative reconstruction, *lʾpm || ʾšʾp mntspʾ ḥlt lmlkt*, "For the two bakers, who baked choice food, loaves for the Queen."

33. Among those who associate the reference in the Kition inscription with the worship of the Queen of Heaven, see Culican, "A Votive Model," *PEQ* 108 (1976): 122; Delcor, "La culte de la 'Reine du Ciel,'" *Von Kanaan bis Kerala*, 110–12; Peckham, "Kition," *Or* 37 (1968): 314–15, and n. 2 on p. 315.

34. Culican, "A Votive Model," *PEQ* 108 (1976), *passim*.

35. Cf. J. Tigay, *Ye Shall Have No Other Gods: Israelite Religion in the Light of Hebrew Inscriptions*, Harvard Semitic Studies 31 (Atlanta: Scholars, 1986); idem, "Israelite Religion: The Onomastic and Epigraphic Evidence," *Ancient Israelite Religion*, 157–94.

36. The G, in addition, reads *Astartę* for MT *ʾăšērâ* in 2 Chr. 15:16 and *Astartais* for MT *ʾăšērîm* in 2 Chr. 24:18. In 2 Chr. 15:16, which describes how Maʾacah, the queen mother, made an abominable image for the goddess, the MT is clearly primitive.

37. Eusebius, *Praeparatio evangelica* 1.10.22, 24.

38. Eusebius, *Praeparatio evangelica* 1.10.31.

39. O. Edzard, "Inanna, Ištar," in "Mesopotamien. Die Mythologie der Sumerer und Akkader," *Wörterbuch der Mythologie*, 81; A. Falkenstein, *Die Inschriften Gudeas von Lagas 1, Einleitung*, AnOr 30 (Roma: Pontificium Institutum Biblicum, 1966), 78–79; W. Helck, *Betrachtungen zur grossen Göttin und den ihr verbundenen Gottheiten*, Religion und Kultur der alten Mittelmeerwelt in Parallelforschungen 2 (Munchen und Wien: R. Oldenbourg, 1971), 73; Held, "Biblical Lexicography," *Eretz Israel* 16 (1982): 80, n. 24; S. N. Kramer, *The Sumerians: Their History, Culture, and Character* (Chicago: University of Chicago, 1963), 153.

40. *šarrat šamê u kakkabāni, šarrat šamê u erṣeti, bēlet šamê (u) erṣeti, etellet šamê (u) erṣetim, malkat šamāmī u qaqqari.* See K. Tallqvist, *Akkadische*

Gotterepitheta, StudOr 7 (Helsinki: Societas Orientalis Fennica, 1938), 39, 64, 129, 239–40; cf. 333–34.

41. Albright, *Yahweh and the Gods of Canaan*, 143, n. 88; F. M. Cross, "The Old Phoenician Inscription from Spain Dedicated to Hurrian Astarte," *HTR* 64 (1971): 192; Helck, *Beziehungen*, 459–60; idem, *Betrachtungen*, 213–16; Stadelmann, *Gottheiten*, 107.

42. For this inscription, see E. von Bergmann, "Inschriftliche Denkmäler der Sammlung ägyptischer Alterthümer des österr. Kaiserhauses," *Receuil de travaux* 7 (1886): 196; also the comments of Culican, "A Votive Model," *PEQ* 108 (1976): 122; H. Ranke, "Ištar als Heilgottin in Agypten," *Studies Presented to F. Ll. Griffith* (London: Oxford University, 1932), 412–18; Stadelmann, *Gottheiten*, 107; John A. Wilson, "The Egyptians and the Gods of Asia," *ANET*, 250, n. 19. Also note a second Memphis inscription in which Hurrian Astarte (Ištar of Nineveh) is called Lady of Heaven. See H. Madsen, "Zwei Inschriften in Kopenhagen," *Zeitschrift für Ägyptische Sprache und Altertumskunde* 41 (1904): 114, and the comments of Culican, "A Votive Model," *PEQ* 108 (1976): 122.

43. See Edzard, "Inanna, Ištar," *Wörterbuch der Mythologie*, 85–86.

44. See T. Jacobsen, "Fourth Millennium Metaphors. The Gods as Providers: Dying Gods of Fertility," *The Treasures of Darkness* (New Haven and London: Yale University, 1976), 23–73.

45. See S. N. Kramer, *Sumerian Mythology* (Philadelphia: American Philosophical Society, 1944), 83.

46. See as representative *AHW*, 430a, s. v. *kamānu; HALAT* 2, 444a, b, s. v. *kawwān;* KB, 428a, s. v. *kawwān*. See also A. Jeremias, *Das Alte Testament im Lichte des Alten Orients*, 3d ed. (Leipzig: J. C. Hinrichs, 1916), 611–12; H. Zimmern, *Akkadische Fremdwörter* (Leipzig: J. C. Hinrichs, 1916), 38; Held, "Biblical Lexicography," *Eretz Israel* 16 (1982): 76–77.

47. The text can be found in J. A. Craig, *Assyrian and Babylonian Religious Texts* 1 (Leipzig: J. C. Hinrichs, 1885), 15:20–22. For transcription, translation, and notes, see E. Ebeling, "Quellen zur Kenntnis der babylonischen Religion, II," MVAAG 23/2 (1918), 4, lines 20–22, and 12.

48. The text can be found in E. Ebeling, *Keilschrifttexte aus Assur religiösen Inhalts* 1 (Osnabrück: Otto Zeller, 1972), 42:25. For transcription, translation, and some notes, see Ebeling, "Quellen, II" MVAAG 23/2 (1918), 22, line 25, and 27.

49. So, for example, *AHW*, 1370b, s. v. *tumru(m);* A. L. Oppenheim, "Mesopotamian Mythology II," *Or* 17 (1948): 36, n. 6; H. W. F. Saggs, *The Greatness that was Babylon* (New York: Hawthorn, 1962), 395; A. Schott and W. von Soden, *Das Gilgamesch-Epos* (Stuttgart: Reclam, 1977), 52; E. A. Speiser, "The Epic of Gilgamesh," *ANET*, 84b. But cf. A. Heidel, *The Gilgamesh Epic and Old Testament Parallels* (Chicago: University of Chicago, 1946, 1949), 51, who translates "charcoals." Against Heidel's translation, see B. Landsberger, *Der Kultische Kalender der Babylonier und Assyrer*, Leipziger Semitistische Studien 6/1-2 (Leipzig: J. C. Hinrichs, 1915), 121, n. 1.

50. Reading *lĕha'ăṣībāh* for MT *lĕha'ăṣībâ*. On suffixal *hē* without *mappiq*, see GKC, 56g and cf. 91e.

51. The molds were first published by A. Parrot, *Mission archéologique de Mari 2. Le palais-documents et monuments* (Paris: Geuthner, 1959), 37–38, and Pl. 19. For a readily accessible photograph of the largest and best-preserved mold, see A. Malamat, "Mari," *BA* 34 (1971), Fig. 9 (p. 21), or Pope, *Song*, Pl. 1 (opposite p. 360).

52. This is proposed by Rast, "Cakes for the Queen of Heaven," *Scripture in History and Theology*, 171–74, and by Pope, *Song*, 379. See also Holladay, *Jeremiah* 1, 254.

53. A. Parrot writes (*Le palais*, 37), "L'identification nous échappe: simple mortelle, femme de haut rang, divinité?"

54. Although seasonal interpretations of ancient Near Eastern myths are often unwarranted, the myths of Tammuz do seem best understood as having agricultural concerns as their main (but not exclusive) focus.

55. See, for example, the laments collected in Jacobsen, *Treasures of Darkness*, 49–50, 53–54.

56. Although facile equations of myth and ritual must be avoided (see, most recently, R. S. Hendel, *The Epic of the Patriarch: The Jacob Cycle and the Narrative Traditions of Canaan and Israel*, HSM 42 [Atlanta: Scholars, 1987], 69–71; in addition to Hendel's references, note W. Burkert, *Homo Necans: The Anthropology of Ancient Greek Sacrificial Ritual and Myth* [Berkeley, Los Angeles, London: University of California, 1983], 29–34), it is acknowledged by all commentators that the Mesopotamian myth of Tammuz is to some degree reflective of and at the same time reflected in Mesopotamian ritual and cult.

57. See CAD K (vol. 8), 111a, s. v. *kamānu*: "Baked in ashes, the *k*.-cake seems to have been a dish of the shepherd"; also note the references listed there.

58. See above; also Helck, *Beziehungen*, 458–60; idem, *Betrachtungen*, 213–16.

59. See Cross, "Hurrian Astarte," *HTR* 64 (1971): 189–95.

60. J. A. Hackett, "In the Days of Jael: Reclaiming the History of Women in Ancient Israel," in *Immaculate and Powerful: The Female in Sacred Image and Social Reality*, eds. C. W. Atkinson, C. H. Buchanan, M. R. Miles (Boston: Beacon, 1985), 15–38.

61. It is perhaps not coincidental that Huldah, the first prophetess reported by the biblical writers since the period of the League, is active at approximately the same time, the last quarter of the seventh century (2 Kgs. 23:14–20).

9 "WHENCE SHALL HELP COME TO ME?": THE BIBLICAL WIDOW*

PAULA S. HIEBERT

In a forward-looking essay Jo Ann Hackett[1] placed contemporary feminist concerns in the field of biblical studies within a larger framework, that of contemporary scholarship on women. What is evident from Hackett's work is that the connection between biblical studies and women is not merely that today there are more women doing advanced degrees in Hebrew Bible and New Testament and thus that there are more women today equipped with the academic credentials to engage in serious biblical research with a feminist perspective. A more accurate assessment of what is presently transpiring between biblical studies and women is that many women doing biblical research are applying the methodologies and interpretive models of such fields as women's history, sociology, and anthropology in order to reconstruct a history of biblical women from written records that are pervaded by an androcentric bias. This new exploration implies that fresh questions are posed to the biblical text with the result that new and diverse insights and understandings are drawn from it.

Doing research on women and the Bible does not mean that past and even more recent biblical studies must be set aside, that they have been negated. As with any other area of scholarly research, and in any other time, the present generation of scholars brings to the task its own assumptions, queries, methods, and worldviews, all of which are influenced by its experience of the world in which it lives. Such is the case with those doing scholarship on women and whose main area of

* I would like to thank Professors John Huehnergard, Nancy Jay, Piotr Steinkeller, and Joan Goodnick Westenholz for their helpful comments.

expertise is biblical studies. There is a new way of doing the work. As Hackett expresses it, biblical scholars must recognize

> that to do it [women's history within biblical studies] one has to retrain, to be willing to move the boundaries of "our field" out a bit to accept some of the new scholarship on women, some sociological and anthropological work, the new women's history. In a field that seems to me only recently to have discovered political history instead of religious or theological or sacred or biblical history, we are now being pushed headlong into social history, especially those of us doing research on women.[2]

The study of widows illustrates the demands required of one who would pursue the place of women in the Hebrew Bible. Most work that has been done to date on the biblical widow (*ʾalmānâ*) consists in gathering the texts in which the word occurs.[3] This is a necessary step in any investigation. What is needed now, and the impetus has been provided by the current interest in women's social history, is to explore more rigorously issues related to the social status[4] of the widow. Looking at a few texts within one corpus in which *ʾalmānâ* occurs can serve to focus our attention on those aspects of the *ʾalmānâ* that will be pursued in this paper.

The Book of Psalms contains five references to the *ʾalmānâ.* This collection of hymns, laments, and songs of thanksgiving constituted the hymnbook of Israel collected over the centuries from the time of David to the post-exilic period. Whereas the task of dating the Psalms and classifying them according to type is a notoriously difficult one and no consensus among scholars has been reached, the picture of the *ʾalmānâ* that emerges from the book is a uniform one. Four of the texts illustrate a phenomenon that occurs in over half of the biblical occurrences of *ʾalmānâ,* namely the grouping together of the widow, the fatherless (*yātôm*), and the client (*gēr*). Ps. 94:4–7 depicts the actions of the wicked (*rĕšāʿîm*) who flagrantly violate the weaker members of society. In v. 6 they are described as slaying the *ʾalmānâ* and the client, and murdering the fatherless. The hymn of praise found at Psalm 146 lists Yahweh's accomplishments in creation and his fidelity to his people. That he guards clients and upholds the fatherless and the *ʾalmānâ* (v. 9) makes good sense in the light of what may befall these groups according to Psalm 94 above. God's beneficence is again extolled in Ps. 68:6 where he is called the father of the fatherless and the judge of *ʾalmānôt.* In a lament that painstakingly enumerates all the vengeance the psalmist wishes to see exacted upon his evildoers, Ps. 109:9 lists this imprecation: "May his children be fatherless, and his wife a widow." Not only does this curse imply that the psalmist desires the death of his enemy, but even more that he wants his enemy's family to experience hardship as a result of that death. The last mention of the *ʾalmānâ* in the Psalms is found in a list of people affected by Yahweh's rage against faithless Israel. Yahweh's rejection results in the defeat of his people at the hand of their enemies. Specific mention is made of the fate of the young men, the maidens, the priests, and the *ʾalmānôt* (Ps. 78:63–64). While the maidens are no longer praised (in wedding songs?), the *ʾalmānôt* no longer lament. In all of these texts it is evident that the *ʾalmānâ* is someone in an unenviable position. She is victimized, by reason of being an *ʾalmānâ,* by the strong and powerful members of the society. This woman, whose lot is a wretched one, stands in need of Yahweh's protection in order that she not be an object of oppression and abuse.

There has been no attempt thus far to delineate a picture of the Hebrew *ʾalmānâ.* Many questions arise about this woman. Just who is this *ʾalmānâ*? Is every widow designated by this term? In a society where the levirate[5] is legislated, why is an *ʾalmānâ* considered so vulnerable and alone? Where are the kin who are obliged to provide for her? What is her financial situation? Why is she grouped with the fatherless and the client? Why is she in need of Yahweh's special protection? What is her connection with lamentation? It is my aim to initiate the process of depicting the Hebrew *ʾalmānâ,* of fleshing out her life, of determining her status. Useful in this endeavor will be comparative ancient Near Eastern data and contemporary studies in sociology and anthropology.

The word *ʾalmānâ* has cognates in the other Semitic languages: Akkadian *almattu,* Ugaritic *ʾlmnt,* Phoenician *ʾlmt,* Aramaic *ʾarmaltāʾ,* and Arabic *ʾarmalat.*[6] The etymology is uncertain, and none of the proposals offered to date is satisfactory.[7] The only thing that can be said with certainty is that *ʾalmānâ* is a very old word with a strange pattern of consonants. The combination of *l, m,* and *n* in one word is unusual in Semitic. Since, however, all the cognates mean "widow," an investigation of the various languages' use of the term is potentially relevant for an understanding of the Hebrew *ʾalmānâ.*

At this point it will be helpful to turn to Mesopotamian literature, for it is here alone that explicit information is found about the ancient Near Eastern widow. Although the word *almattu* occurs in earlier Mesopotamian texts,[8] it is only with the Middle Assyrian laws that a definition of, as well as pertinent information about, the *almattu* is available.[9]

While the clay tablets on which these laws were inscribed date from the time of Tiglath Pileser I in the late twelfth and early eleventh centuries B.C.E., the laws themselves may be several centuries earlier.

The most immediately informative law with respect to the *almattu* is A § 33:

> [If] a woman is still dwelling in her father's house, (and) her husband is dead and [she] has sons, [she shall dwell in a] house [belonging to them where she chooses. If] she has no [son, her father-in-law shall give her] to whichever [of his sons] he likes . . . or, if he pleases, he shall give her as a spouse to her father-in-law. If her husband and her father-in-law are [indeed] dead and she has no son, she becomes (in law) a widow (*almattu*); she shall go whither she pleases.[10]

According to the last few lines of this law certain conditions must exist before a woman is called an *almattu,* namely both husband and father-in-law must be deceased, and there is no son to provide for the widowed mother.[11] From other laws (A §§ 30 and 43) it is clear that a form of levirate existed in Assyria. A § 43 provides for a husband in the case of the deaths of both future father-in-law and betrothed. If the betrothed man had a son of at least ten years of age, that son could be given to the woman to marry. For the woman of A § 33 none of these options appears possible. Furthermore, in the circumstances in which she finds herself—without husband, sons, or father-in-law—responsibility for her does not revert to her paternal family even though, according to the opening lines of the law, she resides in her father's house.[12] As stated by the law, either there is a male within the husband's family, namely son or father-in-law, to take over her maintenance, or she is an *almattu.* In other words, an *almattu* is a woman without males who are responsible for supporting her.

From A § 45, which is concerned with the wife of a prisoner of war, a further noteworthy aspect of the *almattu* is discovered. This law states that after the woman has waited two years for the return of her missing husband "she may go to live with the husband of her choice, (and) they shall write a tablet for her as a widow" (*ṭuppaša kī almatte*). Apparently once a woman was officially declared or considered an *almattu,* she was given or could apply for a document that stated her position as an *almattu.* Presumably she would need such a document to give her access to a world that normally would be mediated for her through the authority of some male.

From this examination of the *almattu* in the Middle Assyrian laws, it is apparent that the English word "widow" does not accurately translate *almattu.*[13] An *almattu* is not a "widow" in the western sense of the word. Our understanding of a widow is a once-married woman whose husband has died. Her conjugal obligations to her husband are now terminated; she is free to marry another if she chooses. The traditional marriage vows express this concept through the words "till death do us part."

This view of death as a severance of the marriage bond is not found in all societies. Michael Kirwen studied four societies of northwest Tanzania that practice levirate marriage.[14] In the Luo society, one of the four that Kirwen studied, the widow considers herself to be a legal, functioning wife; hence she is not free to remarry. The technical term in Luo for widow, *chi liel,* literally means "wife of a grave." A similar phenomenon occurs in the biblical text; a woman whose husband has died continues to be called his wife. Ruth is described by Boaz as *ʾēšet-hammēt,* "the wife of the dead man" (4:5) and *ʾēšet maḥlôn,* "the wife of Mahlon" (4:10).[15] The woman of 2 Kgs. 4:1–7 who entreats Elisha to help her pay off her deceased husband's creditors is introduced in the narrative with the words, "One woman from the wives of the sons of the prophets (*wĕʾiššâ ʾaḥat minnĕšê bĕnê hannĕbîʾîm*) cried out to Elisha" (2 Kgs. 4:1). Even in the levirate law (Deut. 25:5–10) the woman is referred to as "the wife of the dead man" (*ʾēšet-hammēt*).

This belief that death does not dissolve the marriage bond is intelligible when it is placed in the context of a particular society's understanding of marriage. In most traditional societies based on a kinship structure,[16] marriage is not so much the union of two individuals as it is the union of two families.

In a patriarchal society such as ancient Israel was, the woman entered her husband's family at the time of marriage.[17] When her husband died, she was still considered to be part of his family, to be subject to the authority of a male of his kin. Tamar, the daughter-in-law of Judah (Gen. 38), illustrates this point. When Tamar's husband's death left her a childless widow, Judah was obliged by the levirate law to provide another son for her. When this procedure proved futile with his second son and since his third son was under age, Judah told Tamar to return to her own kin.[18] Yet even after Tamar had resumed living with her paternal kin, it was still Judah who claimed control over her. When told she was pregnant, it was Judah who ordered her to be burned. We hear nothing from any member of Tamar's family. So even though death had ended the physical relationship that existed between Tamar and Er, it had not terminated the relationship of Tamar with her husband's family, with the mutual rights and obligations incumbent upon both parties.

The fact that the *ʾalmānâ* is so often linked with the fatherless and the client suggests that these three groups shared something in common. Lawrence Stager in a recent article dealt with the notion of *gēr*[19] and his treatment is relevant to an understanding of *ʾalmānâ*. The *gēr*, commonly translated "sojourner, stranger, resident alien," but more properly "client," was a man who was dwelling outside the geographical area of his own kin. He was, therefore, in need of protection that was not available to him from his own family. The *gēr* needed to attach himself to a patron for this protection and for economic assistance. The *ʾalmānâ*, I would suggest, was like the *gēr* in that she existed in a situation with no supporting kinship ties. Like the *almattu* of the Middle Assyrian laws, her link to her husband's kin has been severed because there is no male of that family who has authority over her. Numbers 30, which concerns vows made by women, illustrates this. Every vow made by a woman is subject to the approval of either her father or her husband. Only the vow of an *ʾalmānâ* or of a divorcée (*gĕrûšâ*) is valid on its own (Num. 30:10). Implicit in the law is the acknowledgment that the *ʾalmānâ* has no male authority figure to pass judgment on the validity of her vow. Tamar has no husband, no son, no father-in-law who will take responsibility for her. When Judah tells her to return to her paternal kin, he says, "Remain an *ʾalmānâ* in your father's house" (Gen. 38:11). Judah here releases Tamar from her bonds with his family until Judah's youngest son is old enough to perform the levirate. Yet because she has been married, she no longer belongs under the authority of her paternal kin, as evidenced by Judah's sentence of burning on Tamar even while she dwelt in her *bêt ʾāb*.

The Hebrew *ʾalmānâ* then, like the *gēr*, existed on the fringes of society. In a society where kinship ties gave one identity, meaning, and protection, both the *ʾalmānâ* and the *gēr* had no such ties. Unlike the *gēr*, however, the *ʾalmānâ* lived in this liminal zone as a woman. Not only was she bereft of kin, but she was also without a male who ordinarily provided a woman with access to the public sphere.

To delineate further this picture of the Hebrew *ʾalmānâ*, a sociological model developed with respect to a cross-cultural study on widows is useful. It was organized and directed by Helena Lopata.[20] In this study of widows from around the world a theoretical framework of support systems was developed in order to analyze how a woman experiences the world as a widow. Lopata defines a support as "any object or action that the giver and/or receiver define as necessary or helpful in maintaining a style of life."[21] A group of similar supports constitutes a support system. The four sets of support systems used by the group included economic, service, social, and emotional supports.

While an exhaustive application of this sociological model involving the widow's support systems to the Hebrew Bible would be a fruitful enterprise, the constraints of this paper have limited the study to the economic support system only. Since survival in any society is dependent on the provision of the basic necessities of food, clothing, and shelter, it seems logical to begin to fill in the picture of the Hebrew *ʾalmānâ* with a look at her economic means. In order to illuminate this area it is necessary to know something about marriage practices and laws of inheritance in ancient Israelite society. Basically the question we need to answer is whether or not the widow owned property.

As mentioned above marriage in most traditional societies based on kinship structure is a union between two families. At the time of the marriage an exchange of goods between the families takes place. This practice is referred to by the terms bridewealth and dowry. Social anthropologists Jack Goody and Stanley Tambiah have studied this institution in African and Asian societies.[22] Their analysis provides a backdrop by which to study this phenomenon as it manifests itself in biblical and other ancient Near Eastern texts.

According to Goody and Tambiah, bridewealth and dowry involve the transmission of property and the transfer of rights at marriage. For both bridewealth and dowry a number of variables must be taken into consideration in order to understand the nature, function, and purpose of each. These include the givers and receivers, the contents, the returnability, the variability (fixed or variable), the control, and the payment schedule. The range of possible combinations of these variables as well as the importance attached to the practice of bridewealth and/or dowry differs from one society to another. With respect to the relationship of this practice to the task of determining the economic resources of the *ʾalmānâ* it will be beneficial to keep certain questions in mind. Who receives what at the time of marriage? What property does the woman own when her husband dies? What conditions, if any, must she satisfy in order to retain control of her property?

In societies that practice bridewealth it is usual for the kin of the groom to give the bridewealth to the kin of the bride, either her father or her brothers. The bridewealth is not destined for her use. Typically the sister's bridewealth is used for the purchase of her brother's wife. Thus the bridewealth constitutes a societal fund that Goody describes as "a circulating pool of resources."[23] Sometimes the bride is the recipient of the bridewealth, in which case either it becomes part of a joint conjugal fund or it remains solely the property of the bride. This latter kind of transaction Goody prefers to designate as "indirect dowry."

According to the Code of Hammurabi, an eighteenth-century B.C.E. Babylonian legal collection, the bridegroom gave the bridewealth (*tirḫātu,* §§ 159–61) to his future father-in-law.[24] The recipient of the bridewealth is not so clear in the Middle Assyrian laws. The problem revolves around the interpretation of the last lines of A § 38, part of which concerns the ownership of the *terḫātu.*[25] Does it belong to the groom's father-in-law or the bride? There is evidence at Nuzi that the bride's father, after having received the *terḫātu,* handed over part of it to his daughter.[26] The Akkadian texts from ancient Ugarit also indicate this practice.[27] Such a procedure resembles Goody's description of the indirect dowry. Perhaps this is the case here in Assyria.

In the Ugaritic literature found at Ras Shamra, *trḫ* appears as a verb meaning "to pay the price for a bride." It is found in two poetic texts, *CTA* 23.64 and 24.18, 33. *Trḫ* can also mean "bridegroom" (*CTA* 14. 100, 189), and the form *mtrḫt* refers to a woman acquired by the payment of bridewealth (*CTA* 14.13; 24.10). The recipient of the bridewealth (*mhr*) is the father also in Ugaritic literature. In the poetic text of the marriage of Nikkal and Yariḫ (*CTA* 24) the latter is told that he must give the bridewealth to Nikkal's father in the amount of a thousand shekels of silver, ten thousand shekels of gold, and lapis lazuli.[28]

Aramaic documents belonging to a fifth-century B.C.E. Jewish community that existed at Elephantine in Egypt contain marriage contracts. R. Yaron[29] has studied these contracts, which specify that the bridewealth (*mōhar*) is given to the head of the girl's family. There also is evidence that the *mōhar* was added to the girl's dowry. If this is the case, then at Elephantine we have another example of indirect dowry.

Through the interplay of two biblical texts (Exod. 22:16–17; Deut. 22:28–29) concerning the rape of a virgin, it is possible to conclude that the recipient of the bridewealth in ancient Israel was the bride's father. While the text from Exodus specifically mentions the word for bridewealth (*mōhar*),[30] it is from Deuteronomy that the recipient can be determined. From the words of Leah and Rachel in Gen. 31:15 we learn that their father, Laban, had received money for them: "Does he not consider us as foreign women to him since he sold us? And he has utterly used up our silver."[31] Surely they are referring to the bridewealth that was given for them at the time of their marriage. Some scholars cite this passage in claiming that the bridewealth belonged to the wife. However, the two women's reference to "our silver" does not necessarily mean the silver that belonged to them; it could just as well mean the silver that was given for them. This latter reading of the text is preferable. Two other observations on this text are relevant here. Leah and Rachel say that their father now regards them as foreign women. This could refer to the fact that once they are married, they are no longer considered his responsibility; they are now part of their husband's family. The use of the verb *mākar* "sell" indicates that Leah and Rachel, at least, understood their marriage to have involved a purchase.[32]

One may conclude from the preceding discussion that ordinarily the bride was not the recipient of the bridewealth in the ancient Near East in general and in Israel in particular. Where the evidence indicates that the bride did receive part of the bridewealth (Nuzi, Elephantine), it is more proper to consider this transaction as indirect dowry. A widow, including the *ʾalmānâ,* would not have access to her bridewealth as a means of economic support.

There is mention in the Bible of other goods that originated from the groom's family and were given to the bride's family at the time of marriage. It is necessary to examine these texts in order to determine first of all if the goods were given to the woman; and if so, whether or not they could provide substantial economic support for her during her widowhood. In the account of the quest for a bride for Isaac in Genesis 24, Abraham's servant on several occasions bestows jewelry and other gifts on Rebekah and her family. When the servant realizes that Rebekah is a potential bride for Isaac, he gives her a gold ring and two gold bracelets (vv. 22, 47). When Rebekah's family agrees to the marriage, again the servant produces gifts. This time Rebekah receives silver and gold ornaments and clothes; her brother and mother receive costly gifts (v. 53). In Genesis 34 Shechem's infatuation with Dinah led him to say to her father and brothers, "Ask of me ever so much as bridewealth (*mōhar*) and gift (*mattān*) and I will give as you say to me" (v. 12). Nothing further is said concerning the contents or the recipient of this *mattān.* What is not clear in any of these texts is whether or not the bride was allowed to keep these gifts throughout her lifetime.

Mesopotamian evidence for such gifts is found in both the Code of Hammurabi and the Middle Assyrian laws. In the Middle Assyrian laws these goods are designated by the terms *dumāqi, biblu,* and *zubullū*. In both the Code and the Middle Assyrian laws a further gift is identified as the *nudunnû*. The *dumāqi* (A §§ 25, 26, 38) are jewels given to the bride by the husband. She enjoys their use during their marriage but the husband retains ownership. When her husband dies, the widow may claim the *dumāqi* only in the absence of heirs of the deceased husband, namely his sons or brothers. The *biblu* (A § 30) and *zubullū* (A §§ 30, 31), which may both be translated as "marriage gift," consisted of movable property, some of which was edible.[33] It is likely that celebrations including banquets accompanied the announcement of betrothals.[34] Part of the function of the *biblu* and *zubullū* would have been to help defray the expenses of these celebrations. They may also have functioned as gifts bestowed on the bride's family by the kin of the groom.

If the custom in Israel with respect to jewels was similar to that in Mesopotamia, one may conclude that a widow could have claimed jewelry as her own only if she had had no sons to whom she could have passed them. It is doubtful that this property would have contributed significantly toward her support throughout her widowhood. Other gifts that came into the bride's family at the time of marriage would seem to have been destined for other members of her family or to have been consumed during the marriage festivities.

A possible source of support for the widow in Mesopotamia was the *nudunnû*, which was given to the wife by her husband at some point during the marriage.[35] The sections of the Code of Hammurabi that speak of the *nudunnû* are §§ 171 and 172; A §§ 27 and 32 are the relevant passages in the Middle Assyrian laws. Its specific purpose was to provide for the wife's maintenance during her widowhood. There is no indication in the biblical text that such a practice existed in Israel. It is, therefore, impossible to know whether or not the wife received from her husband a gift like the *nudunnû* that was to maintain her during her widowhood.

The other large category of property involved in marriage transactions is the dowry. Goody characterizes dowry as "a type of premortem inheritance to the bride."[36] In other words the daughter receives her part of the family estate at the time of her marriage. The dowry is not part of a societal fund but of a familial fund that passes down from parents to daughter. The source of the dowry is usually the woman's parents, or her siblings if the parents are deceased. In some cases the bridewealth may be wholly or partially redirected to the bride as dowry; in this way one may still consider the dowry as coming from the bride's parents albeit indirectly. Hence Goody's term for this kind of dowry, as mentioned above, is indirect dowry. Both movable and immovable property may form part of the dowry. If land comprises part of it, then among farming communities there often is a correlation with a requirement of endogamy, that is, marriage within a defined group of persons. The land would thus remain within that specific group from one generation to the next. The contents of the dowry may vary with the status of the bride. While the bride is the recipient of the dowry, she does not necessarily administer it. The control of the dowry may remain with the woman throughout the marriage, or pass to the husband who functions as its manager, or be shared by both husband and wife.

The Code of Hammurabi contains legislation concerning the dowry (*šeriktu*) a woman received from her father when she entered the house of her husband. According to § 178 land constituted at least part of the *šeriktu*. Since §§ 178–84 of the Code deal with the devolution of the property of priestesses whose dowries would ultimately revert to their paternal families, the inclusion of land in the dowry should not be considered the usual practice. More likely the *šeriktu* consisted of movables.[37]

The Middle Assyrian laws, while not providing information as to the contents of the dowry (*širku*), do verify its existence and disposition. "If a woman has entered her husband's house, her dowry (*širku*) and whatever she brought from her father's house or what her father-in-law gave her on her entry are vested in the sons, with her father-in-law's sons having no claim to (them)" (A § 29). The woman's sons were the beneficiaries of her dowry. Her husband's relatives were not entitled to it and had no right to claim it as property belonging to their dead brother. The mention in this law of goods that the woman's father-in-law gave her when she entered the house is unique here. Just what these were is unknown. Since the *nudunnû* is given by the husband and could easily have been named as such in this law, it is unlikely that that is what is meant.

Evidence for the practice of dowry in the Hebrew Bible is sparse. When the Pharaoh's daughter marries Solomon, she receives from her father the city of Gezer as part of her dowry (*šillūḥîm*, literally "parting gifts;" 1 Kgs. 9:16).[38] Since this is a royal wedding, the transfer of land in the form of an entire city can hardly be considered an example of the typical dowry. No doubt political motives prompted the giving of this present. Moreover this dowry does not illustrate Israelite practice since it comes from an Egyptian family. There is another text that narrates the transfer of land to a woman and that could be interpreted as the giving of a dowry. It is found in Judges 1 with a parallel in Joshua 15. Achsah, the daughter of Caleb, became the wife of Othniel because her father had promised her in marriage to the man who successfully attacked Kiriath-sepher (Judg. 1:11–12). Shortly after the marriage she approaches her father with this request, "Give me a present (literally "a blessing"; *hābâ lî bĕrākâ* Judg. 1:15; cf. Jos. 15:19). She goes on to specify what she has in mind, springs of water. Caleb grants Achsah's request with both upper and lower springs. Since Achsah has just married Othniel, it is possible to regard Caleb's gift of the springs as dowry. The fact that land given to a woman is involved here can be understood if the action is placed in the context of endogamy. Achsah has married someone within her own family (Judg. 1:13; cf. Jos. 15:17). The land will remain within Caleb's patrilineage even though it will be passed through a woman. Finally, dowry in the form of slaves is given to Rebekah when she leaves her homeland (Gen. 24:59, 61) and to Leah and Rachel by their father, Laban, on the occasion of their marriages to Jacob (Gen. 29:24, 29).

Evidence for the practice of dowry in ancient Israel is meager. If viewed in the light of dowry as practiced in traditional societies and in Mesopotamia, some general remarks may be made about it. One may conclude that the dowry was property owned by the woman, her share of the family inheritance. Its contents—slaves or other movable goods, if we imagine the practice to have been similar to Mesopotamian custom—do not indicate that ordinarily it would have been sufficient to provide economic support for a widow for any length of time. Of course, the contents of a dowry would have varied according to the economic condition of the family. Women from wealthy families would most likely have received substantial dowries. Conversely, women from poorer families would have received less. Whether or not even a sizable dowry could have supported a widow is questionable.

Dowry in the form of land was rare. The Hebrew belief that each man possessed his *naḥălâ*, "patrimony" or "inheritance," to be handed down from father to son, was firm. The alienation of any part of the *naḥălâ*, which would have resulted from its being given as dowry to a daughter, was inconceivable. Land remained with the male members of the family. Where the Bible records the transfer of land to women, besides the two cases of Pharaoh's daughter and Achsah already discussed, stipulations were legislated to cover this unique situation. In Num. 27:1–11 the five daughters of Zelophehad inherit his land because there are no sons. Numbers 36:1–9 specifies that these women must marry within the clan (*mišpāḥâ*) of their father in order not to alienate the land.

From an investigation of the resources available to the biblical widow to supply her economic needs a grim picture emerges. A woman's economic well-being was directly related to her link with some male. Though a married woman may have owned some property in the form of her dowry, she could not have supported herself on that alone, if at all, when her husband died. Ordinarily the widow's maintenance would have been the responsibility of either her sons or her father-in-law. When these male persons were nonexistent, then the widow's connection to the kinship structure was severed. She became an *ʾalmānâ.*

While this chapter has dealt with only one of the widow's support systems deserving examination, even at this point the texts in the Psalms with which we began our study can be read with a new consciousness. The wicked take advantage of the *ʾalmānâ* because they fear no reprisals from outraged family members. Yahweh takes special care of the *ʾalmānâ,* supplying the role of the missing male kin who would have been concerned for her well-being and economic support. To wish that an enemy's wife be an *ʾalmānâ* is to wish for her a life of alienation from one of the most basic aspects of existence, namely family and all that kinship means in a traditional society, and a life of destitution that accompanies this alienation.

NOTES

1. Jo Ann Hackett, "Women's Studies and the Hebrew Bible," in *The Future of Biblical Studies. The Hebrew Scriptures,* eds. R. E. Friedman and H. Williamson, Semeia Studies (Atlanta: Scholars, 1987), 143–64.
2. Hackett, "Women's Studies," 144.
3. Examples are the entry "Widow" by O. J. Baab in the *IDB* (it is noteworthy that there is no entry in the IDBSup for "Widow"); J. Otwell, *And Sarah Laughed: The Status of Woman in the Old Testament* (Philadelphia: Westminster, 1977), 123–31; and F. C. Fensham, "Widow, Orphan, and the Poor in

Ancient Near Eastern Legal and Wisdom Literature," *JNES* 21 (1962): 129–39. Otwell goes beyond the other two by pointing out that *ʾalmānâ* is not used of every widow in the Hebrew Bible, a very significant clarification.

4. Following S. R. Johansson ("'Herstory' as History: A New Field or Another Fad," in *Liberating Women's History,* ed. B. A. Carroll [Urbana, Ill.: University of Illinois, 1976], 405–6) I understand status as "a composite of many details about the rights, duties, privileges, disabilities, options, and restrictions that the women of a specific group experience as they move through an inevitable progression of age-group and social roles."

5. According to Deut. 25:5–10, when a man died childless and his brothers still lived together, one of his brothers (in Latin *levir* and hence the name levirate) was obliged to beget a son by the widow. This child was considered to be the dead man's son. Provision is made in the law for the man who did not wish to perform the levirate for his dead brother.

6. The interchange of *l, n,* and *r* is a fairly common phenomenon in Semitic. See S. Moscati, *An Introduction to the Comparative Grammar of the Semitic Languages,* Porta Linguarum Orientalium. Neue Serie 6 (Wiesbaden: Harrassowitz, 1969), 32. C. Brockelmann (*Grundriss der Vergleichenden Grammatik der Semitischen Sprachen,* 2 vols. [Berlin, 1908–13; reprint, Hildesheim: Georg Olms, 1961], 220) cites *ʾalmānâ* as an example of consonantal dissimilation.

7. See *HALAT,* 1. 56; and *TDOT,* 1. 287–88. The etymological analysis in *TDOT* has suffered in its translation from the original. What has been rendered "poor" in the English represents the German "schlecht," which more properly denotes "bad, wicked, evil."

8. In Mesopotamian legal texts *almattu* is found as early as the OB period. See *CAD,* A/1, 362–64.

9. For the most recent treatment of the *almattu* see A. A. Tavares, "L'*almanah* hébraique et l'*almattu* des textes akkadiens," in *La Femme dans le Proche-Orient Antique.* Compte rendu de la XXXIIIe Rencontre assyriologique internationale (Paris, 7–10 juillet 1986), ed. J.-M. Durand (Paris: Editions Recherche sur les Civilisations, 1987), 155–62. I am largely in agreement with his understanding of the *almattu.* Cf. C. Saporetti, *The Status of Women in the Middle Assyrian Period,* Monographs on the Ancient Near East 2/1 (Malibu: Undena, 1979), 17–20.

10. The English translation used here is that of G. R. Driver and J. C. Miles (*The Assyrian Laws* [Oxford: Clarendon, 1935], 403–5); another translation is available in *ANET.* The tablets were originally published by O. Schroeder (*Keilschrifttexte aus Assur verschiedenen Inhalts,* WVDOG 35 [Berlin, 1920]). The most recent translation and commentary is that of G. Cardascia (*Les Lois assyriennes* [Paris: Cerf, 1969]).

11. G. Lerner (*The Creation of Patriarchy* [New York: Oxford University, 1986], 269 n. 53) comments that the class of widows who still live in their father's house "would usually refer to a child-bride only." I find this statement unconvincing. If the widow is a child-bride, then how could the possibility exist that she have a grown son with whom she could choose to live?

12. Cf. the discussion of Driver and Miles (*Assyrian Laws* 217–18).
13. Cf. *CAD,* A/1, 364.
14. Michael Kirwen, *African Widows* (Maryknoll: Orbis, 1979).
15. The RSV and NAB both translate *ʾēšet* in 4:5 as "widow" while the JPSV, NEB, and JB translate accurately as "wife." At 4:10 the RSV and NAB again translate *ʾēšet* as "widow," and this time are joined by the JB. The JPSV and NEB retain the translation "wife."
16. As a general introduction to kinship theory I have found R. M. Keesing's *Kin Groups and Social Structure* (New York: Holt, Rinehart and Winston, 1975) most useful. Cf. R. Fox, *Kinship and Marriage, An Anthropological Perspective,* Cambridge Studies in Social Anthropology 50 (Cambridge: Cambridge University, 1967).
17. See N. Jay ("Sacrifice, Descent and the Patriarchs" *VT* 38 [1988]: 52–70) for an enlightening and provocative analysis, from a sociological perspective, of the tensions in the patriarchal narratives between patrilineal and matrilineal descent. She attempts to identify the different ways in which the three sources (J, E, and P) deal with this tension.
18. Literally "the house of your father" (*bêt-ʾābîkē* Gen. 38:11). L. Stager ("The Archaeology of the Family in Ancient Israel," *BASOR* 260 [1985]: 18–23) discusses *bêt ʾāb,* which he translates "lineage" or "household." Thus the phrase *bêt ʾāb* does not mean that Tamar returned literally to her father, rather she returned to her paternal kin.
19. Lawrence Stager, "Archaeology, Ecology, and Social History: Background Themes to the Song of Deborah," in *Congress Volume. Jerusalem 1986,* ed. J. A. Emerton, VTSup 40 (Leiden: Brill, 1988), 229–32.
20. Helena Lopata, *Widows,* 2 vols. (Durham, N.C.: Duke University, 1987). For a more detailed explanation of the theoretical framework of the study see Lopata's introductory essay, "Widowhood: World Perspectives on Support Systems," 1–23.
21. Lopata, *Widows,* 4.
22. Jack Goody and Stanley Tambiah, *Bridewealth and Dowry,* Cambridge Papers in Social Anthropology 7 (Cambridge: Cambridge University, 1973), esp. 1–21, 61–67.
23. Goody and Tambiah, *Bridewealth,* 5.
24. I am following the critical edition of the Code of Hammurabi found in G. R. Driver and J. C. Miles, *The Babylonian Laws,* 2 vols. (Oxford: Clarendon, 1952–55). A translation is also available in *ANET.*
25. See Cardascia, *Les Lois assyriennes,* 193–95, for a discussion of the various interpretations.
26. K. Grosz has studied the institutions of bridewealth and dowry at Nuzi. The results of her investigation are available in two forms. "Bridewealth and Dowry in Nuzi," in *Images of Women in Antiquity,* eds. A. Cameron and A. Kuhrt (Detroit: Wayne State University, 1983), 193–206, is intended for a more general audience while "Dowry and Brideprice in Nuzi," in *Studies on the Civilization and Culture of Nuzi and the Hurrians,* eds. M. A. Morison and

D. I. Owen (Winona Lake, Ind.: Eisenbrauns, 1981), 161–82, is directed to Assyriologists and other ancient Near Eastern scholars.

27. *PRU III,* 15.92:19–23; 16.141:14–15; 16.158:6. See A. F. Rainey, "Family Relationships in Ugarit," *Or* 34 (1965): 18; and J. Gray, *The Legacy of Canaan,* VTSup 5, 2d ed. (Leiden: Brill, 1965), 251.

28. *wʾatn mhrh l ʾa/bh. ʾalp ksp. wrbt ḫ/rṣ. ʾišlḥ ẓhrm ʾiq/nʾim* (*CTA* 24.19–22).

29. R. Yaron, "Aramaic Marriage Contracts From Elephantine," *JSS* 3 (1958): 1–39 and "Aramaic Marriage Contracts: Corrigenda and Addenda," *JSS* 5 (1960): 66–70.

30. The RSV translates "marriage present"; the NEB, JPSV, and JB "brideprice"; and the NAB "marriage price."

31. *Hălôʾ nokriyyôt neḥsabnû lô kî mĕkārānû wayyōʾkal gam-ʾākôl ʾet-kaspēnû.* Since the *ʾaṭnāḥ* appears under *mĕkārānû,* it is better to read the clause *kî mĕkārānû* with what precedes than with what follows.

32. See also Hos. 3:2; Ruth 4:10. There has been a long debate about whether or not marriage in the Bible was marriage by purchase, i.e. marriage with bridewealth. It seems to me that the reluctance to classify biblical marriage as marriage by purchase stems from an inability on the part of biblical commentators (the vast majority of whom have been male) to correlate the practice of purchasing a wife with the high ideals associated with the Judaeo-Christian tradition. To say that marriage in the Bible was marriage by purchase does not exhaust what can be said of marriage in the Bible. It is merely a descriptive category, not a judgmental one.

De Vaux's comment on the Genesis text under discussion here is telling. (See Roland de Vaux, *Ancient Israel: Its Life and Institutions* [New York: McGraw-Hill, 1961].) He cites the passage in the context of arguing against marriage by purchase. "But one need not give a formal, juridical sense to words spoken by women in a moment of anger" (p. 26). One can infer from this statement that Père de Vaux was among those who characterize women as speaking more from emotions than from reason.

33. *CAD* (Z, 152) states that *tirḫātu, biblu,* and *zubullū* denoted at first the bringing of edibles into the house of the bride for the marriage banquet. As early as the OB period *tirḫātu* came to denote brideprice, while *zubullū* and *biblu* preserved the meaning of "marriage gift" throughout all periods.

34. Judg. 14:10 describes a banquet (*mišteh*) given by Samson in Timnah on the occasion of his marriage to a Philistine woman. While no technical terms that refer to marriage transactions appear in the text, it may be assumed that the feast was part of the marriage celebrations (Judg. 14:15).

35. Driver and Miles translate *nudunnû* as "settlement" in the Code of Hammurabi; Meek in *ANET* translates it as "marriage gift" in the Middle Assyrian laws. *Nudunnû* also had the meaning "dowry" in the OB period. See

CAD N/2, 310–11. In the OB law codes, however, *nudunnû* has the meaning put forward in this paper.

36. Goody and Tambiah, *Bridewealth,* 1.

37. §138 refers to "the dowry which she brought from her father's house" (*šeriktam ša ištu É abiša ublam*).

38. *CTA* 24.47 contains *t̲lḫ(h),* which Gordon translates "her dowry." He suggests (*UT* Glossary #2682) that the Hebrew *šillūḥîm* is probably related to this root.

10 | WOMAN AND THE DISCOURSE OF PATRIARCHAL WISDOM: A STUDY OF PROVERBS 1–9

CAROL A. NEWSOM

A casual reader asked to describe Proverbs 1–9 might reply that it was the words of a father talking to his son, mostly about women. While that might be a naive reading, its very naiveté brings into focus some of the features of Proverbs 1–9 that have not always been sufficiently attended to in scholarly discussions. First, these chapters are virtually all talk. They are, to use a currently fashionable word, discourse. But even more importantly, discourse, the dialogic, social dimension of language, becomes a central topic of these chapters. Second, the cast of characters is severely limited, and the privileged axis of communication is that from father to son. The reader's locus of self-identification, that is, the subject position established for the reader, is that of the son, the character who never speaks. Third, discourse embodies and generates a symbolic world. Consequently, it is significant that though woman is not the sole topic of the chapters, talk about women and women's speech occupies an astonishing amount of the text—men, preoccupied with speech, talking about women and women's speech. What role, then, does sexual difference play in this symbolic world both in making men's speech possible but at the same time rendering it problematic?

PROVERBS 1:2–9

Although it is widely recognized that the father/son address of Proverbs 1–9 is not to be taken literally, very little attention is generally given to the significance of the fictional level established by these terms. It is a rather minimal fiction, but nonetheless important. The father, who speaks, is the "I" of the discourse. The son, addressed in the vocative and with imperative verbs, is the "you." Though other types of speech are occasionally embedded within it, the fiction never moves beyond this repeated moment of address. The linguist Emile Benveniste has drawn attention to the peculiar nature of the pronouns "I" and "you." What is unique to them becomes evident when one asks what they refer to. They don't refer either to a concept (the way that nouns like "tree" do), nor do they refer to unique individuals (the way that proper names do). Instead "I" and "you" are linguistic blanks or empty signs filled only when individual speakers and addressees appropriate them in specific instances of discourse. Their oddity among linguistic signs is related to "the problem they serve to solve, which is none other than that of intersubjective communication."[1] In fact Benveniste claims that it is through language that our subjectivity, our ability to constitute ourselves as subjects, is made possible. "Consciousness of self is only possible if it is experienced by contrast. I use *I* only when I am speaking to someone who will be a *you* in my address. It is this condition of dialogue that is constitutive of person."[2] The striking prominence of the pronouns "I" and "you" and the repeated use of vocative and imperative address in Proverbs 1–9 are clear indicators of what is at stake in these chapters: the formation of the subjectivity of the reader.[3]

Because of the social nature of discourse in which subjectivity is established, it can never be ideologically neutral. There is no Cartesian self that can be established apart from all else, but always a self in relation. The emergence of subjectivity is always in the context of ideology. In a well-known analogy the Marxist theoretician Louis Althusser speaks of the way in which ideology "recruits" subjects, "hails" them as a policeman might: "Hey, you there!" The individual, recognizing himself or herself as the one addressed, turns around in response to the hailing. And with that gesture he or she becomes a subject, takes up a particular subject position in a particular ideology. Althusser uses the term *interpellation* for this process.[4] The actual hailing by ideology is seldom as direct as one finds in the instruction literature of Proverbs 1–9. But here the intent is explicit and self-conscious. The reader of this text is called upon to take up the subject position of son in relation to an authoritative father. Now that would be a rather banal statement if this were a piece of children's literature, used exclusively in a school setting and then outgrown. But clearly it is not. The intended readers identified by the text include not only the naive youth (v. 4) but also the mature sage (v. 5). All readers of this text, whatever their actual identities, are called upon to take up the subject position of son in relation to an authoritative father. Through its imitation of a familiar scene of interpellation the text continually reinterpellates its readers.

The familiar scene, a father advising his son, is important. Proverbs 1–9 takes a moment from the history of the patriarchal family and gives it a privileged status as a continuing social norm.[5] The choice of the patriarchal family as the symbol of the authority structure of wisdom has important implications. Since it is in the family that one's subjectivity is first formed, the malleability called for in the text is made to seem innocent, natural, inevitable. In addition the symbol of the family causes the discourse to appear to stand outside of specific class interests. This is not a landed aristocrat speaking, not a senior bureaucrat, not a member of the urban middle class or a disenfranchised intellectual, but "your father." Families are not ideologically innocent places, but because everyone has one, they give the appearance of being so.

The specific social dimensions of Proverbs 1–9 are also cloaked by the preference for abstract terms, such as "righteousness, justice, and equity" (1:3). The pragmatic meaning of these terms is seldom clear from the text. And yet it is precisely in the struggle to control the meaning of such terms that one finds evidence of ideological conflict between social groups.[6] Occasionally, one can catch a hint as to the social location of wisdom discourse, but the type of speech used in Proverbs 1–9 largely serves to deflect that inquiry. What is important for Proverbs 1–9 is the issue of interpellation and the need for continual reinterpellation.

PROVERBS 1:10–19

The first speech that is addressed to the son is precisely about how to resist interpellation by a rival discourse ("My son, if sinners try to persuade you, do not consent," v. 10). Because the discourse of the "sinners" is presented by the father, their alleged speech is really completely controlled by the father. In fact the sinners' speech is crowded with negative markers: they are made to describe their own victims as "innocent" (v. 12a). Their metaphor for themselves is that of death itself, Sheol swallowing up life (v. 12b). They act gratuitously, "for the hell of it" (Heb. *ḥinnām,* v. 11). Assuming, with many commentators, that verse 16 is a late marginal comment drawn from Isa. 59:7, the father follows an interesting rhetorical strategy in soliciting the son's agreement to his point of view. He first reiterates his admonition (v. 15) and then poses a challenge: "in vain is the net spread in full view of the bird" (v. 17). The wise son, the reader who can "deconstruct" the discourse of the sinners, won't be trapped in their net of words. Since the self-incriminating elements of the hypothetical speech are hard to miss, the reader enjoys a moment of self-congratulation, a moment that bonds the reader closer to the father. The father then confirms the reader's judgment in verse 18, making explicit the self-destructive quality of the sinners.

But what else is going on here? Who and what is the son really being warned against? It seems scarcely credible that the advice should be taken at face value as career counseling. It is much more likely that this depiction of brigands is a metaphor for something else. Indeed, verse 19 confirms it. The summary statement of the address explains that "such are the ways of all who cut a big profit." Here at least is one clue to the social location of the text, though we still do not know precisely what economic activity is identified by the pejorative phrase. A closer look at the sinners' speech offers a different avenue of approach. The structure of authority embodied there is strikingly different from that of the overall discourse of Proverbs 1–9. The persuaders are not fathers hierarchically related to the son, but peers. Their speech uses the cohortative rather than the direct imperative. Featured pronouns are not the counterposed "I-you" pair but the often repeated "us," "we." The egalitarian subtext is made explicit in verse 14b, "we will all share a common purse." The rival discourse against which the father argues can be made visible in its general outlines: it is one with a horizontal rather than a vertical structure of authority, based not on patriarchal family affiliation but on common enterprise, and one that offers young men immediate access to wealth rather than the deferred wealth of inheritance. What lurks under the surface is the generational chasm, the division of power between older and younger men in patriarchal society. The genuine appeal to younger men of the set of values just described is cleverly defused by associating them with what is clearly outside the law.

PROVERBS 1:20–33

Here and in chapter 8 the father's discourse is interrupted by speeches of personified wisdom. These speeches serve to buttress what the father has said, however, and belong to the same cultural voice that speaks through the father. Although the pronouns and inflected verb forms identify wisdom as female, the significance of her gender emerges more clearly in the later part of Proverbs 1–9. Here I want to focus on the relative positions of speaker and addressee established in the speech. That *Ḥokmot* (personified wisdom) is an extension of the cultural voice that speaks through the father can be seen in the complementary authoritative position she occupies. Where the father is the authoritative voice in the family, *Ḥokmot* is the corresponding public voice ("in the streets," "in the public squares," v. 20) who occupies the places that are physically symbolic of collective authority and power ("at the entrance of the gates," v. 21). She also has the power to save from disaster (vv. 26–33). Although she addresses a plurality of listeners, the frequent second-person forms identify the reader as directly addressed. Perhaps the most interesting feature of the text is that it posits a past to the relationship between *Ḥokmot* and the reader. Her first words are "How long will you . . ." (v. 22). The reader's subjectivity is furnished not only with a past but with a guilty one. As one who is "naive," "cocky," and "complacent" (v. 22), he has refused advice and correction. The reader discovers himself in the text as always, already at fault. And the fault is recalcitrance before legitimate authority.

The two paired speeches of chapter 1 have attempted to construct a subject who is extremely submissive: perennially a son, willing to forgo the attractions of nonhierarchical order, and yet despite it all, somehow never quite submissive enough. But one may sense, lurking behind this nearly supine persona, a shadow figure of significant power. A world made of discourse, a symbolic order, an ideology exists only by consensus. If it cannot recruit new adherents and if those whom it reinterpellates do not recognize themselves in its hailing, it ceases to have reality. *Ḥokmot* may threaten the recalcitrant with destruction, but the inverse is also true: enough recalcitrance and *Ḥokmot* ceases to exist.[7]

PROVERBS 2

The problematic aspects of discourse already present in chapter 1 are given a sharper focus in the carefully constructed composition of Proverbs 2. One can summarize the argument as follows: Accept my words and internalize them with the help of God (vv. 1–11), and they will protect you from the man who speaks perversely (vv. 12–15) and from the strange, smooth-talking woman (vv. 16–20). The world is presented as a place of competing and conflicting discourses: the words of the father, the words of the crooked man, the words of the strange woman. One is hailed from many directions, offered subject positions in discourses that construe the world very differently.

Far from valuing the plurality of discourses that intersect a culture, Proverbs 1–9 seeks the hegemony of its own discourse. If one has internalized a discourse, one is insulated from, or as the text more polemically puts it, protected from other voices.

But how is this to occur? How is one's subjectivity formed in that definitive way? Verses 1–11 make the astute observation that allegiance precedes understanding, not the other way around. We should not be surprised that these wisdom discourses do not closely define the pragmatic content of wisdom and contrast it with the competing discourses, seeking to convince the hearer of its superiority. Rather it repeatedly asks first for allegiance ("accept my words," "treasure up my strictures," "incline your ear," "extend your heart," vv. 1–2). Nor is the allegiance passive. It must involve active participation ("call out," "seek," vv. 3–4). Only then does understanding follow ("then you will understand fear of Yahweh," v. 5; "then you will understand righteousness and justice and equity, every good path," v. 9), for at that point habituation to the assumptions, values, and cultural practices of the group will make them seem one's own ("for wisdom will come into your heart and your soul will delight in knowledge," v. 10). As Althusser pungently paraphrases Pascal, "Kneel down, move your lips in prayer, and you will believe."[8]

For this reason it isn't surprising that the metaphors of "way," "path," and "track," which occur throughout Proverbs 1–9, appear in this chapter with particular density (twelve occurrences in vv. 8–20). "Way" or "path" may be a hackneyed metaphor for customary behavior, but its connotations are worth some reflection. A path is a social product, made by many feet over a period of time. But its purely physical record of customary social behavior is often transposed in terms of a teleology and a will ("Where does that path lead?"). A path does not, in fact, exclude movement in any direction. It only makes its own direction the easiest, most natural, most logical way of proceeding. As each individual "freely" chooses to walk the path, that act incises the path more deeply. Finally, a path orders the world in a particular way as it establishes relations between place and place, relations that are not necessarily the shortest distance between two points. It is understandable why, in a chapter that construes the world as a place of conflicting discourses, the metaphor of the path figures so prominently. Customary social behavior, represented by the image of the path, is a type of nonverbal discourse. Manners, dress, food, orientation to time, divisions of labor, and so forth, are all elements of a social group's discourse, alongside its explicit words. Words and ways are related, as the parallelism of verse 12 suggests.

But against whom is the father arguing so strenuously? Who are the man and woman whose speech the son is warned about? Of the man all we learn is that he is associated with inversion of values (he delights in what is bad, v. 14a; his words are all "turned about," v. 12) and with perversion of values ("twisted," "crooked," v. 15), the opposite of the quality of "uprightness" and "perfection" associated with the father's advice (v. 21). His function is definitional. He simply serves to signify whatever stands over against "us," the group of the father's discourse.

It is with the symbol of the strange woman, however, that the text discovers its primary image of otherness. For a patriarchal discourse in which the self is defined as male, woman qua woman is the quintessential other. Much ink has been spilled in attempting to clarify why she is identified as a "strange" or "foreign" woman, whether the terms refer to an ethnic, legal, or social status. But it may not be an either/or question. Whether the terms were originally ambiguous or have only become so after the passage of years, any and all of the possible interpretations underscore the quality of otherness that she already possesses as woman in male discourse. As a foreigner, she would recall the strong Israelite cultural preference for endogamy over exogamy, the choice of same over other. If, as seems to be clearly the case in chapter 7, she is an adulteress, then she may be called strange/foreign because she is legally "off limits."[9] Or, if 2:17 is meant to suggest that she has left her husband ("one who has abandoned the companion of her youth"), then she is strange/foreign because she is an anomaly who no longer has a place in the system of socially regulated sexuality and now belongs on the side of the chaotic. In any case her otherness serves to identify the boundary and what must be repressed or excluded.

Woman is a much more serviceable symbol for this definitionally important "other" than was the man of verses 12–15 because she can be posited as a figure of ambivalence, both frightening and attractive. Her words are described as "smooth," a term that suggests both pleasure and danger (= slippery). Once experienced, the ambivalence has to be tilted in the proper direction, and so she is identified with the ultimate boundary, death. A textual problem in verse 18 provides a clue to the psychological basis for the equation. Judging from the parallelism and the meaning of the verb, one expects the text to read "her path sinks down to death, her tracks are toward the shades." As it stands, it reads "her house sinks down to death. . . ." If the MT is a textual corruption, it is in truth a Freudian slip, for "house" is a common symbolic representation of woman or womb.[10] The ambivalence is the attraction and fear of a return to the womb. The strange woman is the devouring woman, for "none who go in to her will return" (v. 19).

With this text one can begin to see the significance of sexual difference for the existence of patriarchal discourse. Invoking the strange woman as a threat provides a basis for solidarity between father and son. Her difference makes available a shared sameness for father and son that bridges the generational divisions of patriarchy that were visible in Proverbs 1. But more importantly the woman and her discourse exist as a persistent irritant located, to borrow Julia Kristeva's phrase, at the margin.[11] In the following chapters she continues to preoccupy the father's advice. He can never quite be finished with her. The competition she represents is the cause of the father's speech, the incentive for its very existence. The strange woman figures the irreducible difference that prevents any discourse from establishing itself unproblematically. That is to say, she is not simply the speech of actual women, but she is the symbolic figure of a variety of marginal discourses. She is the contradiction, the dissonance that forces a dominant discourse to articulate itself and at the same time threatens to subvert it. Those dissonances can no more be eliminated than can sexual difference itself. And their existence is a source of slow but profound change in symbolic orders.

PROVERBS 3

In giving discourse a privileged position and in representing the world as a place of conflicting discourses, Proverbs 1–9 appears to acknowledge the socially constructed nature of reality and the problematic status of truth. Such reflections were part of the broader wisdom tradition, as the saying in Prov. 18:17 illustrates: "The one who argues his case first seems right, until someone else is brought forward and cross-examines him." The implications are disturbing for the representatives of authority. What can ensure that the content given to the terms "righteousness, justice, and equity" or "wisdom, knowledge, and discernment" can be stabilized according to the values of the tradents of Proverbs 1–9 and not captured by rival discourses? The text has attempted to buttress its authoritative position by claiming the symbol of the patriarchal father and by discrediting other voices as alien and criminal. Thus the signifiers point to the father and to the law. Though powerful, that is not sufficient. What is needed is an anchorage beyond the contestable social world, in short, a transcendental signified to which all terms point and from which they derive their stable meanings.[12] In a provisional way the parallel between the speech of the father and the speech of *Ḥokmot* in chapter 1 provided this anchorage. But that strategy is not fully developed until chapter 8. In chapter 3 we encounter the first sustained effort to provide the transcendental signified that stops the threatening slippage of meaning.

The first indication is in the initial call for hearing: "My son, don't forget my teaching (Heb. *tôrātî*) and let your heart guard my commands" (Heb. *miṣwôtay*). Various paired terms refer to the father's instruction throughout the chapters. But this particular pair has resonances of God's *torah* and *miṣwot* to Israel and so subtly positions the father in association with divine authority. The benefits of long life and peace that are promised (v. 2) also suggest that the father's teaching and commands derive from transcendent power. In verse 4 it is made explicit. The father's advice will be validated both in the social and in the transcendent realms ("before the eyes of God and humankind"). For several further verses the father actually speaks on behalf of God, urging the son to obedience to God and promising rewards. The appeal parallels in structure and motivation the father's call for obedience to himself in vv. 1–4. It comes as no surprise that in the MT the passage concludes in v. 12 with the metaphor of God as a father reproving his son. It is not enough to ground the authority structure of Proverbs 1–9 in the patriarchal father. The authority of the transcendent Father of fathers is needed.

Having claimed access to the transcendent realm through the alignment of the father and God, the chapter next turns to secure the stability of its comprehensive terms of value, "wisdom," and "understanding" (vv. 13–21). A variety of linked images carries the argument. First wisdom is compared with riches. Then it is personified as a woman holding riches and honor in one hand, long life in the other. The tableau may well be an evocation of the Egyptian goddess Maat, but the meaning of the image does not require knowledge of the allusion. A figure who holds life in her hand belongs to the transcendent. References to her pleasant ways and safe paths recall the paths of the strange woman of chapter 2 and establish this figure as her opposite. As death belongs to one, life belongs to the other. The chain of association completes itself with another mythic image, wisdom as the tree of life. Such a phrase sets up an intertextual play with Genesis 2–3. Here the two trees of Genesis are condensed into one—knowledge that gives life. In the Genesis narrative the quest for knowledge was marked as rebellion and resulted in exclusion from the source of life. Here it is submissive obedience that is correlated with wisdom and with life. In Genesis the desire "to be like God" with respect to wisdom ("knowing good and evil") was a mark of hybris. Here the one who finds wisdom (v. 13) is blessed precisely because he is like God, having found that by which God created the world (vv. 19–20). Wisdom is not one discourse among others but the stuff of reality itself. The values of the father are built into the structures of the world.

PROVERBS 4

In Prov. 4:3–4 the father speaks and says "I was a son to my father; a precious only son to my mother. And he taught me and said to me. . . ." In part this is a strengthening of the claim to authority, as fathers quote earlier fathers. But there is another function. I made the point earlier that the subject position of the reader in Proverbs 1–9 is that of the son, established through the fiction of direct address by the father. But the situation is somewhat more complex than that. There is always a measure of identification between father and son, so that a son understands and thinks "when I grow up, that's what I will be." The father-status already exists as potentiality in the son. That identification is, of course, vital in negotiating the intergenerational divide of patriarchal society. For the young male deferral is not endless. So, in Proverbs 1–9, where the reader is continually reinterpellated in the subject position of the son, chapter 4 speaks of the transformation of sons into fathers in the chain of tradition. The male subject is to a certain degree apportioned between father and son. One is always a subordinate son to the collective authority of the symbolic order. But its transcending father-status is what underwrites the father-status of those who occupy positions of authority within it.

Each of the following poetic sections of Proverbs 4 is built up by a playful use of one or more metaphoric conceits that employ various cultural codes. Despite the apparent heterogeneity, the various sections all relate to the familiar issues of subjectivity, discourse, and allegiance. In vv. 5–9 what appears to be an economic code ("acquire wisdom," "with all of your acquisition, acquire understanding") is combined with an erotic code ("don't abandon," "love," "embrace"). What seems to connect the two is the notion of the relationship as a transaction between the son and wisdom, an exchange of value. Verses 10–19 develop a code of movement: way, lead, walk, paths, steps, run, stumble, go, come, road, go straight, avoid, cross over, etc. At least some of the possible connotations have been discussed above in connection with chapter 2.

The most curious of the codes is the rewriting of the self as a series of body parts in verses 20–27: ear, eyes, heart, flesh, mouth, lips, eyes, pupils, feet. Intertwined with this inventory of the body are terms from a code of physical orientation (incline, extend, twist away, turn aside, twistedness, crookedness, make distant, straight, in front, straight before, swerve to right or left). The values associated with straightness and twistedness were made explicit in chapter 2. What is of more interest is the subdivision of the body. There are two other similar poems in 6:12–15 and 6:16–19. In the first of these we are introduced to the man "who goes about with a twisted mouth." What is wrong with his speech is made evident in v. 13. He allows other body parts to act, improperly, as speaking mouths, setting up commentaries or other discourses that invert the words of the mouth. "He winks with his eyes, communicates with his feet, instructs with his fingers." No wonder his speech is duplicitous. In the numerical poem that follows there is a catalog of the crucial body parts and their characteristic misuses: arrogant eyes, a lying tongue, hands shedding innocent blood, a scheming heart, feet that speed to whatever is bad. The self is not presented as a simple entity. Or perhaps it is better to say that various parts of the body can represent the whole by synecdoche. The individual's subjectivity can be seen as invested in each of these parts, any of which has the power to work his ruin. But it seems odd that one part of the body, that part that males traditionally have considered to be the privileged representation of their subjectivity, is not mentioned. Although the phallus is never referred to explicitly, the problems of that important but unruly member are taken up in chapters 5–6.

PROVERBS 5–6

If the image of the woman has figured importantly in the first chapters of Proverbs 1–9, it utterly dominates the second half of the text. The most vivid and extensive representations are those of the strange woman. As in chapter 2, her sexuality is repeatedly associated with speech. She has "a smooth tongue" (6:24), "smooth words" (7:5), "smooth lips" (7:21). In the most explicitly erotic description it is said that "her lips drip with honey" and the inside of her mouth is "smoother than oil" (5:3). That she figures as the father's chief rival for the allegiance of the son would be clear simply from the length and intensity of the attack on her, but in 7:21 it is even said that she misleads the naive youth with her "teaching," a term used of the father's instruction as well (4:2). The fear that the father has of her is revealed in one of the images used to describe her deceptiveness. In patriarchal thinking it is woman's lack of the phallus and the privilege that the male associates with its possession that grounds woman's inferiority. In the father's phantasm the danger is that behind that reassuring smoothness, that visible absence of the phallus, there lurks something "sharp as a two edged sword" (5:4). The fantasy is that she not only possesses a hidden super potency but that it is a castrating potency as well. She threatens to reverse the body symbolism on which the father's authority is established.

The simple opposition between male and female is fundamental to the symbolic order of patriarchy, but it does not exhaust the role of woman in the symbolic economy. The triple association of sexuality, speech, and authority needs to be followed a bit further. The association of authority with speech is clear. In Proverbs 1–9 the father speaks, the son is spoken to. The father's control of speech is further indicated in that the speech of the sinners and of the strange woman does not reach the son directly but only as filtered through the father's speech. And in general, the silencing of women in patriarchal society is both symbol and result of the inferior status based on their perceived sexual "lack." On the other hand sexuality is by its nature dialogical, as the term "intercourse" well suggests. Culturally, it is closely associated with speech: courting speech, seductive speech, love songs, whispered sweet nothings. The point at which the horizontal speech of the woman's sexuality comes into conflict with the vertical speech of the father's authority is precisely at the point of generational transition, when the boy becomes a man. In her provocative study of the Samson story Mieke Bal makes reference to the moment of sexual maturity as the point at which "the trinity of the nuclear family is sacrificed to the alienating relationship with the other, the fourth person."[13] The sexual maturation of the son is a critical moment not only in psychoanalytic terms but also a critical moment for the social and symbolic order. It is the moment at which the patriarchal family will be successfully replicated or threatened. The system of approved and disapproved sexual relations forms a language through which men define their relations with one another. Proverbs 5:7–14, 15–20; and 6:20–35 set up three parallel situations: the woman outside the group/ the proper wife/ the wife of another man inside the group.[14]

It is interesting to see how the benefits and consequences of each are described. Sexual relations with the first woman ("approaching the door to her house," 5:8) are described in terms of depletion: ". . . lest you give to others your wealth and your years to the merciless; lest strangers batten on your strength and your labors in the house of a foreigner. You will be sorry afterwards when your flesh and body are consumed" (5:9–11).[15] Although there is an obvious element of psychosexual fantasy here, it is overwritten by social references. The others/ the merciless/the strangers/the foreigner who are the devourers here are all masculine nouns and imply the community of males to whom the woman belongs. Exogamy is deplorable because it results in the alienation of wealth. The communal context is further indicated by the concluding lament: "I was quickly brought to ruin in the midst of the congregation and the assembly." Going outside deprives a man of standing in his own group as well.

By contrast appropriate sexual relations have a centripetal direction. In 5:15–20 sexual connections are described under the figure of water contained and dispersed. "Drink water from your own cistern and running water from your own well. [Don't] let your springs overflow outside, streams of water in the public squares. Let them be for yourself alone, not for strangers with you."

Because there is a considerable subjective investment in one's own proper wife ("your cistern, your well, for yourself alone"), the selfhood of individual males and the solidarity of the community is severely threatened by adultery. The "foreign" woman of 6:20–35 is not ethnically foreign but off limits because she is "the wife of one's neighbor." As in the first example, the code of property crops up, here in a comparison between theft and adultery (vv. 30–31). The point of comparison is not between the rights of the male to the woman or property but to the social rather than the merely private dimensions of the offense. The criminal is in each case the object of contempt or scorn, though much more so in the case of the adulterer.[16] Not only will the wronged husband refuse an offered settlement; the entire community is implacable in its judgment of "his reproach which can never be effaced" (v. 33). The code of behavior between men and women is raised up in these passages as an important code of signifying behavior among groups of men. Metaphorically, in the social fabric of patriarchy woman is the essential thread that joins the pieces. But equally she indicates the seams where the fabric is subject to tears.

Although much of the advice offered in Proverbs 5–6 about relations with women appears to be strictly pragmatic, one often has a sense of a curious slippage between the literal and the symbolic. When one understands from Prov. 5:15–20 that a good marriage will protect a man from foreign women and "thy neighbor's wife," one also remembers the themes of protection associated with personified wisdom in 4:6–9. When the ruined son recollects in Prov. 5:12–13 how he "hated discipline," "despised criticism," and never listened to his teachers, his regrets seem to refer to more than just the lesson on sex. Is the strange woman not a problem in sexual mores after all, but an allegory of folly? The final pairing in chapter 9 of the allegorical women *Ḥokmot* and *Kesilut* (Wisdom and Folly) would seem to point in that direction. But it would be a mistake to pose the pragmatic and the allegorical as either/or alternatives. When symbolic thinking is carried forward by means of concrete objects or persons, statements and actions pertaining to these concrete entities can never be merely pragmatic on the one hand or simply metaphorical on the other. All customary praxis involving women is nonverbal symbolic construction. All use of the feminine in symbolic representation implicates behavior. So long as a society's discourse is carried on by males alone, that fact is scarcely noticeable. But as women enter into public discourse as speaking subjects, the habit of patriarchy to think symbolically by means of woman is thrown into confusion. Woman cannot occupy the same symbolic relation to herself that she does to man. With that change the long, slow crisis of the symbolic order is at hand.

PROVERBS 7–9

Something of the both/and, pragmatic/symbolic totality of woman in the discourse of Proverbs 1–9 can be seen in the two great paired poems of Proverbs 7 and 8. Although very different in style and content, these poems of the strange woman and of personified wisdom form a diptych. Chapter 8, with its strong mythic overtones, is written largely in the symbolic register; chapter 7 largely in the realistic. But in the framing of chapter 7 there are certain elements that establish its relationship to chapter 8 and disclose its mythic dimensions. In the father's account of the meeting between the vapid youth and the strange woman the words are ominous and negative. The woman is associated with many of the wisdom tradition's bad values, yet appears to be an ordinary, mundane character. The setting is twilight, so that the woman arrives with the onset of "night and darkness" (v. 9). She is associated with concealment and with the appearance of what is illicit (v. 10). Where wisdom tradition values quietness, she is "noisy" (v. 11), and her movement is characterized as restless, vagrant, and flitting. When she is still, she is "lying in wait" (v. 12), a predatory quality that is made explicit in verses 22–23. Her smooth speech "turns" the young man (v. 21). The symbolic register is more explicitly evoked in the introductory and concluding remarks of the father. Calling wisdom "sister" and "kinswoman" (v. 4) introduces explicit personification. Those words also set up a relation of equivalence between wisdom and "the wife of your youth" from chapter 5, instilling actual marriage with the protective values of wisdom. Similarly, the father's concluding words in verses 24–27 expose the monstrous, mythic dimension of the strange woman. She is not just a woman who has seduced a simple-minded young man. She is a predator who has slain multitudes. Indeed, her vagina is the gate of Sheol. Her womb, death itself.

Chapter 8 is radically different in style. Where the strange woman's speech is passed through the father's admonitory speech, wisdom speaks autonomously. Although there are traces of the erotic associated with her ("love" in v. 17, perhaps the reference to "delighting" in vv. 30–31, and the allusion to the man waiting and watching at her gate in v. 34), her speech and self-presentation are thoroughly unlike the strange woman's. Her movement is public, direct, and authoritative. Unlike the smooth, seductive, but deceptive speech of the strange woman, wisdom's is like that of the father: "straight," "right," and "true," not "twisted," or "crooked." Her voice, of course, is the cultural voice that speaks through the father, the voice that grounds the social fathers: the kings, rulers, princes, nobles of verses 15–16. Hers is the voice that mediates between the transcendent father and his earthly sons.

But how can it be, when so much energy has been invested in disclosing the terrifying dangerousness of woman as represented in the strange woman, that Proverbs 1–9 turns to woman also for its ideal representation of the central term of value, wisdom itself? In fact it is not surprising at all. Thinking in terms of sexual difference, of woman as man's other, difference serves to articulate both what is inferior and what is superior. Toril Moi develops Julia Kristeva's understanding of women's position of marginality in patriarchal thinking in a way that precisely explains the symbolic projection of Proverbs 7–8:

> If patriarchy sees women as occupying a marginal position within the symbolic order, then it can construe them as the limit or borderline of that order. From a phallocentric point of view, women will then come to represent the necessary frontier between man and chaos; but because of their very marginality they will also always seem to recede into and merge with the chaos of the outside. Women seen as the limit of the symbolic order will in other words share in the disconcerting properties of all frontiers: they will be neither inside nor outside, neither known nor unknown. It is this position that has enabled male culture sometimes to vilify women as representing darkness and chaos, to view them as Lilith or the Whore of Babylon, and sometimes to elevate them as the representatives of a higher and purer nature, to venerate them as Virgins and Mothers of God. In the first instance the borderline is seen as part of the chaotic wilderness outside, and in the second it is seen as an inherent part of the inside: the part that protects and shields the symbolic order from the imaginary chaos.[17]

Wisdom's self-presentation as a divine figure in chapter 8 not only serves to anchor wisdom discourse in the transcendent realm. It also positions her as the counterpart of the strange woman. One is the gate of Sheol, the other the gate of Heaven. Together they define and secure the boundaries of the symbolic order of patriarchal wisdom. Chapter 9 draws the conclusion self-consciously with its explicit parallel of personified wisdom and folly.

CONCLUSION

Analyzing the symbolic structure of Proverbs 1–9 is not merely an antiquarian exercise. Phallocentric constructions of the world continue to be deeply dependent on such uses of sexual difference for their articulation. A good illustration of the profound psychic attachment to this mode of thinking as well as the symbolic dimensions of apparently "realistic" speech is the recent film *Fatal Attraction.* Its subtitle could easily have been "cling to the wife of your youth, and she will save you from the strange woman." In the film the viewer's subjectivity is rigorously identified with that of the male character, Dan. He is consistently depicted as a good but naive and occasionally impulsive man, an object of seduction. The "strange woman," Alex, is portrayed as belonging to the margin in many ways. Her family background is obscure, her employment with the company recent. She has no husband or recognized lover. She stands outside the realm of socially ordered sexuality. Her apartment is located in an ambiguous commercial/residential neighborhood, where workers ominously carry about large pieces of butchered animals ("like an ox to the slaughter," 7:22). Like the strange woman of Proverbs 7 she has a brilliant power of speech, always more than a match for her male victim. But also like the strange woman of Proverbs, it is only an illusion that we encounter her and her speech directly. She is not a speaking subject but rather is an effect of someone else's speech, the paternal speech of the film itself.[18]

When the predatory seduction has been accomplished, the chaotic, monstrous dimensions of Alex become evident: madness, violence, an uncanny unstoppable will. In an allusion to the tradition of horror films, Alex is drowned (we see her staring eyes and parted lips) and yet comes back from the dead. Against the inbreaking of chaos, the male character proves himself to be finally helpless. It is "the wife of his youth" who must rescue him. The wife has been presented, as is the wife of Proverbs 5, as herself a deeply erotic, desirable woman. Equally, she is the center of the domesticity of the patriarchal family. Her symbol is the house, where, more than once, we see the brightly burning kitchen hearth. It is in her climactic appearance, however, that we glimpse her mythic status. In contrast to the frantic, ineffectual, and messy struggle of the husband, her single shot is decisive. But it is her bearing when the camera turns to view her that has such an effect on the viewer. She stands framed in the doorway, quiet, impassive, erect, authoritative. She is a dea ex machina and, for one familiar with Proverbs 1–9, a figure evocative of *Ḥokmot.*

As is well known, the original end of the film was changed by the director in response to the reaction of the audience in test screenings.[19] He had originally filmed an ending that was a twist on the Madam Butterfly theme, in which Alex's suicide would implicate Dan as her murderer. Preview audiences, however, disliked the ending. They recognized the mythic structure of the film and insisted on its "proper" conclusion. The version of the film as we have it is thus the result of a collective writing. The extraordinary emotional reaction from subsequent audiences, especially among men, confirms how deep is the investment in the patriarchal positioning of women as the inner and outer linings of its symbolic order.

Although the similarity of the symbolic positioning of woman in *Fatal Attraction* and Proverbs 1–9 is unmistakable, it is the difference in their manner of presentation that makes Proverbs 1–9 of particular interest to feminist analysis. Where the film skillfully attempts to naturalize its discourse, to conceal its speaking subject, and mask its interpellation of the viewer, Proverbs 1–9 emphasizes precisely these features. Certainly Proverbs 1–9 also makes its own claims to universality and transcendent authority, but its explicit self-consciousness about the central role of discourses in competition provides an internal basis for questioning its own claims. Having learned from the father how to resist interpellation by hearing the internal contradictions in discourse, one is prepared to resist the patriarchal interpellation of the father as well. For the reader who does not take up the subject position offered by the text, Proverbs 1–9 ceases to be a simple text of initiation and becomes a text about the problematic nature of discourse itself. Not only the dazzling (and defensive) rhetoric of the father but also the pregnant silence of the son and the dissidence that speaks from the margin in the person of the strange woman become matters of significance. Israel's wisdom tradition never examined its patriarchal assumptions. But its commitment to the centrality of discourse as such and its fascination with the dissident voice in Job and Qohelet made it the locus within Israel for radical challenges to the complacency of the dominant symbolic order.

NOTES

1. E. Benveniste, *Problems in General Linguistics,* Miami linguistics series no. 8 (Coral Gables, Fla.: University of Miami, 1971), 219.
2. Benveniste, *Problems in General Linguistics,* 224–25.
3. Because of the masculine subject position offered to the reader, I will refer to the reader as "he."
4. L. Althusser, *Lenin and Philosophy,* trans. B. Brewster (London: Monthly Review, 1971), 174–75.
5. I say "family" because the mother's authority as well as the father's is invoked (1:8; 4:3; 6:20). In no way is she seen as constituting an independent voice, however, but serves as a confirmer of what is presented as essentially patriarchal authority.
6. Both the Soviet Union and the United States use the term "human rights." Only when the term is precisely defined does one become aware of the assumptions of totalitarian socialism implicit in the use of this term by Soviet speakers and bourgeois liberalism and capitalism by American speakers.
7. J. Crenshaw has drawn attention to the problematic nature of authority in ancient instruction literature. "Sapiential Rhetoric and Its Warrants," VTSup 32 (1981): 16.
8. Althusser, *Lenin and Philosophy,* 168.

9. Mieke Bal observes that "there is a verb in Dutch for 'to commit adultery,' which is literally 'to go strange,' to go with a stranger (*vreemd gaan*)." *Lethal Love,* Indiana studies in biblical literature (Bloomington and Indianapolis: Indiana University, 1987), 43.

10. We can be certain that the error is not a meaningless one since the image of the house recurs in chapters 5, 7, and 9. For a discussion of the house/female body symbolism in the Samson story see Mieke Bal, *Lethal Love,* 49–58.

11. See J. Kristeva, "Women's Time" (187–213), and "A New Type of Intellectual: The Dissident" (292–300) in *The Kristeva Reader,* ed. Toril Moi (New York: Columbia University, 1986). Ironically, Roland Barthes entitled an early review of Kristeva's work "L'Etrangere," the strange or foreign woman, referring to her Bulgarian nationality and the unsettling quality of her work. See Toril Moi, *Sexual/Textual Politics: Feminist Literary Theory* (London: Methuen, 1985), 150.

12. The illusory nature of the transcendental signified is argued by Jacques Derrida in *Writing and Difference,* trans. Alan Bass (Chicago: University of Chicago, 1978), 278–80.

13. Bal, *Lethal Love,* 57.

14. Not all commentators understand 5:7–14 to refer to social or ethnic outsiders. Some argue that adultery is at issue. The language is probably intentionally ambiguous and polyvalent. But the contrast between "others, strangers, foreigner" in 5:9–10 and "your neighbor" in 6:29 (where adultery is explicitly at issue) suggests that the connotations of social or ethnic alienness are to the fore in 5:7–14. There is also a sharp contrast in the relation between improper sex and money in 5:9–10 and 6:35, implying different social situations.

15. Reading *wĕniḥamtā* in v. 11. Cf. LXX. The Greek text also suggests that "your wealth" in v. 9 may be an error for "your life," which would fit the parallelism better.

16. I read v. 30 as an implied question.

17. Toril Moi, *Sexual/Textual Politics,* 167.

18. For an excellent discussion of the problem of enunciation and subjectivity in film see chap. 5 of Kaja Silverman, *The Subject of Semiotics* (New York: Oxford University, 1983).

19. Myra Forsberg, "James Dearden: Life After 'Fatal Attraction,'" *New York Times,* 24 July 1988, p. 21.

11 ESTHER: A FEMININE MODEL FOR JEWISH DIASPORA

SIDNIE ANN WHITE

The book of Esther, found among the Writings (or *kĕtûbîm*) in the Hebrew Bible, has suffered an ambiguous reputation in the history of Judaism and Christianity. Written sometime during the Persian period,[1] its place in the canon was still a matter of debate in the third century C.E. when Rabbi Samuel ben Judah opined that Esther did not defile the hands, that is to say, was not sacred Scripture.[2] On the other hand, Josephus, the first century C.E. Jewish historian, clearly regards Esther as canonical, since he paraphrases the book in his *Jewish Antiquities*, and probably counts it in his canonical list.[3]

The book of Esther early on holds an equally ambiguous position among Christians. The Eastern church did not completely accept the book of Esther as canonical until the eighth century C.E., while it was accepted in the west by the fourth century.[4]

The reasons for all the ambiguity regarding the book of Esther, we feel, are the result of misunderstandings concerning its purpose. The primary concern of this essay will be to clarify the purpose of the book through an investigation of the main character, Esther, and her actions and reactions in regard to the power structures of Persian society. But first we will discuss some general introductory matters that will serve to explain the parameters within which the main thesis of this essay was constructed.

The religiosity of the book of Esther has been the source of much debate. As is well known, God is never mentioned in the book of Esther. In addition, the Law and the Covenant are never alluded to; there are no prayers; and Esther, as a Jew, seems to have no scruples about being married to a Gentile or living in a completely heathen environment. These problems were felt at least as early as the second century B.C.E. when the Greek additions to Esther were composed, adding prayers and explicitly stating that Esther loathes being married to a Gentile and has scrupulously followed the dietary laws.[5] The commentaries by the rabbis in the Mishnah and the Talmud also attempt to deal with this problem. According to Rabbi Johanan, Esther obtained vegetables, as did Daniel, and Rab held that she was given kosher food.[6] However, there is no hint in the text that Esther refused Persian food, or that she received any sort of special food. In fact, in verse 10 we are told that she hid her Jewish origins, obviously impossible to do if she had requested special food. We may assume that the dietary laws were not an issue for the author of the book of Esther. It is clear that in the Masoretic text there is no concern for what we may call Jewish piety, as there is, for example, in the book of Daniel. As Carey Moore states, "Esther seems to be Jewish in a sense more ethnic than religious."[7] Wilhelm Vischer correctly observes that Esther is concerned with the Jewish question as a political and cultural, rather than religious problem.[8]

In spite of these observations, however, we believe that the element of piety in Esther, though veiled, is present. First of all, Esther, when faced with the consequences of going to the king unsummoned, calls on the Jews in Susa to join her in a fast. Fasting is, in the later Jewish tradition, a religious act.[9] Second, in 4:14 Mordecai tells Esther, "For if you keep silence at such a time as this, relief and deliverance will arise for the Jews from another place, but you and your father's house will perish." It has been suggested, in both the interpretive tradition of Esther and in modern scholarship, that the Hebrew word for place, *maqôm,* is a veiled reference to God.[10] While this is not entirely clear, since there is no other place in the biblical literature where *maqôm* has this meaning, it seems clear that the verse as a whole is referring to what we may call Divine Providence. In fact, Mordecai goes on to say "Who knows if for a time like this you attained royal power?" God's control of events seems to be assumed in this verse, and the status of the Jews as God's chosen people is also assumed. However, the God of the book of Esther does not take center stage as a deus ex machina, as in the book of Daniel. Rather, this God appears to act through human beings, allowing them to take center stage and act as the instruments of their own salvation. The human element is thus all-important.

The book of Esther purports to be an account of the events that led to the inauguration of the Jewish festival of Purim. The Persian king

Ahasuerus has deposed Vashti, his queen, and decides to find a new one. A young Jewish girl named Esther wins his favor and becomes the new queen. Her adopted father Mordecai becomes involved in a quarrel with the king's vizier, Haman. Haman plots to slaughter all the Jews in the empire to revenge himself against Mordecai. His plot is discovered and, by the efforts of Esther, Haman is executed and the enemies of the Jews destroyed. Mordecai becomes the king's vizier and institutes the festival of Purim to celebrate this great victory.

The plot hangs together well, and yet different sources have been discerned within the book of Esther. The most famous source theory is Henri Cazelles's two-source theory.[11] Cazelles hypothesizes that the Masoretic text of the book of Esther is a conflation of two independent texts, basing his theory on the occurrence of pairs throughout the book. The first text is liturgical, centers around the character of Esther, is about the relationship between Jews and Gentiles in the provinces, and explains the origin of the festival of Purim. The second text is historical and centers on the court intrigues of Mordecai and the persecution of the Jews in Susa.[12] Hans Bardtke, on the other hand, finds three separate tales in the book of Esther.[13] The first story concerns Queen Vashti, the second involves Mordecai, court intrigues, and the avoidance of persecution, and the third involves Esther, the king's favorite, and the avoidance of persecution. Elias Bickerman discovers two separate plots: in the first, Esther becomes queen and the enmity of Haman endangers her; in the second, Mordecai, a royal courtier, is hated by Haman.[14]

The difficulty with these source theories is that the sources do not separate cleanly, but instead overlap a great deal. The most obvious overlap is the fact that each tale (if we use Bardtke's three-source analysis) shares the character of the king. This is easily explained, however, by saying that there are always many tales circulating involving kings, and it would be quite easy to combine two or three of these into one tale. A more serious difficulty is that the tales of Esther and Mordecai share the same villain, Haman. While it is possible to isolate separate conclusions for the adventures of Esther and Mordecai, it is more difficult to separate two strands for the character of Haman. There is no motive for Haman to persecute the Jews in the plot line that involves Esther alone. That motive comes solely from his hatred of Mordecai. In addition, there are several factors in the Esther tale that become pointless without the tale of Mordecai. For example, why does Esther hide her identity as a Jew? For these reasons Larry Wills suggests that it is difficult to isolate a self-contained Esther story, and that the story of Esther came into existence as an expansion of an original Mordecai source.[15]

What all these differing theories finally show, however, is that it is difficult, if not impossible, to divide the book of Esther into separate sources. While it seems clear that two or three different tales lie behind our present book of Esther, the author of the present book was not a mere editor, but truly deserves the title of author, having combined his sources with a skill the result of which is that the whole is greater than the sum of its parts. For this reason, we will consider the story of Esther and Mordecai as a whole, rather than attempt to distinguish source material from editorial material.

The connection of the tale of Esther and Mordecai to the festival of Purim is highly dubious. The only connection between the tale and the festival is the word *pûr*, or "lot," which Haman casts to determine the date for the slaughter of the Jews (3:7).[16] Some sort of festival is connected with the name of Mordecai in 2 Maccabees 15:36 ("the day of Mordecai") but the name Purim is not mentioned. D. J. A. Clines argues cogently that chapters 9–10 should be separated from chapters 1–8 as the work of a different redactor.[17] For the purposes of this paper, we will follow Clines's conclusion that the story of Esther and Mordecai, in its Masoretic version, originally ended with chapter 8.

Esther 1–8, or what we shall call the story of Esther and Mordecai, is a fast-paced, suspenseful tale. The tale clearly is meant to entertain, but it has a didactic purpose as well. It is meant to teach Jews how to live a productive life in the Diaspora. Jones, in "Two Misconceptions about the Book of Esther," argues that the scroll's purpose is "the reconciliation of Jewish audiences to their minority status among gentiles whose attitudes toward Jews varied unpredictably from honor to persecution."[18] Other books in the Hebrew Bible address this problem, both directly and indirectly.[19] In the historical figure of Nehemiah, we have a portrait of a Jew who has risen to prominence in the Persian court while keeping his religious identity intact (Neh. 1–2). The character of Daniel, in chapters 1–6 of the book of Daniel, is a Jew who rises to prominence in a gentile court while maintaining his religious integrity, engenders hostility because of his prominence, and overcomes the danger and regains his prominence through the help of divine providence.[20] Daniel 1–6 has been correctly identified as a series of court tales, a well-known type of wisdom tale in which a wise courtier rises to prominence, is persecuted, suffers a fall, and is finally vindicated.[21] This sort of tale enjoyed great popularity in the post-exilic period.

The book of Esther also has the basic elements of the court tale: the setting in the royal court, the wise heroine/hero representing a "ruled ethnic group," and the persecution of the protagonists and their ultimate vindication.[22] However, the story of Esther and Mordecai is more complicated than the normal court tale, with two protagonists and a conflict much broader in its implications than the persecution of one protagonist.

S. Talmon has attempted to place the book of Esther within the corpus of wisdom literature.[23] He characterizes the book as a "historicized wisdom tale" and sees in the characters of the book the types common to wisdom literature. Ahasuerus is the foolish king, Mordecai is the wise and virtuous courtier, and Haman is the wise but wicked courtier. Esther herself represents the motif of the orphan adopted by a wise man who makes good. The point of the narrative is to portray "applied" wisdom, that is, how a wise man [*sic!*] may lead a successful life in the world. This explains the "disturbing lack of . . . religiosity in the book." Ultimately, Talmon would say that "in the last analysis the Persian setting is of secondary importance."[24]

Here, however, we disagree. The Persian setting is of primary importance, because the book is attempting to teach its audience how to lead a successful life *in the Diaspora.* The question of how to live successfully in exile had been asked since the time of Jeremiah, who said,

> Thus says the LORD of hosts, the God of Israel, to all the exiles whom I have sent into exile from Jerusalem to Babylon: Build houses and live in them; plant gardens and eat their produce. Take wives and have sons and daughters; take wives for your sons, and give your daughters in marriage, that they may bear sons and daughters; multiply there, and do not decrease. But seek the welfare of the city where I have sent you into exile, and pray to the LORD on its behalf, for in its welfare you will find your welfare (Jer. 29:4–7).

This is a course of action that is espoused in the book of Esther. Esther and Mordecai function in a completely heathen environment: Esther becomes the spouse of a Gentile king; Mordecai "sits in the king's gate," a technical term for a royal courtier; and there is a large Jewish population living permanently in the capital and in the provinces. As Berg has pointed out, this is "a story which does not envision or promote the return of the Jews to Palestine."[25]

Most commentators have focused on Mordecai as the paradigm for Diaspora life. We have already seen that Talmon views Mordecai as the type for the wise and virtuous courtier.[26] Carey Moore states, "Between

Mordecai and Esther the greater hero is Mordecai, who supplied the brains while Esther simply followed his directions."[27] Paton places Esther in a completely negative light:

> Esther, for the chance of winning wealth and power, takes her place in the herd of maidens who became concubines of the king. She wins her victories not by skill or by character, but by her beauty. She conceals her origin, is relentless toward a fallen enemy, secures not merely that the Jews escape from danger, but that they fall upon their enemies, slay their wives and children, and plunder their property.[28]

He assigns to her the worst of character and motives, and then does not even allow her the intelligence to further her own plot.[29]

As will be seen, I disagree with all of these characterizations. I believe Esther is the true heroine of the tale, and the traits in her character and her actions that make her successful are those that a Jew must emulate if she or he is to be successful in the precarious world of the Diaspora. Mordecai, while certainly a sympathetic character, is not successful because he refuses to fit into the situation in which he finds himself. Esther unravels the plot of Haman and strengthens her position, while affirming, in the end, her ethnic identity as a Jew.

The method of this essay is ostensibly simple: to make a detailed analysis of the character and the actions of Esther, and to investigate their impact on the story of Esther and Mordecai. However, this method is not as straightforward as it appears at first glance. Elisabeth Schüssler Fiorenza has warned that we must be cautious "in adopting the standard scholarly interpretations of texts, which are often androcentric."[30] We have found that androcentrism abounds in most of the commentaries on the book of Esther, with the author either ignoring the character of Esther or relegating her to a secondary position behind Mordecai. I hope, by giving a more sympathetic reading of the character and role of Esther, to show Esther's real status as the heroine of the book which is, after all, called by her name. I also will be using new studies on the psychology of women that show that women function differently in the world than men, and that therefore their actions must be judged according to their own standards.

As Elizabeth Janeway states in her book *Powers of the Weak*, the variety of lives that women have led at different times and in different sorts of society make up a dictionary of survival techniques.[31] There are two groups in any society, the powerful and the weak, or as Jean Baker Miller terms them, the dominants and the subordinates. A subordinate group has to concentrate on basic survival, not on attaining power.[32] However, in order for the powerful to maintain their power, the weak must acquiesce to the relationship. Maintaining power by force does not work for long. Women have nearly always been among the weak in any society, and the adjustments that women have made during centuries spent as subordinate partners in a power relationship illuminate the whole range of power situations.[33]

The Jews in the Diaspora also are in the position of the weak, as a subordinate population under the dominant Persian government. They must adjust to their lack of immediate political and economic power and learn to work within the system to gain what power they can. In the book of Esther, their role model for this adjustment is Esther. Not only is she a woman, a member of a perpetually subordinate population, but she is an orphan, a powerless member of Jewish society. Therefore, her position in society is constantly precarious, as was the position of the Jews in the Diaspora. With no native power of her own owing to her sex or position in society, Esther must learn to make her way among the powerful and to cooperate with others in order to make herself secure.

Esther first appears in 2:7, where she is introduced as the cousin of Mordecai. She is described as very beautiful, but no hint of her character is given. In verse 8, Esther is taken, along with all the other unmarried women in the capital, into the king's house.[34] In verse 9, we finally begin to learn something about Esther beyond her physical beauty. We are told that "the maiden (Esther) pleased him (Hegai, the eunuch in charge of the king's harem) and won his favor." It has been pointed out by others that the phrase *wattiśśā' ḥesed,* "and she won favor," is active in meaning, as opposed to the more usual phrase *mṣ' ḥesed,* "to find favor."[35] Esther is not a passive character; she takes steps, within the situation in which she finds herself, to place herself in the best possible position. And her strategy works. Her beauty treatments are hastened, she receives good food, and is given seven maidservants.

Verse 10 informs us that Esther does not reveal that she is a Jew, because Mordecai had instructed her not to do so. This has been taken as reaffirming Mordecai's dominance over Esther. Moore states that the emphatic position of the proper name Mordecai in the verse shows Esther's subordination.[36] However, a more sympathetic interpretation would be that she sensibly follows the advice of the more seasoned courtier Mordecai, who, after all, "sits in the king's gate." Again, she is adapting herself to the situation in which she finds herself. R. Gordis suggests that Esther does not reveal her nationality so that there are no known legal impediments to her ascension. He bases his surmise on the fact that we know from Herodotus that the Persian kings could only select queens from seven noble Persian families. However, wouldn't the king, in that case, make sure that he knew Esther's background? It must finally be said, however, that no motive for Esther's silence is given in the text. It is, again, simply stated as a fact. The most obvious function of her silence is to serve as a plot device to heighten the tension, since Haman, when he resolves to destroy the Jews, obviously does not know that the queen is a Jew.

Esther 2:15–18 explains how Esther wins the favor of Ahasuerus and becomes the queen. Again, her actions in this situation show her taking advantage of the opportunities around her to improve her position. She wisely follows the advice of Hegai, who knows what the king prefers. At this point, it may be necessary to comment on some of the presuppositions of the story and our own prejudices. To our modern ears, becoming a member of a harem and attempting to win the favor of a man by sexual means sounds degrading, and it would be so in our society. However, if we think in terms of the historical period and the acceptable means of winning power, Esther's actions become less problematic. Her behavior is no more reprehensible than the sycophantic responses of Xerxes' counselors and the behavior of Haman in trying to obtain power; her actions simply contain a sexual element. And it must be emphasized that there is no note of censure in the Hebrew text; in fact, Esther's behavior is applauded in the statement, "Now Esther found favor in the eyes of all who saw her" (2:15). Once we accept the worldview of the text, Esther immediately becomes a much more sympathetic character. By her actions, Esther shows herself to be cooperative, an important characteristic for a successful court life.

And Esther certainly does succeed. The king is smitten by her and makes her his queen. Her last act before the main events of chapter 4 is to inform the king that Mordecai had uncovered the plot of the eunuchs to murder Ahasuerus (2:22). Again, she is using her influence to enhance the position of her relatives. Nothing immediately comes of her actions, but it is the action of a wise courtier.

Esther's next appearance is in chapter 4, the turning point of the story. At 4:4, Esther is informed that Mordecai is wailing in sackcloth at the palace gate. The actions of the main characters are very important here, for they illustrate more and less constructive ways of dealing with disasters. Janeway points out that basic to survival is the avoidance of shock, for shock precipitates panic.[37] We see the victim of shock in Mordecai, who goes into a panic, putting on mourning and wailing through the city streets (4:1). These actions are, of course, acceptable means of expressing grief in the ancient Near East, but they do not help to avert the crisis. Mordecai's one idea seems to be to bring the crisis to the attention of Esther. Esther's first reaction to the news of Mordecai's appearance is nurturing; she sends him clothes.[38] Mordecai then sends word to Esther of the disaster that has befallen the Jews and charges her to go to the king. Although we are investigating the character of Esther, it would be helpful at this point to look at the character of Mordecai and to determine how calamity has come upon the Jews. The text states that Mordecai earned the enmity of Haman by refusing to bow down to him (3:2, 5). What the text does not tell us is why Mordecai refuses obeisance to Haman. Commentators, beginning with the rabbis, have sought to supply the reason: Midrash Rabbah says that 1) Haman pinned an idol to his breast, and 2) Mordecai would not bow down to anything except God.[39] We have examples, however, of Jews doing obeisance to rulers all the time with no censure attached to the action (e.g., in the Joseph story Joseph's brothers bow down to him as the ruler of Egypt). Paton sees in Mordecai's action a "spirit of independence."[40] However, the fact remains that the text itself gives us no reason for the refusal. In verse 4, the other servants wait to see who would prove stronger, Haman or Mordecai, for Mordecai "had told them that he was a Jew." But this is not the reason for the refusal to bow down. One can make the assumption that Mordecai had a good reason for refusing to bow down, but this remains an assumption.[41] On the face of it, however, Mordecai's refusal appears foolish. He seems to have nothing to gain by it and a great deal to lose. Surely this is not the action of a wise courtier! Mordecai is refusing to accept and work with his subordinate position. As Miller points out, it is practically impossible to initiate open conflict when you are totally dependent on the other person or group for the basic material and psychological means of existence.[42] Yet this is precisely what Mordecai attempts to do. Then, having precipitated this crisis, he must rely on Esther to undo the damage. Her reaction, as described below, is much more the action of the wise courtier. As Talmon states: "she ascends from the role of Mordecai's protégée and becomes her mentor's guardian."[43]

Esther now speaks directly for the first time in the narrative:

> All the king's servants and the people of the king's provinces know that if any man or woman goes to the king inside the inner court without being called, there is but one law; all alike are to be put to death, except the one to whom the king holds out the golden sceptre that he [*sic!*] may live. And I have not been called to come in to the king these thirty days (4:11).

Esther's reaction is not a sign of cowardice, but a statement of fact. If she appears before the king, the chances are good that she will die. In addition, what influence does she have with the king if he has not wished to see her for thirty days? As Moore notes, even after being queen for five years, Esther still occupies a weak and precarious position.[44] This is normal for women; circumstances have accustomed women to expect a considerable amount of unpredictability to come their way.[45] In spite of Esther's objections, however, Mordecai sends back another message:

> Think not that in the king's palace you will escape any more than all the other Jews. For if you keep silence at such a time as this, relief and deliverance will arise for the Jews from another place (*RSV* "quarter"), but you and your father's house will perish. And who knows whether you have not come to royal power (*RSV* "the kingdom") for such a time as this (4:13–14)?

Mordecai's speech, as mentioned above, contains a veiled reference to God, but it also emphasizes the importance of human action in accomplishing God's purpose. It also serves to remind Esther that she possesses power in her own right.[46] Mordecai's reply rallies Esther. She realizes that she must act for the good of the community, and she springs into action. Carol Gilligan has stated that men's social orientation is positional while women's is personal. That is, men define themselves in terms of their position in society, while women define themselves by their relationship to others.[47] This seems to hold true for Esther. When she first objects to going to the king, her reason is her status in relation to the king. However, when Mordecai reminds her of her relationship to her family and the Jewish community as a whole, she is willing to take risks and act for their benefit.

Esther now becomes the initiator of events. She orders a fast, which, as we have already mentioned, is of religious significance, and prepares to go to the king. The final verse of chapter 4 sums up the dramatic force of Esther's actions: "Mordecai then went away and did everything as *Esther* had ordered him [emphasis mine]." The powerless has become the powerful.

In her decision to confront the king, Esther continues on the same wise course she has taken up until now. She does not risk direct confrontation without first taking all the steps possible to safeguard herself. This is not cowardice, but a realistic assessment of the situation. The best chance she has of obtaining her goals is by appealing to the king's emotions, rather than by cool logic. In our (androcentric) society, emotion has not been seen as an aid to understanding and action, but rather as an impediment to understanding. Because of this, it is one of the few weapons the dominants allow the subordinates to use.[48] We have already seen, however, that Ahasuerus reacts emotionally rather than rationally. He banishes Vashti in a rage, then later regrets it; makes Esther queen because he loves her; and allows Haman to manipulate him unthinkingly. So Esther's best way to appeal to this king is clearly through his emotions.

After her fast, Esther appears unsummoned before the king. She has put on her royal robes in order to appear as attractive and queenly as possible.[49] Her strategy works, for she "earns favor" in his eyes.[50] Ahasuerus offers to grant any request of hers up to half of his kingdom. This might seem like the right time to ask the king to save the Jews. However, that would not neutralize Haman, as Esther appears to realize. So, rather than making her request and leaving the results to the discretion of this mercurial king who is very easily influenced, she sets out to lull Haman into a false sense of complacency and to place the king in a position where a strong emotional response from him is guaranteed. She invites the king and Haman to a private dinner party. This places the king in her territory, the women's quarters, where she can more easily control the situation. It also puts Haman off his guard. It is difficult to believe that a person who invites you to a dinner party is your enemy. The strategy again is successful: the king is further inclined to do Esther's will, and "Haman went out that day joyful and glad of heart" (5:9).

Many commentators have raised the question of why Esther gives a second banquet. The proponents of the two-source theory (e.g., Cazelles) see this as part of the evidence for two sources. The first banquet is part of the Mordecai source and the second is part of the Esther source.[51] The problem with this division, which Cazelles acknowledges, is that Esther gives both banquets. If we take the text as we have it, the second banquet may be viewed as a device to heighten the tension of the plot,[52] or as mere foolishness on the part of Esther.[53] However, as Clines points out, by using the first banquet as a purely social occasion she has lulled Haman into such a false sense of security that he tries pleading for his life from her after she reveals who she really is. In addition, at the first banquet Esther requests the king to affirm publicly that he means to grant her request by attending the second banquet. "If I have found favor in the sight of the king and if it please the king, *let the king and Haman come* to the dinner which I will prepare for them, *and tomorrow I will do* as the king has said" (5:8 [emphasis mine]). By coming to the second banquet, Ahasuerus is agreeing in advance to Esther's still unheard petition.[54]

Finally, at the second banquet, Esther makes her request. It should be noted that although we have the benefit of chapter 6 and know of Haman's humiliation before Mordecai, there is no indication in the text that Esther knows anything about it. She views Haman as "as powerful and as dangerous as before."[55] So when she makes her request, she must convince the king of the rightness of her position and the wrongness of Haman's. First she appeals to Ahasuerus' emotions by the raw urgency of her plea: "Let my life be given me at my petition, and my people at my request" (7:3). Then she disarms Haman by answering his argument that "it is not to the king's profit" to tolerate the Jews (3:8). She argues that the destruction of the Jews would mean a great loss to the king. This argument stems from a woman's sense of the interrelatedness of people's lives.[56] Later in the scene, when Haman pleads for his life, some commentators have taken her to task for not attempting to save him. For example, Paton says, "It must be admitted that her character would have been more attractive if she had shown pity toward a fallen foe."[57] However, Esther must act on her primary loyalty to her community. Haman, after all, does not repent; he simply begs for his life. Haman left alive would still constitute a threat to the Jewish community. Haman must die if the Jews are to be safe, and Esther acknowledges this by her silence.

Chapter 8 brings us the conclusion of the tale of Esther and Mordecai. Esther receives from Ahasuerus the property of Haman, and recommends Mordecai to the king. Mordecai is then made the vizier in place of Haman. Esther now controls wealth, court appointments, and access to the king.

However, the main problem of the story still remains. Haman has issued an edict in the king's name for the destruction of the Jews, and it cannot be annulled, for "an edict written in the name of the king and sealed with the king's ring cannot be revoked" (8:8). Something must be done to avert the consequences of the edict.[58] Esther again petitions the king; she makes a strong appeal to his emotions. She falls at his feet and weeps. The king holds out his sceptre to her again, and she begins her petition. As Clines has pointed out, her speech in 8:5–6 is a masterpiece of courtier's rhetoric.[59] She prefaces it with four conditional clauses: "If it please the king, and if I have found favor in his sight, and if the thing seems right before the king, and I be pleasing in his eyes. . . ." The first two are familiar from earlier speeches of Esther (5:4, 5:8, and 7:3), the third and fourth are newly composed for the occasion. In these third and fourth clauses she shifts the responsibility for overturning Haman's decree onto the king ("if the thing seems right before the king") and again appeals directly to her relationship with him ("and I be pleasing in his eyes"). Although on the surface her speech is merely that of a polite courtier, underneath she is giving the reasons why her request should be granted. In the body of the speech she uses an appeal to the king's emotions rather than cool logic to drive her point home and to get what she needs. She is careful not to put the king on the defensive by referring to a royal decree; instead she refers to "the letters devised by Haman the Agagite." Then in verse 6, she plays what Clines refers to as her "trump card": her favored position with the king (how can I endure . . . ?).[60] And the king grants her carte blanche: "And you may write as you please with regard to the Jews, in the name of the king, and seal it with the king's ring" (8:8).

Esther now disappears from our original story, leaving the final business to Mordecai. Her conduct throughout the story has been a masterpiece of feminine skill. From beginning to end, she does not make a misstep. While in the harem, she earns the favor of Hegai, and follows his advice and the advice of Mordecai, both experienced in the ways of the court. She wins the king's heart, becomes queen, and then, when danger threatens, skillfully negotiates her tricky course. She is a model for the successful conduct of life in the often uncertain world of the Diaspora. The fact that she is a woman emphasizes the plight of the Jew in the Diaspora: the once-powerful Jewish nation has become a subordinate minority within a foreign empire, just as Esther, as a woman, is subject to the dominant male. However, by accepting the reality of a subordinate position and learning to gain power by working within the structure rather than against it, the Jew can build a successful and fulfilling life in the Diaspora, as Esther does in the court of Ahasuerus.

NOTES

1. Most commentators on Esther are agreed that the core of the book was written at some time during the period of Persian dominance in the ancient Near East (i.e., 539–332 B.C.E.). The reasons most often cited for this dating are the Persian setting and local coloring, the absence of all Greek coloring, and the sympathetic attitude toward the gentile king. In the Persian period, Jews were often willing servants of the Persian kings (Nehemiah is a good example of this phenomenon). As for the setting, we would argue that the lack of interest in Judah or its cultic institutions, along with the familiarity with the Persian royal court and gentile lifestyle, favors a setting in the Eastern Diaspora. See further Lewis Bayles Paton, *A Critical and Exegetical Commentary on the Book of Esther,* ICC (New York: Scribner, 1908); Carey A. Moore, *Esther, AB* (Garden City: Doubleday, 1971); and Sandra Beth Berg, *The Book of Esther: Motifs, Themes and Structure,* SBL Dissertation Series 44 (Missoula, Mont.: Scholars, 1979). All quotations from the book of Esther in this paper will be according to *The New Oxford Annotated Bible: Revised Standard Version,* unless otherwise noted.

King Ahasuerus has been identified as Xerxes, the fourth Achaemenian monarch (486–465 B.C.E.). The portrait of the king in Esther coincides with what we know about Xerxes from extra-biblical sources: his empire extended from India to Ethiopia, he had a winter palace at Susa, he gave lavish drinking parties, made extravagant promises and gifts, and had a nasty and irrational temper (Moore, *Esther,* xli).

2. Megilla 7a, tr. by Maurice Simon, in *The Babylonian Talmud,* ed. Isidore Epstein (New York: Soncino, 1938), 35–36.

3. In *Against Apion,* I, 38–41, Josephus states that there are twenty-two books in the Hebrew canon, which he unfortunately does not enumerate. However, it appears that Josephus counted Judges and Ruth as one book, as well as Jeremiah and Lamentations. Thus Esther could be included in his list of twenty-two.

4. Moore, *Esther,* xxviii.

5. The additions to Esther may be found in the *New Oxford Annotated Bible.* For commentary, see *Jewish Writings of the Second Temple Period,* in *Compendia Rerum Iudaicarum ad Novum Testamentum*: Section 2, ed. Michael E. Stone (Philadelphia: Fortress, 1984) and G. W. Nickelsburg, *Jewish Literature between the Bible and the Mishnah* (Philadelphia: Fortress, 1981).

6. Paton, *Commentary,* 174.

7. Moore, *Esther,* xxii.

8. Wilhelm Vischer, *Esther,* TEH 48 (Munich: C. Kaiser, 1937), 15.

9. See Matt. 6:16–18.

10. Cf. the A text of the Greek Esther, Josephus' *Antiquities,* and the 1 and 2 Targums to Esther. For further commentary, see, for example, Moore, *Esther,* 50.

11. Henri Cazelles, "Note sur la composition du rouleau d'Esther" in *Lex*

Tua Veritas, eds. Heinrich Gross and Franz Mussner (Trier: Paulinus, 1961), 17–30.

12. D. J. A. Clines, *The Esther Scroll,* JSOTSup 30 (Sheffield: *JSOT,* 1984), 123, revises Cazelles's source analysis, dividing the sources slightly differently.

13. Hans Bardtke, *Das Buch Esther,* KAT 17/5 (Gütersloh: Gütersloher, 1963).

14. Elias Bickerman, *Four Strange Books of the Bible* (New York: Schocken, 1967), 172.

15. Lawrence Wills, "The Jew in the Court of Foreign Kings: Ancient Jewish Court Legends" (dissertation, Harvard University, 1987), 260–61.

16. Julius Lewy has shown that the word *pûr* stems from the Babylonian word *pūrū,* which means "lot" or "fate," (*RHA* 5 [1939]: 117–24). It is interesting to note that the Greek text and Josephus contain the word *phrourai* (A text *phoudaia*), which evidently springs from the Aramaic word *pûrrāyā'* (C. C. Torrey, "The Older Book of Esther," *HTR* 37 [1944]: 6).

17. Clines, *Esther Scroll,* 39 ff. He argues on the basis of both linguistic and literary data. Wills draws heavily on Clines in his analysis of the sources of Esther, and also does away with the Purim connection. C. C. Torrey ("Older Book," 14) notes that Esther A ends at exactly the end of the folktale of Esther and Mordecai, arguing for an originally shorter story. The story ends quite satisfactorily at chap. 8, with the danger to the Jews averted and Esther and Mordecai firmly in power. The inclusion of the actions of the Jews after Mordecai issues his decree and the institution of Purim is extraneous to the original tale. For an opposing viewpoint, see Berg, who argues for the inclusion of Purim in the original narrative on the basis of stylistic traits.

18. B. W. Jones, "Two Misconceptions about the Book of Esther," *CBQ* 39 (1977): 171. I would add that the author's message is also that by following the book's program one would gain honor regularly (not unpredictably).

19. As R. Gordis points out, "anti-semitic encounters with a dominant non-Jewish majority were recurring phenomena in the history of Diaspora Jewry" ("Religion, Wisdom and History in the Book of Esther—A New Solution to an Ancient Crux," *JBL* 100 [1981]: 381).

20. It is clear that Daniel 1–6 are merely selections from a much larger cycle of Daniel tales, as witnessed by the "Prayer of Nabonidus" and the unpublished "4QpseudoDan" found at Qumran.

21. For an excellent discussion of this type of tale, see Susan Niditch and Robert Doran, "The Success Story of the Wise Courtier," *JBL* 96 (1977): 179–93, and Wills, "Court Legends," 205 ff.

22. Wills, "Court Legends," 205.

23. S. Talmon, "Wisdom in the Book of Esther," *VT* 13 (1963): 419–55.

24. Talmon, "Wisdom," 441.

25. Berg, *Esther,* 68.

26. Talmon ("Wisdom," 451) does list prototypes for Esther: Delilah, Naomi, Ruth, Michal, Jael, Rachel, Bathsheba, the wise women of Tekoa and

Abel beth Maacah, Tamar, and Potiphar's wife, and notes that women are prolific in the practical employment of wisdom maxims. The list is eclectic: there are both positive and negative characters in it, and the actions and goals of the women listed tend to be quite different. This eclecticism, or more negatively, the lumping together of women without differentiation, may stem from Talmon's attempt to identify the character of Esther as a type.

27. Moore, *Esther,* lii.

28. Paton, *Commentary,* 96.

29. He also is not sensitive to the situation of the Jews living under Persian dominance. Esther, in fact, has no choice about going into Ahasuerus' harem; she is not trying to gain "wealth and power," but preserving her life! I owe this observation to Peggy Day.

30. Elisabeth Schüssler Fiorenza, "Interpreting Patriarchal Traditions," in *The Liberating Word,* ed. Letty M. Russell (Philadelphia: Westminster, 1976), 61.

31. Elizabeth Janeway, *Powers of the Weak* (New York: Alfred A. Knopf, 1980), 210.

32. Jean Baker Miller, *Toward a New Psychology of Women* (Boston: Beacon, 1976), 10.

33. Janeway, *Powers,* 4.

34. The verb *tillāqaḥ* is a Niphal, with a passive meaning, so again the text gives no hint of Esther's reaction or character. Paton's assertion that she "takes her place in the herd of maidens" (p. 96), an active role, is certainly not borne out by the text. Nor does the author wish to cast any negative light on Esther's entering the harem of Ahasuerus. It is simply a fact.

35. For example, Moore, *Esther,* 27.

36. Moore, *Esther,* 22.

37. Janeway, *Powers,* 210.

38. Janeway, *Powers,* 272, lists nurturing as a quintessential feminine trait.

39. H. Freedman & Maurice Simon, eds. *The Midrash Rabbah,* vol. 4, (London: Soncino, 1977), 82, 107.

40. Paton, *Commentary,* 62.

41. Many commentators have noted that Mordecai is a descendant of Kish, the father of Saul, and that Haman is an Agagite, a descendant of the bitter enemy of Saul, Agag. Therefore Mordecai's behavior is the result of this ancient feud. While possible, this is not explicitly stated in the text. For further comment, see Moore, *Esther,* 42.

42. Miller, *Psychology,* 127.

43. Talmon, "Wisdom," 449.

44. Moore, *Esther,* 18.

45. Janeway, *Powers,* 210.

46. Berg, *Esther,* 60.

47. Carol Gilligan, *In a Different Voice* (Cambridge, Mass.: Harvard University, 1982), 16.

48. Miller, *Psychology,* 38.

49. Moore (*Esther,* 55) notes that this is not only a matter of feminine strategy but also of court etiquette. In 4:2 Mordecai must stay outside the palace complex, for "no one might enter the king's gate clothed in sackcloth."

50. Again, the verb used is *nāśē'āh,* with its active connotation.

51. Cazelles, "Esther," 27.

52. Paton (*Commentary,* 236) states that the author needs time for the disgrace of Haman.

53. W. Lee Humphreys calls it a "dangerous overconfidence." See Humphreys, "The Story of Esther and Mordecai: An Early Jewish Novella," in *Saga, Legend, Tale, Novella, Fable,* ed. G. W. Coats, JSOT Sup 35 (Sheffield: JSOT, 1985).

54. Clines, *Esther Scroll,* 144.

55. Moore, *Esther,* 73.

56. Janeway (*Powers,* 272) calls the "greater recognition of the essential cooperative nature of human existence" a feminine trait. The fact that the king originally allows Haman to arrange the destruction of the Jews can also be explained as part of the dominant-subordinate relationship. Janeway (4) notes "a general tendency of governors to ignore the humanity and even the presence, of groups whose lives fall within the category of the weak." Thus, Ahasuerus does not even inquire after the identity of the group that Haman is seeking to destroy!

57. Paton, *Commentary,* 264.

58. Clines, (*Esther Scroll,* 15–21) gives a good discussion of the theme of the irreversibility of Persian law. The law of the Medes and the Persians is taken very seriously by the book of Esther; the law is never disobeyed by a Jew except by dire necessity (the exception to this is Mordecai's refusal to bow before Haman). Esther in particular is the exemplar of this; the disobedience of Esther is the direct result of her membership in the larger Jewish community (Berg, *Esther,* 77). Loyalty to the Jewish community is valued above allegiance to the civil government; however, in normal circumstances no conflict should result. It is, according to the book, perfectly possible to be a loyal Jew and a loyal subject of the Persian king.

59. Clines, *Esther Scroll,* 101.

60. Clines, *Esther Scroll,* 102.

12 WOMEN OF THE EXODUS IN BIBLICAL RETELLINGS OF THE SECOND TEMPLE PERIOD

EILEEN SCHULLER

In few places in the Old Testament do as many women appear as in the opening chapters of the book of Exodus. There is no doubt that the hero of the story is Moses; the text is primarily concerned with his birth and his role in the deliverance of the Hebrew people from the bondage of Egyptian slavery. But Moses is surrounded by six women and, in fact, owes his very life to them: the two midwives Shiphrah and Puah who thwart Pharaoh's design to destroy all male babies at birth; his biological mother who gives him birth and then fashions the ark that will give him a chance for survival; his sister who cleverly ensures that the baby's nursemaid will be his mother; his adoptive mother, the daughter of Pharaoh, who looks with compassion on the child and takes him as her son; and Zipporah, his wife, who saves his life when "the Lord met him and sought to kill him" (Exod. 4:24). Later in the story, at the climax of the Exodus deliverance when the people stand in freedom on the shore to sing their hymn of thanksgiving, beside Moses is his sister Miriam, leading the company of women with timbrels and dance (Exod. 15:20–21). Finally, there is a passing cryptic reference to yet another woman in the life of Moses, his unnamed Cushite wife (Num. 12:1). Truly, "the text is as full of women as Egypt seemed full of Hebrews."[1]

Although these are some of the most familiar and most studied chapters of the Bible, the women have received little explicit attention. Often, their stories have simply not been heard. The Common Lectionary, which sets the Scripture texts to be used on Sundays in many Protestant churches, prescribes the reading of all of Exod. 1:6—2:22 with the exception of 1:15–21, the story of the midwives;[2] at the celebration of the Easter Vigil, the song of Moses is read but not the song of Miriam.

Recently, a number of studies from a feminist perspective have invited us to look again, and in a new way, at these texts in which women play a crucial role in the central events of the drama of Israel's salvation.[3] It is important to review briefly the stories of these women in the biblical text as a prelude to the main work of this paper, an examination of how these stories were retold and interpreted centuries later.

The story of the midwives forms a contained unit, the second stage in Pharaoh's threefold intensification of his plan to wipe out this people who have become "too many and too mighty" (Exod. 1:9). The two midwives are named, Shiphrah and Puah, a significant detail in a story in which only one other name (Moses) appears. They defy his command to kill the male babies at birth; challenged by Pharaoh, they cleverly (and ironically) explain that "the Hebrew women are not like the Egyptian women" (Exod. 1:19) and do not need their services. The ancient Hebrew consonantal text is ambiguous on one key point—are these Egyptian women ("the [Egyptian] midwives of the Hebrews") or Hebrew women ("the Hebrew midwives")? Certainly when the Rabbis added vowels to the text in the early centuries of the Christian era, they read it as "the Hebrew midwives," but that may not have been the original intent. Whether Egyptian or Hebrew, the midwives refuse to be party to Pharaoh's assumption that women could be used against women, as agents of death rather than life.

The role of Moses' mother is central to the story although she never speaks and is not named in this text (in the biblical genealogies she is identified as Jochebed, Exod. 6:20; Num. 26:59). While the earlier matriarchs (Sarah, Rebekah, Rachael) were "barren wives" who waited long for children, now, at a time when pregnancy is fraught with danger for any Hebrew woman, the mother of Moses immediately conceives. After birth, she hides her baby for three months and when "she could hide him no longer," she prepares an "ark" (the rare Hebrew word is used only here and in Gen. 6–9; RSV "a basket") in which to expose him. Unlike Noah who himself builds the ark that saves him, here the baby is dependent upon his mother to provide the means of his rescue. It is the mother who makes all the decisions; the father, introduced only as "a man from the house of Levi" (Exod. 2:1), does not appear again after the conception of the child. As wet-nurse hired for her own child, Moses' mother continues to nourish him.

The appearance of the sister in the story is somewhat unexpected; Exod. 2:1–2 gives the impression that Moses was the first born. The sister here is unnamed, although later tradition will consistently identify her with Miriam. She watches over the baby at a distance, and courageously and cleverly approaches the princess with her suggestion for nursing the baby. Here, as throughout the whole story, when we look for God's providential action, it is to be found not in direct divine intervention but through the sagacity and resourcefulness of these women.

The final rescuer is an Egyptian woman, the daughter of the very king seeking to destroy the baby. Pharaoh's daughter embodies a compassion that goes beyond natural feelings of pity for a crying infant; it is compassion for one whom she recognizes as the child of the enemy, "one of the Hebrews' children" (Exod. 2:6). In many ways she is another mother-figure in the story; she arranges for Moses' care and names him. He "became her son" (Exod. 2:10).[4] Once again a woman makes mockery of the plans of the mighty; the child whom Pharaoh wanted destroyed at birth grows up in the king's own house!

But Pharaoh's daughter is not the only foreign woman to save Moses' life. After killing an Egyptian, Moses flees to the land of Midian where his safety is assured when he marries Zipporah, one of the seven daughters of Reuel, the Midianite priest. After Moses speaks to God directly in the burning bush and receives his mandate to bring the people out of Egypt, there is yet another attack on his life: "at a lodging place on the way the Lord met him and sought to kill him" (Exod. 4:24). The passage is difficult, "very obscure in several respects."[5] However, with all the unresolved questions in the text, one thing is clear: it is Zipporah who acts. She circumcises either her son or Moses, and it is her action that resolves the crisis and saves her husband's life.[6] After the incident, biblical tradition took little interest in Zipporah. Apparently she did not participate in the deliverance through the Red Sea, for at some earlier stage Moses had sent her and her two sons back to his father-in-law (Exod. 18:1–4); when she is reunited with Moses, the focus is entirely on the men in the story (Exod. 18:1–12).

The sister of Moses appears once again after the crossing of the Red Sea. Here she is called "the prophetess" (Exod. 15:20), although the title is probably anachronistic and not particularly helpful in understanding her role and position.[7] The biblical text gives us three major stories about Miriam: in Exod. 15:20–21 she takes an active and cultic role in the celebration of the foundational event of Israel's faith as she sings a parallel song to Moses while the women join with timbrels and dancing; in Num. 12:1–16 (a complex text with many layers of tradition) she joins with Aaron in challenging Moses' leadership and becomes "leprous, as white as snow" for seven days until she is restored; and in Num. 20:1 there is a brief account of her death at Kadesh. Historically, Miriam may have been an independent figure, only secondarily brought into the text as "sister" of Aaron and Moses. There are at least hints that she exercised a much more prominent position of leadership than the final form of the text allows;[8] we can note, for instance, how the people refuse to go on until she is restored (Num. 12:15) and how her death, like that of Moses and Aaron, is arranged to coincide with one of the last three stops on the wilderness route. In later prophetic tradition, Miriam is remembered as one of the leaders given by God to Israel as a mark of divine favor, "I sent before you Moses, Aaron and Miriam" (Mic. 6:4).

Although our survey of these biblical stories has necessarily been brief,[9] it is clear that in these texts women play an absolutely essential role; they are presented as "defiers of oppression . . . givers of life . . . wise and resourceful."[10] But when we raise the question of how these powerful stories have touched women and men down through the centuries who have considered them as foundational and sacred, it is essential to recall that reading the book of Exodus is not the only way that people have "heard" these stories. Even in our own day, the biblical text per se is never the sole fashioner of our imagination; whether we are aware of it or not, our "picture" of the Exodus story is shaped at least as much (if not more perhaps!) by the way the story has been retold in the words and pictures of Sunday school books, in hymns, and in the well-known Negro Spirituals that draw so powerfully on this imagery; we *know* how the water swelled up in walls to allow the people to walk through dry-shod because we have seen it in the Cecil B. DeMille movie!

Thus, although we can point to the prominent role given to women in the biblical text, we need to ask the question: what happened when these stories were told and retold in subsequent centuries? What about the mother and sister of Moses, Shiphrah and Puah, the daughter of Pharaoh, Zipporah, and Miriam—were their stories also told?[11] In the embellishment and enlargements, the additions and the deletions that are part of any retelling, was the role of women expanded and amplified, or were they, directly or in subtle ways, edited out of the story? As the position of women became more restricted in post-exilic Judaism,[12] did contemporary social reality influence how these foundational stories were remembered and refashioned?

We are justified in raising this question with a certain hermeneutic of suspicion because within the Bible itself there are examples of how the sacred history could be retold without women. In the liturgical and formulaic language and style of the "historical psalms" (Pss. 105, 106, 135, 136) and deuteronomistic-style prayer (Neh. 9), the Exodus events are often celebrated as God's activity alone with no human agency (Ps. 106:8–12; 136:10–16); in other places Moses and Aaron are remembered (Ps. 105:26) but not the third leader "which I have sent" (Mic. 6:4).

The same bracketing out of biblical women can be observed in the Wisdom hymn of Ben Sira 44–50. Written by a priest/teacher in Jerusalem in about 180 B.C.E. this hymn sets out to praise "famous men, and our fathers in their generations" (Sir. 44:1) from Adam right up to the current high priest Simon. Moses and Aaron are among the illustrious examples cited, but not Miriam. In fact, the only women mentioned in this recital are those blamed for Solomon's downfall;[13] all the "mothers in their generation" have disappeared. While Ben Sira may have been influenced by the conventions of the Hellenistic genre of the *encomium* (a highly stylized rhetorical form for praising heroes, kings, and commanders on public occasions), his own undisguised misogynist attitude would not dispose him to include women in a hymn of praise.[14] Similarly, in the *Wisdom of Solomon,* a work in Greek from a Hellenistic-Jewish author living in Alexandria in the first century B.C.E., salvation history from Adam to Exodus is retold as a series of stylized examples of how "men were taught what pleases you, and were saved by wisdom" (Wis. 9:18). Ironically, although the figure of Wisdom is female, all other women have disappeared from the story. It was through texts such as these that young men in the wisdom schools in the first century learned their biblical history!

From the Second Temple period, there has survived a corpus of literary works that we can group together under the general term "rewritten Bible." Although extremely diverse in many ways, all of these works "take as their literary framework the flow of the biblical text itself and apparently have as their major purpose the clarification and actualization of the biblical story."[15] The existence of such a genre of writing attests both to the growing sense of "sacred text" and to the conviction that the Word of God can and must be reinterpreted to respond to exegetical problems, fill in narrative gaps, smooth out inconsistencies, and make the text relevant in a new context. These works do not fit the criteria of midrash as the term is technically used,[16] and clearly predate even the earliest tannaitic midrashim and the Targums. Yet the fact that exegetical traditions in these texts can be traced through to the Targums and much later works such as *Shemot Rabbah* suggests that these rewritten Bible-style narratives are not expressing the idiosyncratic inventions of an individual author but rather a common body of tradition. Three such works, *Jubilees*, the *Biblical Antiquities*, and the *Jewish Antiquities*,[17] enable us to glimpse something of how the biblical stories of the Exodus were understood and retold in the late Second Temple period in Palestine.[18] We turn to these specifically to ask how the women of the Exodus fared in these retellings.

The book of *Jubilees* is a retelling of Gen. 1—Exod. 14, divided into a series of jubilees (forty-nine year periods) and presented as the revelatory experience of Moses on Mount Sinai. The work was written around 170–150 B.C.E. (making it the earliest of the texts we are discussing) by a priestly scribe concerned with issues of election, Law, calendar, and covenant identity in the face of Hellenism.[19] The author gave particular attention to the stories of the Jacob cycle; Exodus 1–14 is retold very succinctly in the final four chapters (46–50), with none of the lengthy elaborations that characterized earlier chapters.

Although the author of *Jubilees* can be very harsh in his treatment of women, especially foreign women (*Jub.* 25:1–2), he does devote an unusual amount of attention to Rebekah, developing for her a role that goes far beyond the biblical text (she counsels Jacob about his marriage 25:1–3, gives a lengthy maternal blessing 25:11–23, and speaks a final testament 35:1–27); although the revised picture of Rebekah is shaped by certain theological and exegetical concerns, the result is that "a woman has taken her place in the company of men; a matriarch has joined the patriarchs."[20] Elsewhere in *Jubilees* other women are highlighted (the praise of Leah at her death 36:21–24), or elements of the biblical story that could be perceived negatively are simply omitted (Rachael's theft of the teraphim Gen. 31:33–35).

Thus, we might expect that the author of *Jubilees* would take a real interest in the women of the Exodus story and develop at some length the material already there in the biblical text, but we are disappointed. Partly this may be simply a function of the very concise nature of these final chapters of the book (all of Exod. 1–12 is treated in thirteen verses). Some new material is added but it is about Moses' father, Amram;[21] the story is told of his journey to Canaan (46:9–10) and return to Egypt (47:1). Amram surfaces again when the boy grows up; in contrast to Exod. 2:10 where the boy's mother is the sole actor, in

Jub. 47:9 "they" bring Moses to the daughter of Pharaoh, and Amram is credited with teaching him writing.

In contrast to the emphasis on Amram, the mother of the child is unnamed until her very last appearance. In other ways, however, the author of *Jubilees* takes an interest in Jochebed. As in the biblical version, she is the main actor; she alone hides the baby, makes the ark and places Moses in it; even then she is not really abandoning the child, for "your mother came in the night and suckled you" (*Jub.* 47:4). The author of *Jubilees* is sensitive to the problem implicit in the biblical text—why did Jochebed suddenly expose the baby after managing to hide him for three months, and is she blameworthy? Exodus 2:3 says only "and when she could hide him no longer;" *Jubilees* explains her actions by elaborating that "they reported concerning her." In this retelling, the midwives have disappeared completely; the command to throw the male children into the river is given to the Israelites and they obey for seven months "until the day when you were born" (*Jub.* 47:3). Jochebed alone has the courage to disobey.

In keeping with its tendency to supply names lacking in the biblical text, *Jubilees* clearly identifies Moses' sister as Miriam; she is made to share in the motif of the well-cared-for child in the ark with the cryptic statement "Miriam, your sister, guarded you from the birds" (*Jub.* 47:4). Pharaoh's daughter is named, Tharmuth;[22] there is little elaboration beyond the biblical text, although it is not explicitly stated that she recognized the child as a Hebrew.

The chronology of Moses' stay in Midian is included (*Jub.* 48:1) but in keeping with the author's abhorrence of marriage to foreign women, there is no mention of Zipporah. *Jubilees* is the only "rewritten Bible" to include the problematic story of the attack on Moses' life (*Jub.* 48:2–4), but the biblical narrative is carefully reworked to fit the author's theological convictions: the attack does not come from God but from Prince Mastema; the precipitating issue is not Moses' failure to circumcise his son but Mastema's desire to protect the idolatrous Egyptians. God claims direct responsibility for rescuing Moses, "I delivered you from his hand" (*Jub.* 48:4); Zipporah, the Midianite wife who acts to save his life, has been completely edited out from the story.

Let me turn now to our second example of "rewritten Bible," the *Biblical Antiquities,* a fascinating, though at times puzzling, retelling of selections of sacred history from Adam to David.[23] Its unknown author has been dubbed Pseudo-Philo simply because the text was transmitted along with the Latin translations of Philo of Alexandria; the work dates from the first century C.E. but not much more can be said with any certainty about authorship. The lack of any strong sectarian or esoteric tendencies that would link it to a specific group (Pharisees, Samaritans, or Essenes), plus the fact that it shares many traditions with later midrashim and often treats texts that were subsequently part of the lectionary readings in the Palestinian synagogues, all suggest that *Biblical Antiquities* was a "popular" history, a text that reflects how the biblical story was understood within "mainstream" late Second Temple Judaism.

Throughout the book, Pseudo-Philo frequently included women in his retelling, even where they are not in the biblical text.[24] In only two incidents (43:5 and 44:2) are these stories in which the women are cast negatively. In three instances the birth of a hero is announced by or to a woman (the birth of Abraham by Melcha 4:11, the birth of Moses by Miriam 9:10; the birth of Samson to Eluma 42:1–10). Lengthy prayers and laments are placed on the lips of Deborah, "a woman of God" (32: 1–17), Seila, the daughter of Jephthah (40:5–7), and Hannah (51:3–6).

However, when it comes to retelling Exodus 1–2, one is immediately struck by how much it has become Amram's story. He is the dominant character, simply by virtue of the amount of material included about him. When the elders of the people refuse to approach their wives lest the children they bear be defiled and serve idols, Amram gives a lengthy speech (9:3–8) protesting his faith in God's promise, his refusal to obey Pharaoh, and his determination to take his wife and bear children.[25] God's reply reinforces the role of Amram by establishing a causal relationship "because Amram's plan is pleasing to me . . . so behold now he who will be born from him will serve me forever" (*Bib. Ant.* 9.7). The story continues to be told from his perspective ("and this man had one son and one daughter"); later he joins Jochebed in placing the baby in the river and he is the one to speak to the elders who come to utter reproaches.[26]

Moses' mother is a much-less-developed character. In what appears to be a non sequitur, Pseudo-Philo joins together the phrase from Exod. 2:3 "for she could conceal him no longer" with the explanation "because the king of Egypt appointed local chiefs who, when the Hebrew women gave birth, would immediately throw their male children into the river" (*Bib. Ant.* 9:12).[27] These local chiefs have replaced the midwives at the birth. In this version of the story, Jochebed does not nurse her son, but she does bestow on him a name (Melchiel).

Pharaoh's daughter comes to the river to bathe, not by chance as might be assumed from the biblical text but "as she had seen in dreams" (*Bib. Ant.* 9:15). Similarly, it is not by chance that she recognizes that the child is Hebrew; Pseudo-Philo follows a tradition, repeated often in later writings, that Moses was born circumcised. This is the only version of the retelling in which Pharaoh's daughter nurses the baby herself.

Twice Pseudo-Philo chooses to highlight the role of Miriam, in both instances with additions to the biblical text that are repeated and developed in later midrashim.[28] It is to Miriam that the birth of the deliverer of the people is announced in a dream, "Go and say to your parents, 'Behold he who will be born from you will be cast forth into the water; likewise through him the water will be dried up'" (*Bib. Ant.* 9.10). But Miriam is more than the recipient of a dream; the language Pseudo-Philo uses is the language of prophecy, "the spirit of God came upon Miriam one night."[29] Perhaps the understanding of Miriam as a prophet developed from the odd conjunction of "prophetess" and "sister of Aaron" in Exod. 15:20; that is, she exercised her prophetic role in announcing the birth of Moses. It is difficult to see the precise function of Miriam's prophecy in Pseudo-Philo's narrative;[30] it seems to be intended to encourage Amram and Jochebed to have another child, although her message is not believed ("when Miriam told of her dream, her parents did not listen"). Still, in this retelling Miriam is given a new and striking role in the preparations for the birth of Moses.

Miriam appears only once more in *Biblical Antiquities,* in a comment on Josh. 5:12 about the cessation of the manna on entering the land: "there are three things that God gave to his people on account of three people: that is, the well of Marah for Miriam, the pillar of cloud for Aaron and the manna for Moses. And when these came to their end, these three things were taken away from them" (*Bib. Ant.* 20:8). This is the earliest (though very brief) attestation of a rich tradition[31] about "Miriam's well" that was derived from the association of Miriam with water in almost all her appearances in the biblical story and the juxtaposition of her death in Num. 20:1 with the next verse "now there was no water for the congregation" (20:2). This formulation of "the three gifts" is one of the few traditions that carries on the memory of Miriam as an equal with Moses and Aaron.

In the final text we will examine, Josephus retells the story of the Exodus in book II of *The Jewish Antiquities.* In this lengthy work, completed in 94 C.E. while on an imperial pension in Rome, Josephus retells biblical history according to the canons of Hellenistic historiography and rhetoric so that "the whole Greek-speaking world will find it worthy of attention" (*Ant* I i 2). Conscious of current anti-Semitic sentiments, Josephus' basic stance is both apologetic and confident; if the Greeks have their heroes, "our own great heroes are deserving of winning no less praise" (*Con. Ap.* II 136). Josephus' relationship to the biblical text is complex;[32] he claims to be setting forth "precise details" of the Scriptures "neither adding nor omitting anything" (*Ant* I i 3) and at times follows it quite closely; his additions often are rooted in Palestinian oral traditions, many of which appear elsewhere.

Josephus' attitude toward women in the *Antiquities* has not been studied in any comprehensive way.[33] A number of passing remarks throughout his work reveal a misogynist attitude towards the capabilities of women: for example, evidence is not to be accepted from a woman "because of the levity and temerity of their sex" (*Ant* IV 219); he damns with faint praise in his description of his third wife (all of them left unnamed) "in character she surpassed many of her sex as her subsequent life showed." Yet whatever Josephus' views on contemporary women, he does rework the stories of the matriarchs in Genesis so as to make them "understandable, attractive and even exemplary to Hellenistic readers."[34]

Given that Josephus sets out to portray Moses as a Hellenistic hero,[35] it is not surprising that his birth is predicted by a "sacred scribe" (*Ant* II ix 2). It is this prediction of one who would "abuse the sovereignty of the Egyptians and exalt the Israelites" that initiates the slaughter of every male child; the story has been reshaped so that the single focus of attention is the birth of Moses. The midwives are "Egyptian midwives," chosen precisely because "as compatriots of the king they were not likely to transgress his will" (*Ant* II ix 2); the courageous defiance of the midwives of the biblical text has disappeared completely. Jochebed escapes their ministrations only because of "the gentleness of her travail" (*Ant* II ix 4).

Yet Josephus does choose to develop the role of Amram. He is of noble birth;[36] there is no mention of Jochebed's lineage. The story is told solely from his perspective: his great anxiety because his wife is pregnant, his prayer to God, and the divine reassurance given in a dream. It is only in Josephus that the dream comes to Amram and not to Miriam (as in Pseudo-Philo and all the later midrashim); one suspects that Josephus may have modified the tradition at this point.[37] It is Amram who makes the decision to expose the child "fearing that he would be detected and . . . would perish himself" (*Ant* II ix 4); once he has made the decision, Jochebed joins in fashioning the basket and placing the baby in the river, all actions that in the Hebrew text were at her initiative alone.[38]

In contrast, it is striking how much attention Josephus devotes to Pharaoh's daughter. It is hard to get a sense of her supposed age; she is at the river "playing" but is concerned for an heir "being blessed with no offspring of her own" (*Ant* II ix 7). A figure of power and influence even in her dealings with the king, she is the one who takes the initiative to adopt the baby and make him heir; even when grown up, Moses is sent as commander against the Ethiopians only after she gives her consent (*Ant* II x 1). She saves Moses' life a second time by her quick action in snatching him away when the sacred scribe "rushed forward to kill him" after the baby had flung the royal diadem to the ground (*Ant* II ix 7). Undoubtedly it was Josephus' own pragmatic acknowledgment of the power of influential women (such as Poppaea and Domitia) at the Roman court rather than any feminist sentiments that influenced this portrait of Pharaoh's daughter.

Josephus shows little interest in Zipporah. Moses' marriage in Midian is described in the sparest of terms and Zipporah is not even named, "he [Raguel] gave him one of his daughters in marriage" (*Ant* II xi 2). Not only Zipporah's actions but the whole problematic incident of Exod. 4:24–26 is omitted entirely.

Though Zipporah is a minor figure, Josephus shows more interest in the "other woman" in the life of Moses, the Cushite woman of Num. 12:1. In *Ant* II x he adds a lengthy supplement to the biblical text, a Hellenistic-romantic tale of Moses as a mighty military leader heading an expedition into Ethiopia on behalf of the Egyptians.[39] While the army is besieging the capital city, Tharbis, the daughter of the king of Ethiopia, falls madly in love with Moses; "under the mastery of this passion" she offers marriage and he calculatingly accepts on condition that she surrender the town. After chastising the Ethiopians, Moses "rendered thanks to God, celebrated the nuptials, and led the Egyptians back to their land." Josephus undoubtedly included the story, not because of any concern with Tharbis per se, but because it suited so many of his other apologetic interests; however, the appeal of this erotic tale of a woman's betrayal of her city for the love of the general of a conquering army ensured that the "the Cushite woman" of Num. 12:1 lived on in the popular imagination.

Finally, Josephus shows little interest in Miriam. Having given the dream of Moses' birth to Amram, not to Miriam, he makes no mention of her at the Reed Sea; Moses alone composes his songs in hexameter verse (*Ant* II xvi 4). In contrast to rabbinic texts that establish (through complex manipulation of certain texts in Chronicles) that Caleb was her husband, Josephus makes only a passing reference to Ur as her husband (*Ant* III ii 4). In view of the repeated charge in Egyptian-Hellenistic anti-Semitic propaganda that Moses and the Israelites were lepers, the whole incident in Numbers 12 of Miriam's leprosy is omitted. Rather surprisingly, the account of her death, its date, and her burial "at public expense in state" is treated in some detail (*Ant* IV iv 6); she is honored by the people with the same thirty-day period of mourning as they observe at the death of Aaron and Moses.

Our search for the women in the retelling of the Exodus stories in *Jubilees, Biblical Antiquities,* and *Antiquities* has yielded limited results. Even more than in our reading of the biblical texts, we have been looking for the "lost token of faith—the remnant that makes the difference;"[40] it is obvious that none of these works are written from a perspective that would guarantee the preservation of the visibility and essential role of women.

Though the very nature of the genre "rewritten Bible" demands that the key elements of the biblical story be preserved, in point of fact the strong female presence that we noted in our examination of the biblical stories has been muted when these stories were retold. The midwives have disappeared except in Josephus where they are Egyptian and ready minions to do Pharaoh's bidding. The father of Moses has become a key figure in the story; the single reference in Exod. 2:1, "a man from the house of Levi went and took to wife a daughter of Levi," has been expanded so that Amram dominates. Interest is taken in his lineage and activities prior to the decree of Pharaoh; he prays and is reassured by God in a dream; in some versions he is the one who makes the decision to expose the baby and his wife only joins him in preparing the ark and placing the baby in the river; he teaches the boy writing. There is little comparable embellishment of Moses' mother, except perhaps in *Jubilees* where there is some concern to soften her abandonment of the baby. It is only in Pseudo-Philo that special interest is taken in Miriam; she is a recipient of a dream about Moses' birth and is remembered as a co-leader with Moses and Aaron, responsible for the well of water for the people in the wanderings. The puzzling story of Zipporah's saving of Moses' life has disappeared completely and where included at all, she is a minor figure. The Cushite wife of Moses becomes a stereotypical romantic figure.

While recognizing that many and diverse factors influenced the authors in their choice to retell the biblical story in precisely the way they did, the end result is that the readers of these books "heard" the story in a very different way from that presented in the biblical text. The strong female presence that has often been lauded in this section of the Bible did not survive for the most part in the Second Temple period. Thus, when we ponder the potential of the stories of the women of the Exodus to influence the life and imagination of people down throughout the centuries, we must realize that many of these women and their active role in the key event of Israel's salvation had already disappeared when these stories were retold.

NOTES

1. Robert B. Lawton, "Irony in Early Exodus," *ZAW* 97 (1985): 414.

2. See *Common Lectionary*, Consultation on Common Texts, Sunday lections for Proper 9,A and 10,A. In the *Lectionary for Mass* (revised 1981) of the Roman Catholic Church, none of Exodus 1–2 or Exodus 15 is read within the Sunday cycle. For weekdays, the selected text (#389) is Exod. 1:8–14 and verse 22, omitting verses 15–21 about the midwives.

3. The bibliography for a study of the women in Exodus includes: J. Cheryl Exum, "'You Shall Let Every Daughter Live': A Study of Exod. 1:8—2:10," *Semeia* 28 (1983): 63–82; Carol A. Newsom, "Retelling the Story of the Exodus: Homiletical Resources for the Season after Pentecost," *Quarterly Review* 7 (1987): 71–100; Alice Laffey, *A Feminist Introduction to the Old Testament* (Philadelphia: Fortress, 1987), 46–55; Athalya Brenner, *The Israelite Woman: Social Role and Literary Type in Biblical Narrative* (Sheffield: JSOT, 1985), 51–56, 61–62, 71–72, 98–100; Rita J. Burns, *Has the Lord Indeed Spoken Only Through Moses? A Study of the Biblical Portrait of Miriam*, SBL Dissertation Series 84 (Atlanta: Scholars, 1987).

4. It is not clear whether the Hebrew wording can be taken to describe formal adoption in the strict legal sense. See the discussion by B. S. Childs, "The Birth of Moses," *JBL* 84 (1965): 114, and in other commentaries.

5. Martin Noth, *Exodus*, OTL (London: SCM, 1962), 49. For a survey of how later interpreters tried to make sense of the text, see Geza Vermes, "Circumcision and Exodus IV 24–26," in *Scripture and Tradition in Judaism* (Leiden: Brill, 1973), 178–92.

6. When the text was translated into Greek (with many variations from the Hebrew), the causal relationship between her act and Moses' deliverance became even more obvious: the Septuagint of Exod. 4:26 reads "and he departed from him *because* she said . . . ."

7. See the lengthy discussion by R. Burns, "Miriam: Prophetess?" in *Has the Lord Indeed Spoken Only Through Moses?* 41–79.

8. The suspicion that there may be more to the Miriam tradition than was preserved in the biblical text was first suggested by Elisabeth Schüssler Fiorenza in "Interpreting Patriarchial Traditions," *The Liberating Word,* ed. Letty M. Russell (Philadelphia: Westminster, 1976), 49–51; the evidence has been more extensively developed by Phyllis Trible in oral addresses at the Third Fosdick Convocation on Preaching and the "Biblical Scholarship in the 21st Century Lecture" at the Society of Biblical Literature meeting in Boston, 1987. R. Burns suggests that the historical Miriam may have "officiated as a mediator of the divine will in the cult at Kadesh," *Has the Lord Spoken Only Through Moses?* 128.

9. For reasons of space, only specific female figures have been included. Note also the women who despoil the Egyptians (Exod. 3:22), the women's contribution to the tabernacle (Exod. 35:20–29), and "the ministering women who minister at the door of the tent of meeting" (Exod. 38:8).

10. J. C. Exum, "'You Shall Let Every Daughter Live,'" *Semeia,* 82. This is not, however, to deny or overlook the essentially patriarchial character of these stories; see the perceptive comments and warning by Exum in her later article "'Mothers in Israel': A Familiar Story Reconsidered," in *Feminist Interpretation of the Bible,* ed. Letty M. Russell (Philadelphia: Westminster, 1985), 81–82.

11. As far as I have been able to ascertain, the question has not been asked in quite this way before. Not surprisingly, most studies have focused on the reinterpretation of Moses, and the women are mentioned peripherally, if at all; for example, Wayne A. Meeks, "Moses in Non-Rabbinic Jewish Sources," *The Prophet-King* (Leiden: Brill, 1967), 100–175; David Lenz Tiede, "Images of Moses in Hellenistic Judaism," *The Charismatic Figure as Miracle-Worker,* SBL Dissertation Series 1 (Missoula: Scholars, 1972), 101–240: Geza Vermes, "La Figure de Moïse au Tournant des deux Testaments," in *Moïse: L'homme de l'Alliance,* eds. H. Cazelles et al. (Paris: Desclee, 1955), 63–92. A few studies have focused specifically on the retellings of the birth narratives; for example, Charles Perrot, "Les recits d'enfance dans la Haggada anterieure au 11e Siècle de notre ère," *RScR* 55 (1967): 481–518; John Dominic Crossan, "From Moses to Jesus: Parallel Themes," *Bible Review* 2 (1986): 18–27.

12. For an overview, see Leonard Swidler, *Women in Judaism; The Status of Women in Formative Judaism* (Metuchen, N.J.: Scarecrow, 1976). However there is some evidence that women exercised a greater leadership role than often assumed; see, for example, the epigraphic material from synagogue inscriptions studied by Bernadette Brooten, *Women Leaders in the Ancient Synagogue,* Brown Judaic Studies 36 (Chico: Scholars, 1982), and the differing perceptions of the role of women reflected in the Testament of Job (Peter W. Van der Horst, "The Role of Women in the Testament of Job," *Nederlands Theologisch Tydscrift* 40 (1986): 278–89, esp. pp. 288–89). The whole question of what can be known about the role of women in post-exilic Judaism now needs re-examination.

13. Sir. 47:19, "you laid your loins beside women and through your body you were brought into subjection." Sir. 48:19 and 49:7 mention women only in a comparison and a biblical quotation.

14. For a comprehensive, though very harsh survey of Ben Sira on this point, see Warren C. Trenchard, *Ben Sira's View of Women: A Literary Analysis*, Brown Judaic Studies 38 (Chico: Scholars, 1982). Note especially Sir. 25:24: "from a woman sin had its beginning and because of her we all die."

15. Daniel J. Harrington, "Palestinian Adaptations of Biblical Narratives and Prophecies. I. The Bible Rewritten (Narratives)," in *Early Judaism and Its Modern Interpreters*, eds. Robert A. Kraft and George W. E. Nickelsburg (Philadelphia: Fortress, 1986), 239. This is probably the clearest and most helpful state-of-the-art discussion on the complex issue of the nature and classification of this type of writing.

16. Although midrash (plural: midrashim) can be defined very generally as "something written for the purpose of interpreting the Bible, usually homiletical," a technical definition has been difficult to establish. Much of the basic work was done by Renée Bloch in two seminal essays in the 1950s, both of which are now available in English translation: "Midrash" and "Methodological Note for the Study of Rabbinic Literature," in *Approaches to Ancient Judaism: Theory and Practice*, ed. William Scott Green, Brown Judaic Studies 1 (Scholars, 1978). Recently the question has been formulated anew from both a literary and a form-critical perspective; for example, Geoffrey H. Hartman and Sanford Budick, *Midrash and Literature* (New Haven: Yale University, 1986) and Jacob Neusner, *Comparative Midrash: The Plan and Program of Genesis Rabba and Leviticus Rabbah*, Brown Judaic Studies (Atlanta: Scholars, 1986). There is a growing sense that "midrash" and "rewritten Bible" should be kept as distinct categories.

17. Translations of *Jubilees* and *Biblical Antiquities* are available in *The Old Testament Pseudepigrapha* Vol. 2, ed. James H. Charlesworth (Garden City: Doubleday & Company, 1985); the *Jewish Antiquities* is available in the Loeb Classical Library, translated by H. St. J. Thackeray (Cambridge, Mass.: Harvard University, 1978).

18. Because of space, we are not able to treat relevant examples from Diaspora Judaism, in particular *De Vita Mosis* by Philo of Alexandria, and *Exagoge* by Ezekiel (a fascinating recounting of the Exodus story in the literary form of Greek tragic drama in which the mother of Moses plays a prominent role).

19. For general background to the book of *Jubilees*, see the introduction and bibliography by O. S. Wintermute in Charlesworth, *The Old Testament Pseudepigrapha*, 35–51. The most comprehensive treatment of biblical interpretation is by John C. Endres, *Biblical Interpretation in the Book of Jubilees*, *CBQ* Monographs 18 (Washington: The Catholic Biblical Association, 1987); this study treats only *Jub.* 19–45.

20. John Endres, *Biblical Interpretation*, 25–26; see also 211–12, 217–18. The unusual interest in Rebekah was noted earlier by Piet Von Boxel, "The God of Rebekah," *SIDIC* 9 (1976): 14–18.

21. The name of Moses' father comes from the biblical genealogies (Exod. 6:20; Num. 26:58–59). There is evidence of a fair amount of interest in the figure of Amram in the Second Temple period, particular in texts from Qumran; see J. T. Milik, "4Q Visions de 'Amram et une citation d'Origène," *RB* 79 (1972): 77–97. No comparable texts exist about Jochebed.

22. This name seems to be part of a common tradition since it appears in Josephus as Thermuthis; there might be some relationship to the Egyptian goddess of wet nursing.

23. For background information, see D. J. Harrington, "Pseudo-Philo," in Charlesworth, *The Old Testament Pseudepigrapha,* 297–303, and the full-length commentary by Charles Perrot and Pierre-Maurice Bogaert, *Pseudo-Philon. Les Antiquités Bibliques,* Vol. 2, Sources Chrétiennes 230 (Paris: Cerf, 1976).

24. For example, the daughters of Adam, 1:4; Melcha, 4:11; Dinah the wife of Job, 8:8; Tamar "our mother," 9:5; the daughters of Kenaz, 29:1–2; Deborah, 30–33; Seila, the daughter of Jephthah, 40:1–9; Eluma, the wife of Manoah, 42:1–2; Hannah, 50–51; the wife of Phinehas, 54:6; Sedecla, the witch of Endor, 64:1–7.

25. To some degree Pseudo-Philo has shaped this incident according to a set pattern that he uses elsewhere (see Frederick J. Murphy, "Divine Plan, Human Plan: A Structuring Theme in Pseudo-Philo," *The Jewish Quarterly Review* 78 (1986): 5–14). In some later midrashim, it is Amran's plan that the couples actually divorce and he later remarries Jochebed. To find the divorce motif per se in Pseudo-Philo seems to be reading more than necessary into the text (but for a contrary view, see John Dominic Crossan, "From Moses to Jesus: Parallel Themes," *Bible Review* 2 [1986]: 18–27).

26. One Latin manuscript reads, "Jochebed did not listen to those who were saying these words" while the other manuscripts have Amram as the subject. Bogaert (*Pseudo-Philon: Biblique Antiquities,* 107) suggests that the name may have been missing in the original.

27. The Latin text is difficult in this section. *Bib. Ant.* 9:12a reads "and hid him in her womb for three months." Louis Feldman (*Prolegomenon* to the revised version of M. R. James's translation [New York: Ktav, 1971] xciii) was the first to suggest a lacuna here due to homoeoteleuton so that the three months refers to the hiding of the baby, as in the biblical text. Perhaps the reference is really back to Amram's speech (9.5) where he points out that all Hebrew women, like Tamar, will not show their pregnancy for three months.

28. For later rabbinic traditions about Miriam see R. Le Déaut, "Miriam, soeur de Moïse, et Marie, mère du Messie," *Biblica* 45 (1964): 198–219; Norman J. Cohen, "Miriam's Song: A Modern Midrashic Reading," *Judaism* 33 (1984): 179–90; Devora Steinmetz, "A Portrait of Miriam in Rabbinic Midrash," *Prooftexts* 8 (1988): 35–65.

29. Compare Pseudo-Philo's use of the phrase "the spirit of God came upon . . ." for other prophets, for example, Balaam 18:11 and Saul 62:2.

30. In many Targums and midrashim, it is Pharaoh or Pharaoh's astrologers who have a dream warning about the birth of a child; for a collection of these texts see Renée Bloch, "Traditions Concerning the Proclamation

of Moses' Birth: Pharaoh's Dream," *Approaches to Ancient Judaism,* 61–67. Josephus has both a scribe predicting the birth and a dream of reassurance to Amram.

31. For a study of these traditions, see Germain Bienaime, *Moïse et le don de l'eau dans la tradition juive ancienne: Targum et Midrash,* Analecta Biblica 98 (Rome: Pontifical Biblical Institute, 1984), 88–113.

32. For fuller discussion of Josephus' relationship to the Bible, see Harold Attridge, *The Interpretation of Biblical History in the Antiquitates Judaicae of Flavius Josephus,* Harvard Dissertations in Religion 7 (Missoula: Scholars, 1976), and Thomas Franxman, *Genesis and the Jewish Antiquities of Josephus* (Rome: Pontifical Biblical Institute, 1979).

33. It is striking to note that in Louis Feldman's massive bibliography (*Josephus and Modern Scholarship 1937–1980* [Berlin, New York: Walter de Gruyter, 1984]) the only topic with a single entry is the one on "Women" where he mentions a few pages in the semi-popular study by Evelyn and Frank Stagg, *Woman in the World of Jesus* (Philadelphia: Westminster, 1978). Recently three studies of Josephus' treatment of female biblical figures have appeared: Louis H. Feldman, "Josephus' Portrait of Deborah," in *Hellenica et Judaica,* ed. A Caquot, M. Hadas-Lebel, J. Riaud (Paris: Leuuen, Peeters, 1986), 115–28; James L. Bailey, "Josephus' Portrayal of the Matriarchs," in *Josephus, Judaism and Christianity,* ed. Louis H. Feldman and Gohei Hata (Detroit: Wayne State University, 1987), 154–79; Betsy Halpern Amaru, "Portraits of Biblical Women in Josephus' Antiquities," *JJS* 39 (1988): 143–70.

34. Bailey, "Josephus' Portrayal of the Matriarchs," 169.

35. I have purposefully used the more general term "hero" in light of the long-standing debate about which precise Hellenistic categories have been determinative in Josephus' portrayal of Moses and particularly the influence of the *theios aner* motif.

36. For the importance of good birth in the motif of the hero and in Josephus' characterization of biblical heroes, see Louis H. Feldman, "Josephus' Portrayal of Saul," *HUCA* 53 (1983): 59–62.

37. This would be in keeping with Josephus' general attitude to women and his treatment of other incidents, such as *Ant* I xviii 1 where the Lord speaks about the pregnancy to Isaac, not to Rebekah (compare Gen. 25:23).

38. In the Septuagint translation, certain verbs are already made plural: "they hid him for three months" (Exod. 2:2b, 3a); however, the mother still remains the sole actor in the next four verbs "she took . . . daubed . . . put . . . placed."

39. The story (minus the romantic element) was already known by Artapanus, a second-century B.C.E. Alexandrian historian. For discussion of the possible origins of this chapter, see Tessa Rajak, "Moses in Ethiopia: Legend and Literature," *JJS* 29 (1978): 111–22; Donna Runnalls, "Moses' Ethiopian Campaign," *JSJ* 14 (1983): 135–56.

40. Phyllis Trible, *God and the Rhetoric of Sexuality* (Philadelphia: Fortress, 1978), 202.

SELECTED BIBLIOGRAPHY

DEBRA A. CHASE

Rather than provide a compendium of works cited in this volume, the following bibliographies present those sources that our contributors have found to be particularly helpful in their own critical inquiries. The General bibliography offers a collection of the works that were instrumental in shaping the methodologies of the individual authors. For the most part, these entries are drawn from disciplines other than biblical studies—anthropology, sociology, archaeology, folklore, history, literary criticism, women's studies, and psychology. Their unifying feature is attention to gender as a significant variable. The bibliography on the Hebrew Bible consists of works dealing with women's issues within the framework of biblical studies. In neither case should the entries be considered comprehensive. We hope that these bibliographies will provide models of critical scholarship and will also encourage the formulation of new questions.

In order to reach a wide audience, references in languages other than English have not been included.

A. GENERAL

Ardener, Edwin. "Belief and the Problem of Women." In *The Interpretation of Ritual: Essays in Honour of A. I. Richards,* edited by J. S. La Fontaine, 135–58. London: Tavistock, 1972.

Bamberger, Joan. "The Myth of Matriarchy." In *Woman, Culture and Society,* edited by Michelle Z. Rosaldo and Louise Lamphere, 263–80. Stanford: Stanford University, 1974.

Bourguignon, E. *et al. A World of Women: Anthropological Studies of Women in the Societies of the World.* New York: Praeger, 1980.

Bridenthal, Renate; Koonz, Claudia; and Stuard, Susan, eds. *Becoming Visible: Women in European History.* Boston: Houghton Mifflin, 1987.

Brooten, Bernadette. *Women Leaders in the Ancient Synagogue.* Brown Judaic Studies 36. Chico, Calif.: Scholars, 1982.
Bullough, Vern, and Bullough, Bonnie. *Women and Prostitution: A Social History.* Buffalo: Prometheus Books, 1987.
Cameron, Averil and Kuhrt, Amélie., eds. *Images of Women in Antiquity.* Detroit: Wayne State University, 1983.
Carroll, Berenice A., ed. *Liberating Women's History.* Urbana, Ill.: University of Illinois, 1976.
Conkey, M., and Spector, J. "Archaeology and the Study of Gender." In *Advances in Archaeological Method and Theory,* edited by Michael B. Schiffer, vol. 7, 1–38. New York: Academic Press, 1984.
Culham, Phyllis. "Ten Years After Pomeroy: Studies of the Image and Reality of Women in Antiquity." In *Rescuing Creusa: New Methodological Approaches to Women in Antiquity, Helios* 13, edited by Marilyn Skinner, 9–30. Lubbock, Tex.: Texas Tech, 1987.
Degler, Carl N. *Is There a History of Women?* Oxford: Clarendon, 1975.
———. "Women and the Family." In *The Past Before Us: Contemporary Historical Writing in the United States,* edited by Michael Kammen, 308–26. Ithaca, N.Y.: Cornell University, 1980.
De Lauretis, Teresa, ed. *Feminist Studies/Critical Studies.* Bloomington, Ind.: Indiana University, 1986.
Douglas, Mary. *Purity and Danger: An Analysis of the Concepts of Pollution and Taboo.* London: Routledge and Kegan Paul, 1966.
———. *Cultural Bias.* London: Royal Anthropological Institute, 1978.
Falk, N. A. and Gross, R. M., eds. *Unspoken Worlds: Women's Religious Lives in Non-Western Cultures.* Belmont, Calif.: Wadsworth, 1989.
Fernea, E. W. *Guests of the Sheik: An Ethnography of an Iraqi Village.* Garden City, N.Y.: Doubleday & Co., 1969.
Flynn, E. A. and Schweickart, P. P., eds. *Gender and Reading: Essays on Reader, Texts, and Contexts.* Baltimore: Johns Hopkins, 1986.
Fox, Robin. *Kinship and Marriage. An Anthropological Perspective.* Cambridge: Cambridge University, 1967.
Freidl, E. *Women & Men: An Anthropologist's View.* New York: Holt, Rinehart & Winston, 1975.
Gilligan, Carol. *In a Different Voice.* Cambridge, Mass.: Harvard University, 1982.
Gold, Penny Schine. *The Lady and the Virgin.* Chicago: University of Chicago, 1985.
Goody, Jack and Tambiah, S. J. *Bridewealth and Dowry.* Cambridge Papers in Social Anthropology, No. 7. Cambridge: Cambridge University, 1973.
Gordon, Ann D.; Buhle, Mari Jo; and Dye, Nancy Schrom. "The Problem of Women's History." In *Liberating Women's History,* edited by Berenice A. Carroll, 75–92. Urbana: University of Illinois, 1976.
Gordon, Linda. "What's New in Women's History." In *Feminist Studies/Critical Studies,* edited by Teresa de Lauretis, 20–30. Bloomington, Ind.: Indiana University, 1986.

Greene, G. and Kaplan, C., eds. *Making a Difference: Feminist Literary Criticism*. New York: Methuen, 1983.

Janeway, E. *Powers of the Weak*. New York: Knopf, 1980.

Jason, Heda. "The Fairy Tale of the Active Heroine: An Outline for Discussion." In *Le conte pourquoi? comment?* edited by G. Calame-Griaule, 79–97. Paris: Centre Nationale de la Recherche Scientifique, 1984.

Johansson, Sheila Ryan. "'Herstory' as History: A New Field or Another Fad?" In *Liberating Women's History*, edited by Berenice A. Carroll, 400–430. Urbana, Ill.: University of Illinois, 1976.

Keesing, Roger M. *Kin Groups and Social Structure*. New York: Holt, Rinehart & Winston, 1975.

Kelly-Gadol, Joan. "The Social Relation of the Sexes: Methodological Implications of Women's History." *Signs* 1 (1976): 809–23.

Kristeva, Julia. *The Kristeva Reader*. Edited by Toril Moi. New York: Columbia University, 1986.

La Fontaine, J. S. "Ritualization of Women's Life-Crises in Bugisu." In *The Interpretation of Ritual: Essays in Honor of A. I. Richards*, edited by J. S. La Fontaine. London: Tavistock, 1972.

Leacock, Eleanor Burke. "Introduction." In *The Origin of the Family, Private Property and the State* by Frederick Engels, 7–67. New York: International, 1972.

Lesko, Barbara F., ed. *Women's Earliest Records from Ancient Egypt and Western Asia*. Brown Judaic Studies, vol. 166. Atlanta: Scholars Press, 1989.

Lewis, I. M. *Ecstatic Religion*. Harmondsworth, Eng.: Penguin, 1971.

Lincoln, Bruce. *Emerging from the Chrysalis: Studies in Rituals of Women's Initiation*. Cambridge, Mass.: Harvard University, 1981.

Lundell, Torborg. "Gender-Related Biases in the Type and Motif Indexes of Aarne and Thompson." In *Fairy Tales and Society: Illusion, Allusion, and Paradigm*, edited by Ruth B. Bottigheimer, 151–63. Philadelphia: University of Pennsylvania, 1986.

McNamara, JoAnn and Wemple, Suzanne F. "Sanctity and Power: The Dual Pursuit of Medieval Women." In *Becoming Visible: Women in European History*, 90–118. Boston: Houghton Mifflin, 1977.

Martin, M. K. and Voorhies, B. *Female of the Species*. New York: Columbia University, 1975.

Meese, Elizabeth A. *Crossing the Double Cross: The Practice of Feminist Criticism*. Chapel Hill, N.C.: University of North Carolina, 1986.

Miller, Jean Baker. *Toward a New Psychology of Women*. Boston: Beacon, 1976.

Moi, Toril. *Sexual/Textual Politics: Feminist Literary Theory*. London: Methuen, 1985.

Ortner, Sherry B. "Is Female to Male as Nature is to Culture?" In *Women, Culture and Society*, edited by Michelle Zimbalist Rosaldo and Louise Lamphere, 67–78. Stanford: Stanford University, 1974.

Ortner, S. and Whitehead, H., eds. *Sexual Meanings*. Cambridge: Cambridge University, 1981.

Paige, Karen and Jeffery. *The Politics of Reproductive Ritual*. Berkeley: University of California, 1981.

Pitt-Rivers, Julian. "The fate of Shechem or the politics of sex." In *The Fate of Shechem or the Politics of Sex. Essays on the Anthropology of the Mediterranean,* Cambridge Studies in Social Anthropology, vol. 19, edited by Julian Pitt-Rivers, 126–71 and 182–86. Cambridge: Cambridge University, 1977.

Quinn, N. "Anthropological Studies on Women's Status." *Annual Review of Anthropology* 6 (1977): 182–222.

Reiter, Rayna R., ed. *Toward an Anthropology of Women.* New York: Monthly Review, 1975.

Rogers, Susan C. "Woman's Place: A Critical Review of Anthropological Theory." *Comparative Studies in Society and History* 20 (1978): 123–62.

Rosaldo, Michelle Zimbalist. "Women, Culture, and Society: A Theoretical Overview." In *Women, Culture, and Society,* edited by M. Z. Rosaldo and L. Lamphere, 17–42. Stanford: Stanford University, 1974.

———. "The Use and Abuse of Anthropology: Reflections on Feminism and Cross-cultural Understanding." *Signs* 5 (1980): 389–417.

Rosaldo, Michelle Zimbalist, and Lamphere, Louise, eds. *Woman, Culture and Society.* Stanford: Stanford University, 1974.

Rubin, Gayle. "The Traffic of Women: Notes on the Political Economy of Sex." In *An Anthropology of Women,* edited by Rayna R. Reiter, 157–210. New York: Monthly Review, 1975.

Ruether, Rosemary Radford, ed. *Religion and Sexism: Images of Women in the Jewish and Christian Traditions.* New York: Simon and Schuster, 1974.

Ruether, Rosemary Radford, and McLaughlin, Eleanor, eds. *Women of Spirit: Female Leadership in the Jewish and Christian Traditions.* New York: Simon and Schuster, 1979.

Sanday, P. R. *Female Power and Male Dominance: On the Origins of Female Inequality.* New York: Cambridge University, 1981.

Schaberg, Jane. *The Illegitimacy of Jesus.* San Francisco: Harper & Row, 1987.

Schüssler Fiorenza, Elisabeth. *Bread Not Stone: The Challenge of Feminist Biblical Interpretation.* Boston: Beacon, 1984.

———. *In Memory of Her. A Feminist Theological Reconstruction of Christian Origins.* New York: Crossroad, 1987.

———. "The Ethics of Interpretation: De-Centering Biblical Scholarship." *JBL* 107 (1988): 3–17.

Shapiro, Judith. "Anthropology and the Study of Gender." In *A Feminist Perspective in the Academy: The Difference It Makes,* edited by Elizabeth Langland and Walter Gove, 110–29. Chicago: University of Chicago, 1981.

Skinner, Marilyn, ed. *Rescuing Creusa: New Methodological Approaches to Women in Antiquity.* Special issue of *Helios* (New Series 13). Lubbock, Tex.: Texas Tech, 1987.

———. "Introduction." In *Rescuing Creusa: New Methodological Approaches to Women in Antiquity,* edited by Marilyn Skinner, 1–8. Lubbock, Tex.: Texas Tech, 1987.

Smith, Hilda A. "Feminism and the Methodology of Women's History." In

Liberating Women's History, edited by Berenice A. Carroll, 368–84. Urbana, Ill.: University of Illinois, 1976.
Smith-Rosenberg, Carroll. "The New Woman and the New History." *Feminist Studies* 3 (1975): 185–98.
Spivak, Gayatri Chakravorty. *In Other Worlds: Essays in Cultural Politics.* New York: Methuen, 1987.
Tiffany, S. W., ed. *Women and Society: An Anthropological Reader.* Montreal: Eden Press Women's Publications, 1979.
Weigle, Marta. *Spiders and Spinsters. Women and Mythology.* Albuquerque, N. Mex.: University of New Mexico, 1982.
Whyte, M. K. *The Status of Women in Preindustrial Societies.* Princeton: Princeton University, 1978.

B. HEBREW BIBLE

Ackroyd, Peter R. "Goddesses, Women and Jezebel." In *Images of Women in Antiquity*, edited by Averil Cameron and Amélie Kuhrt, 245–59. Detroit: Wayne State University, 1983.
Amaru, Betsy Halpern. "Portraits of Biblical Women in Josephus' *Antiquities.*" *JJS* 39 (1988): 143–70.
Aschkenasy, Nehama. *Eve's Journey: Feminine Images in Hebraic Literary Tradition.* Philadelphia: University of Penn., 1986.
Bailey, James L. "Josephus' Portrayal of the Matriarchs." In *Josephus, Judaism and Christianity*, edited by Louis H. Feldman and Gohei Hata, 154–79. Detroit: Wayne State University, 1987.
Bal, Mieke. *Lethal Love.* Indiana Studies in Biblical Literature. Bloomington, Ind.: Indiana University, 1987.
———. "Tricky Thematics." *Semeia* 42 (1988): 133–55.
———. *Murder and Difference: Gender, Genre, and Scholarship on Sisera's Death.* Indiana Studies in Biblical Literature. Bloomington, Ind.: Indiana University, 1988.
Baltzer, Klaus. "Women and War in Qohelet 7:23–8:1a." *HTR* 80 (1987): 127–32.
Bass, Dorothy C. "Women's Studies and Biblical Studies: An Historical Perspective." *JSOT* 22 (1982): 6–12.
Berlin, Adele. "Characterization in Biblical Narrative: David's Wives." *JSOT* 23 (1982): 69–85.
Bird, Phyllis A. "Images of Women in the Old Testament." In *Religion and Sexism*, edited by Rosemary R. Ruether, 41–88. New York: Simon and Schuster, 1974.
———. "Male and Female He Created Them: Genesis 1:27b in the Context of the Priestly Account of Creation." *HTR* 74 (1981): 129–59.
———. "The Place of Women in the Israelite Cultus." In *Ancient Israelite Religion: Essays in Honor of Frank M. Cross*, edited by Paul D. Hanson, Patrick D. Miller, and S. Dean McBride, 397–419. Philadelphia: Fortress, 1987.

———. "Translating Sexist Language as a Theological and Cultural Problem." *Union Seminary Quarterly Review* 42 (1988): 89–95.

———. "Sexual Differentiation and Divine Image in the Genesis Creation Texts." In *Image of God and Gender Models,* edited by Kari Børresen. Oslo: Solum, forthcoming.

———. "The Harlot as Heroine: Narrative Art and Social Presupposition in Three Old Testament Texts." *Semeia* 46 (1989): 119–39.

———. "Women's Religion in Ancient Israel." In *Women's Earliest Records from Ancient Egypt to Western Asia,* edited by Barbara F. Lesko, 283–98. Atlanta: Scholars Press, 1989.

Brenner, Athalya. *The Israelite Woman: Social Role and Literary Type in Biblical Narrative.* JSOTSup 21. Sheffield: JSOT, 1985.

———."Female Social Behavior: Two Descriptive Patterns within the 'Birth of the Hero' Paradigm." *VT* 36 (1986): 257–73.

Burns, Rita J. *Has the Lord Indeed Spoken Only Through Moses? A Study of the Biblical Portrait of Miriam.* SBL Dissertation Series 84. Atlanta: Scholars, 1987.

Camp, Claudia. "The Wise Women of 2 Samuel: A Role Model for Women in Early Israel?" *CBQ* 43 (1981): 14–29.

———. *Wisdom and the Feminine in the Book of Proverbs.* Decatur: Almond, 1985.

———. "Wise and Strange: An Interpretation of the Female Imagery in Proverbs in Light of Trickster Mythology." *Semeia* 42 (1988): 14–36.

Collins, Adela Yarbro. "An Inclusive Biblical Anthropology." *Theology Today* 34 (1978): 358–69.

———, ed. *Feminist Perspectives on Biblical Scholarship.* Chico, Calif.: Scholars, 1985.

Coogan, Michael D. "Canaanite Origins and Lineage: Reflections on the Religion of Ancient Israel." In *Ancient Israelite Religion,* edited by Patrick D. Miller, Jr., Paul D. Hanson, S. Dean McBride, 115–24. Philadelphia: Fortress, 1987.

Darr, Katheryn Pfisterer. "Like Warrior, Like Woman: Destruction and Deliverance in Isaiah 42:10–17." *CBQ* 49 (1987): 560–71.

Dever, William G. "Asherah, Consort of Yahweh? New Evidence from Kuntillet Ajrud." *BASOR* 255 (1984): 21–37.

Donaldson, Mara E. "Kinship Theory in the Patriarchal Narratives: The Case of the Barren Wife." *JAAR* 49 (1981): 77–87.

Dutcher-Walls, Patricia. "The Text in Context: A Sociological Model for Women's Roles in Ancient Israel." *Journal of Feminist Studies in Religion,* in press.

Exum, J. Cheryl. "'You Shall Let Every Daughter Live': A Study of Ex 1:8–2:10." *Semeia* 28 (1983): 63–82.

Exum, J. Cheryl, and Bos, Johanna W. H., eds. *Reasoning with the Foxes. Female Wit in a World of Male Power. Semeia* 42. Atlanta: Scholars, 1988.

Fontaine, Carole. "The Deceptive Goddess in Ancient Near Eastern Myth: Inanna and Inaraš." *Semeia* 42 (1988): 84–102.

Frymer-Kensky, Tikva. "Pollution, Purification, and Purgation in Biblical Israel." In *The Word of the Lord Shall Go Forth. Essays in Honor of David Noel Freedman*, edited by Carol L. Meyers and M. O'Connor, 399–414. Winona Lake: Eisenbrauns, 1983.

———. "The Strange Case of the Suspected Sotah (Num V 11–31)." *VT* 34 (1984): 11–26.

Fuchs, Esther. "Structure and Patriarchal Functions in the Biblical Betrothal Type-Scene: Some Preliminary Notes." *Journal of Feminist Studies in Religion* 3 (1987): 7–13.

———. "'For I Have the Way of Women': Deception, Gender, and Ideology in Biblical Narrative." *Semeia* 42 (1988): 68–83.

Furman, Nelly. "His Story Versus Her Story: Male Genealogy and Female Strategy in the Jacob Cycle." In *Feminist Perspectives on Biblical Scholarship*, edited by Adela Yarbro Collins, 107–16. Chico, Calif.: Scholars, 1985.

Glazier-McDonald, Beth. "Intermarriage, Divorce, and the *bat- 'ēl nēkār*: Insights into Mal 2:10–16." *JBL* 106 (1987): 603–11.

Hackett, Jo Ann. "In the Days of Jael: Reclaiming the History of Women in Ancient Israel." In *Immaculate & Powerful: The Female in Sacred Image and Social Reality*, edited by Clarissa W. Atkinson, Constance H. Buchanan, Margaret R. Miles, 15–38. Boston: Beacon, 1985.

———. "Women's Studies and the Hebrew Bible." In *The Future of Biblical Studies. The Hebrew Scriptures*, edited by Richard Eliot Friedman and Hugh Williamson, 143–64. Semeia Studies. Atlanta: Scholars, 1987.

Higgins, Jean M. "The Myth of Eve: The Temptress." *JAAR* 44 (1976): 639–47.

Horowitz, Maryanne Cline. "The Image of God in Man—Is Woman Included?" *HTR* 72 (1979): 175–206.

Jay, Nancy. "Sacrifice as Remedy for Having Been Born of Woman." In *Immaculate and Powerful: The Female in Sacred Image and Social Reality*, edited by Clarissa W. Atkinson, Constance H. Buchanan, Margaret R. Miles, 283–309. Boston: Beacon, 1985.

———. "Sacrifice, Descent and the Patriarchs." *VT* 38 (1988): 52–70.

Lanser, Susan S. "(Feminist) Criticism in the Garden: Inferring Genesis 2–3." *Semeia* 41 (1988): 67–84.

Lipinski, Edward. "The Syro-Palestinian Iconography of Woman and Goddess (Review Article)." *IEJ* 36 (1986): 87–96.

———. "The Wife's Right to Divorce in the Light of An Ancient Near Eastern Tradition." *The Jewish Law Annual* 4 (1981): 9–27.

Meyers, Carol. "Gender Imagery in the Song of Songs." *Hebrew Annual Review* 10 (1986): 209–23.

———. *Discovering Eve: Ancient Israelite Women in Context.* New York: Oxford, 1988.

Miller, Patrick D. "The Absence of the Goddess in Israelite Religion." *Hebrew Annual Review* 10 (1986): 239–47.

Muntingh, L. M. "The Social and Legal Status of a Free Ugaritic Female." *JNES* 26 (1967): 102–12.

Niditch, Susan. "The Wronged Woman Righted: An Analysis of Genesis 38." *HTR* 72 (1979): 143–49.

———. "The 'Sodomite' Theme in Judges 19:20: Family, Community, and Social Disintegration." *CBQ* 44 (1982): 365–78.

Oden, Robert A., Jr. "Religious Identity and the Sacred Prostitution Accusation." Chapter 5 in *The Bible without Theology.* San Francisco: Harper and Row, 1987.

Ruether, Rosemary R. "Feminism and Patriarchal Religion: Principles of Ideological Critique of the Bible." *JSOT* 22 (1982): 54–66.

Russell, Letty M. *Feminist Interpretation of the Bible.* Philadelphia: Westminster, 1985.

Sakenfeld, Katharine D. "Old Testament Perspectives: Methodological Issues." *JSOT* 22 (1982): 13–20.

Segal, J. B. "Popular Religion in Ancient Israel." *JJS* 27 (1976): 1–22.

Setel, T. Drorah. "Prophets and Pornography: Female Sexual Imagery in Hosea." In *Feminist Interpretation of the Bible,* edited by Letty M. Russell, 86–95. Philadelphia: Westminster, 1985.

Steinberg, Naomi. "Gender Roles in the Rebekah Cycle." *Union Seminary Quarterly Review* 39 (1984): 175–84.

———. "Gender Roles in the Monarchy." Paper read at the Society of Biblical Literature Annual Meeting, Atlanta, Seminar on Sociology of the Monarchy, Nov. 1986. Mimeographed.

———. "Israelite Tricksters, Their Analogues and Cross-cultural Study." *Semeia* 42 (1988): 1–13.

Tolbert, Mary Ann, ed. *The Bible and Feminist Hermeneutics. Semeia* 28. Chico, Calif.: Scholars, 1983.

———. "Defining the Problem: The Bible and Feminist Hermeneutics." In *The Bible and Feminist Hermeneutics, Semeia* 28, edited by Mary Ann Tolbert, 113–26. Chico, Calif.: Scholars, 1983.

Trible, Phyllis. *God and the Rhetoric of Sexuality.* Philadelphia: Fortress, 1978.

———. *Texts of Terror: Literary Feminist Readings of Biblical Narratives.* Philadelphia: Fortress, 1984.

Westbrook, Raymond. "Lex talionis and Exodus 21, 22–25." *RB* 93 (1986): 52–69.

———. "The Prohibition on Restoration of Marriage in Deuteronomy 24:1–4." *Scripta Hierosolymitana* 31 (1986): 387–405.

Westenholz, Joan Goodnick. "Towards a New Conceptualization of the Female Role in Mesopotamian Society." *JAOS,* in press.

———. "Tamar, *Qedeša, Qadištu,* and Sacred Prostitution in Mesopotamia. *HTR* 82 (1989).

Williams, James G. *Women Recounted: Narrative Thinking and the God of Israel.* Sheffield: Almond, 1982.

INDEX OF BIBLICAL CITATIONS

OLD TESTAMENT